The Forewarned Investor

The Forewarned Investor

Don't Get Fooled Again by Corporate Fraud

by

Brett S. Messing

and

Steven A. Sugarman

Foreword by

James J. Cramer

CAREER PRESS

Franklin Lakes, NJ

THE FOREWARNED INVESTOR
EDITED AND TYPESET BY ASTRID DERIDDER
Cover design by Jeffrey Bailey/Solaris Design Group
Printed in the U.S.A. by Book-mart Press

To order this title, please call toll-free 1-800-CAREER-1 (NJ and Canada: 201-848-0310) to order using VISA or MasterCard, or for further information on books from Career Press.

CAREER PRESS

The Career Press, Inc., 3 Tice Road, PO Box 687,
Franklin Lakes, NJ 07417
www.careerpress.com

Library of Congress Cataloging-in-Publication Data

Messing, Brett.
The forewarned investor : don't get fooled again by corporate fraud / by Brett Messing and Steven Sugarman.
p. cm.
Includes index.
ISBN-13: 978-1-56414-881-0
ISBN-10: 1-56414-881-5
1. Investments. 2. Securities fraud. 3. Corporations—Corrupt practices. 4. Finance. Personal. I. Sugarman, Steven, 1959- II. Title.

HG4521.M4555 2006
332.6--dc22

2006042603

Acknowledgments

While most authors save the best for last in the acknowledgments section of their books, we do not want to take the chance that the reader may get bored and bail out before reaching the end of this page. Thus, we want to start by thanking our families for their tremendous support. They endured long days, late nights of researching and writing, and piles of books and papers scattered throughout our homes. They edited unintelligible early drafts and rallied us when laziness threatened to overtake us. To Marla, Natalie, Samantha, and Morgan Messing, and Ainslie and Sierra Sugarman, thank you and we love you.

We would also like to extend special thanks to our mothers, Sandy Messing and Hilda Sugarman, and our fathers, Brian Messing and Michael Sugarman, for making possible our lives, careers, and this book. We know that you are proud of what we've created. Now you must read it!

We would like to thank Jim Cramer for his Foreward, inspiration, and the entertainment and education that his show, *Mad Money*, provides our office every afternoon.

Our careers and lives have been touched by too many people to mention. A true forewarned investor would not even try as there is positive expectancy that we will leave people out and unnecessarily upset them. But it is not every day that you write a book. We would like to extend special thanks, in alphabetical order, to Ray Alfano, John Atkeson, Rich Atlas, Karl Austen, Bill Buckley, Rick Camp, John Durrett, Sara Eagle, Ben Van de Bunt and Laura Fox, James Freeman, Glenn Fuhrman, Steve Gribben, Bill Gruver, Kevin Handwerker, Drew and Julie Hanson, Ben Helvey, Doug and Noreen Herzog, Jeff Karish, John Kim, Phil Jackson, Darell Krasnoff, Senator Joe Lieberman, Michael Lifrak, Joel Levine, Ben Mackay, John and Susie Mackay, Alan Marantz, Bob Matza, Geoffrey Michael, Neal Moritz, Heidi Murdy, Matthew Parlow, Norman Pattiz, David and Gina Pearlstein, Sonny and Marsha Pearlstein, John Pike, Jeff and Maya Pinkner, J.B. Pritzker, Alan and Georgina Rothenberg, Rob Sarazen, Anthony Scaramucci, Steve Sidel, Pete Smith, Gary Speciale, Amelia Sugarman, Jason Sugarman, John Svolos, John and Carolyn Tipton, Chad Tons, Jeremy Turk, Bobby and Lauren Turner, Richard Yeh, Debra Messing and Daniel Zelman, Roy Zuckerberg, and the memory of Theresa Krug, Richard Krug, and Harold Sugarman.

We would also like to thank the team at GPS Partners for all their hard work. Kudos to Jeff Farron, Chuck Hastings, Chad FitzGerald, and Oshan Wickramanayake.

This book would not have happened without the endurance and patience of our agent, Esmond Harmsworth, or the fine editing of Shelley Neumeier and Mark Wallace. We would also like to extend our thanks to all the people at Career Press. We hope this book is a winner for you.

And finally, we would like to once again thank our wives, Marla and Ainslie, as it is the prudent, low risk thing for a forewarned investor (or smart husband) to do. We are both very blessed.

Contents

Foreword by James J. Cramer

Those of us who've been around the block have learned some important lessons, often the hard way. As I wrote in Jim Cramer's *Real Money: Sane Investing in an Insane World*, I keep a Post-It note on my quote machine that reads, "Accounting Irregularities = Sell," to remind myself of the massive losses caused by cooked books. But how do you spot those accounting irregularities before it's *too late to sell*? That's the hard part—or it was until this book came along. *The Forewarned Investor* explains—in plain English—how to protect yourself, teaching the kind of lessons you and I both need to have on hand before we commit to owning any stock.

I have seen this painful movie over and over again. You've piled your savings into the latest hot growth stock. The thing is flying. You're already seeing massive paper profits, and according to the brilliant CEO whose new business model is driving it all, there's no place to go but up. If things continue the way they've been going, your kid's college education is paid for, and your retirement is secure. Of course, you're not surprised. You did your homework, you followed the news, and read the analysts' reports. Of course you picked a winner, you're not stupid.

But then one day the whole thing starts to fall apart. The numbers, it seems, may not add up. The CFO resigns, and short-sellers start pushing down the share price for, what the CEO says is, no reason at all except pure unadulterated greed. According to him, the business itself is still as sound as always. But then the SEC starts poking around and the share price falls further. Some pesky reporter uncovers a few less than savory details of the CEO's past. The business climate still looks favorable though, according to your fearless leader. Then the lawsuits hit. Before you know it, the CEO is in jail, the company is bankrupt, and your kid's college education has disappeared in a puff of smoke.

It's the kind of thing you might think can't happen to you, but I've seen it happen all too many times. The fact is, the kind of investment homework most people do just isn't enough to protect themselves from corporate fraud that can cost investors billions of dollars. That's why stock picking makes experienced guys like me nervous. We've seen this kind of thing happen again and again. In many ways, investing is a game of trust. It can take a lot of courage to invest even in a large, stable company with a good track record. Even at companies like those, fraud can end up costing a lot of people a lot of money.

The good news is that you don't have to be one of those people. The world is filled with bad guys, and the corporate world has as many of them as anywhere else. But that doesn't mean you have no defense against the rogues and crooks of the boardroom. All you have to do to protect yourself is learn to spot the warning signs of executive treachery—and then be willing to sell before those warnings turn into a full-fledged emergency.

Don't be fooled by that CEO's impenetrable rhetoric. As veterans of the stock markets already know, the warning signs haven't changed much over the last century. You can learn important lessons about the early indicators of fraud by looking back at the great frauds of the early 20th century, like the original Ponzi scheme, as well as the more immediately painful episodes such as the Lincoln Savings & Loan scandal and the collapse of Enron. Whether it's 1920s postal coupons, 1970s retail loans, or 21st century energy-trading schemes, big corporate fraud often unravels the same way: first with a series of danger signs, then with a precipitous collapse that leaves unwary investors reeling and that promising company in a shambles. It's the kind of thing that could happen to anyone who's not paying attention or who doesn't know what to watch out for.

It doesn't have to happen to you. The best way to avoid getting burned by corporate fraudsters is to learn how to spot those danger signs and then to get out before your investment goes up in smoke. And if you want to become the kind of forewarned investor who knows what to look for, a good way to do it is to read this book. Brett Messing and Steven Sugarman have delved into corporate rogues and fraudulent companies from Charles Ponzi to ZZZZ Best to Charles Keating and the Bre-X gold mine scandal. The warning signs repeat themselves, and they are the kinds of things that set off ear-splitting alarm bells for guys like me. When I hear them, I get out fast because I know that disaster may be right around the corner. It's just a matter of tuning your ears to the right frequencies. So listen up.

Introduction

The Eight Danger Signs of Financial Fraud

The point is ladies and gentlemen that greed, for lack of a better word, is good. Greed is right. Greed works. Greed clarifies, cuts through and captures the essence of the evolutionary spirit. Greed, in all of it's forms—greed for life, for money, knowledge—has marked the upward surge of mankind and greed—you mark my words—will not only save Teldar Paper but that other malfunctioning corporation called the USA. Thank you.

—Gordon Gekko, *Wall Street* (1987)

While money may make the world go round, the greed that fuels the modern capitalist system regularly produces characters so destructive that they can shake a nation's economy to its very foundations. Corporate fraud, pulled off by executives thinking only of themselves, produces losses that extend well beyond those incurred directly by shareholders. Such scandals sap investor confidence, savage the stock market, make it more difficult for companies to raise money, and often deal a blow to the economy as a whole. So far-reaching are their effects that it's sometimes hard to see how anyone could avoid them.

These days, the risk posed by executive misconduct has never been greater. As Wall Street and Main Street have converged, more people than ever have become vulnerable to the misdeeds of the financial elite. More than 80 million Americans now own stock directly; through pension funds, mutual funds, and 401k programs, the retirement plans of millions hinge on the fortunes of the stock market. As the Enron debacle made abundantly clear, white-collar fraud is not a victimless crime. It strikes at the heart of America. The fall of the infamous "Big 6"—Enron, Global Crossing, WorldCom, Tyco, Qwest, and Adelphia—wiped out $340 billion of equity market capitalization between 2000 and 2002. Those six companies alone accounted for 8.5 percent of the $4 trillion lost during that period. While it would be unfair to blame that bear market entirely on corporate misbehavior, there is no question that fraud contributed mightily to the loss of investor confidence and the resulting stock market sell-off.

And yet, it still goes on today. Despite the experience of recent years, corporate rogues continue to find their way to positions of power at the top companies. Thousands of people every year are fooled into investing in companies that turn out to be dishonest, unethical, or even downright criminal. When that happens, nine times out of 10, your money is lost long before the companies' problems are widely acknowledged. You read yesterday's stock price close in *The Wall Street Journal* and you're sitting pretty; then you turn on CNBC and find that your hot stock has crashed even before the market opened. We've seen it happen, and it may even have happened to you.

The good news is, it doesn't have to. In almost every case of major corporate fraud over the last century, sharp-eyed investors could have picked out warning signs and exited before the crash. What it requires, though, are two things that the individual investor often doesn't have a lot of: the experience and knowledge to know where to look for the signs of danger, and the willingness and strategy to get out of a risky investment before disaster strikes.

The purpose of this book is to give you both of those tools. We look at eight of the biggest financial frauds of the last 100 years and show you who perpetrated them, how they were executed, and where the danger signs could have been seen, as well as where those same signs have cropped up in the stock-market scandals of recent years.

History Repeats Itself

As we looked at the recent history of corporate fraud, we found ourselves asking one question: How do investors keep getting duped? How does it happen—again and again and again—that a small group of corporate crooks cheat a large number of people out of vast sums of money?

What we found was that, while the swindles of the last decade may seem sophisticated from the outside, the truth is that the rogues of recent years haven't been up to any new tricks. Throughout history, con artists repeatedly have found their way to positions of great power at large, public top companies—often working from the same play-book as the rogues of more recent years. The use of off-balance-sheet partnerships to hide debt at Enron is eerily similar to the multiple holding company structure employed by Samuel Insull in 1931. Tyco CEO Dennis Kozlowski's misuse of acquisitions to pump up earnings was identical to the tactics of Equity Funding CEO Stanley Goldblum in the 1960s. Using corporate accounts filled with investors' money to finance an unbelievably lavish personal lifestyle—as Kozlowski did until he was indicted in 2002—is also nothing new. Charles Ponzi, who had the dubious distinction of having a whole class of frauds named after him, was doing it soon after the turn of the last century. Populating your executive suite with friends and family who wouldn't dare say no to underhanded schemes—as John Rigas did at Adelphia Communications in the late 1990s—is not exactly a new trick either. Insull used the same technique in the 1930s to allow him to profit from a business being run in deeply unethical, if not downright fraudulent, ways.

The fact is, the basic techniques of corporate fraud have changed little over time. The danger signs that cropped up around Ponzi and Insull's companies are the same ones that developed at Kozlowski's. This book gives a look at how those frauds have worked, and shows how the lessons of yesterday can be applied to the investments of today.

History does, in fact, repeat itself. The parallels between the major bull markets of the last century, particularly the 1920s and 1990s, are striking. In the 1920s, insider trading was common and legal. New securities were sold at discounted prices to a "preferred list" of customers before the issues went public. Syndicated stock pools manipulated share prices. At least 100 stocks were openly rigged. While 90 percent of the NYSE firms had audits of some form in 1926, financial reporting was voluntary, and there was no uniform standard. The quality of the financial reporting was further diluted by lawyers, accountants, and bankers, who worked to aid their corporate clients rather than investors.

Fast forward to the 1990s. Internet and telecom CEOs dumped massive amounts of stock while continuing to espouse the wonderful and transforming futures that lay ahead for their companies. Hot initial public offerings were dished out to corporate CEOs who could return the favors with investment banking business. Hedge funds and market makers manipulated the movements of Internet stocks to establish unsustainable opening prices for IPOs. Companies resorted to "pro-forma" earnings reports to spiff up their operating numbers. Research analysts swapped investment recommendations for banking fees. Accounting firms and law firms such as Arthur Andersen and Vinson & Elkins, blinded by huge client fees, failed to fulfill their fiduciary duties to the investment community.

Like Charlie Brown—who tumbles onto his back every autumn no matter how many times Lucy promises not to pull the football away—investors have fallen for the same bag of tricks again and again. This occurs despite the fact that every business rogue leaves tracks in the sand. In isolation, these signs are usually minor and can be explained away. But viewed in their totality, a damning picture emerges.

This book will show you how to recognize the common manifestations of fraud, and danger signs that are readily visible to investors who do their homework. If you see a number of these danger signs at a specific company, it should alert you that there's probably something amiss behind the scenes, and your investment is at substantially greater risk. That increase in risk means your attractive investment probably has become one that's not only unattractive, but downright dangerous. When you do encounter a collection of these warning signs in a single company, no matter how promising it looks from a distance, you probably should follow the lead of a poker player with a lousy hand, and fold.

The losses that result from fraud can debilitate an investor's portfolio. If your holdings decline by 50 percent, for instance, they then have to appreciate by 100 percent to get you back to where you started. Wouldn't it be easier if you hadn't had to bear the loss in the first place? By simply avoiding the "Big 6" frauds of the early 21st century and investing in the remaining stocks in the Standard & Poors 500 index, investors would have outperformed 90 percent of the professional mutual fund managers in 2001 and 2002. No matter what their style of investing or the kind of assets they buy, great investors are characterized by their ability to identify and manage risk effectively. Identifying and avoiding investments in the stock of high-risk companies run by business rogues can contribute mightily to a portfolio's return. As legendary investment guru Warren Buffet said, "It's easier to avoid the dragon than to slay it." All it takes is a sharp eye, some discipline, and the willingness to get out while the getting's good.

In a sense, this book turns most investment advice on its head. We're not here to tell you how to make a million dollars; we're here to tell you how to hold on to the money your investments have already earned. This book is about how to dodge the losers, a lesson that too many investors never bother to learn.

Gallery of Fraud

This book reviews eight of the biggest frauds of the 20th century. We start with the infamous Charles Ponzi, creator of what's come to be known as the "Ponzi scheme." A host of colorful and edifying rogues have followed in his tracks, and we cover the most important ones in successive chapters of this book. Samuel Insull began his career as Thomas Edison's right hand man and died penniless in a French train station. In between, he carried out an epic fraud that led to massive securities reform and the establishment of the Securities and Exchange Commission. Philip Musica (aka F. Donald Coster, M.D.) of McKesson & Robbins, inflated inventory and receivables that Price Waterhouse & Co. approved without bothering to verify their existence. Modern accounting practices arose largely in response to this audacious fraud.

Investors endured World War II, the global battle against communism, the turbulent 1960s, and a major bear market before the next major scandal broke. Stanley Goldblum, CEO of Equity Funding Corporation of America, carried out a massive multi-year fraud with the help of the infamous Maple Street Gang, a group of employees whose sole function was to create fictitious insurance policies. The pace of major frauds picked up in the 1980s as a new bull market began. The saga of ZZZZ Best recalls how 19 year old Barry Minkow fooled Prudential Bache, Ernst & Whinney, Hughes, Hubbard & Reed, Oprah Winfrey, and Los Angeles Mayor Tom Bradley, defrauding thousands of stock investors in the process.

Minkow was, however, a small fish compared to those who followed. The misconduct of Charles Keating, the poster child for the savings and loan crisis, cost shareholders—and taxpayers—billions of dollars. The Bre-X mining scandal illustrated that commodities such as oil and gold make great bait. Rogues prey on investors who hope that they too will stumble upon "the bubbling crude," like a latter day Beverly Hillbilly. The notorious "Chainsaw" Al Dunlap made use of every accounting trick in the book, from "channel stuffing" to "cookie jar reserves" and exemplified how ego and greed can combine to destroy a company. Dunlap pumped Sunbeam stock to new highs, but the company, like those headed by the other rogues, ended in bankruptcy, amid a swirl of shareholder lawsuits and SEC and Justice Department investigations.

While John Kennedy's *Profiles in Courage* presented human nature at its best, this book will examine human nature at its worst. The stories of America's biggest business bad guys are fascinating in their own right, but our goal is more ambitious. We want to learn from these rogues, understand their tactics, identify the manifestations of their misbehavior, and develop strategies for countering them so we can avoid being duped in the future.

Corporate rogues are amazingly talented at evading regulators and others who would defend the public against them, but there are almost always signs to be discerned that can tip you off to the fact that something is amiss. The trick is slowing down enough to spot them. During bull markets, and particularly during bubble markets like the 1920s and 1990s, investors tend to become so blinded by greed, so convinced of their stock-picking prowess, that they ignore what in retrospect were obvious, glaring warnings. The American people, chides economist John Kenneth Galbraith, "display an inordinate desire to get rich quickly with a minimum of effort." But that just doesn't happen, and trying to make it so only leaves you open to being victimized by the kind of fraudsters we profile in this book.

The danger signs take many forms—financial, behavioral, and structural. It's important to understand that these signs aren't necessarily an indication of fraud. A company could be perfectly sound and exhibit one or more of the traits listed on the following pages. However, as the accumulation of clouds in the sky indicates an ever increasing chance of rain, the accumulation of danger signs should be taken by investors as an indication of a heightened level of risk. Given the devastating impact of fraud on a company's stock, investors are probably better off getting out of a company that's showing more than a few of the following eight danger signs:

Lesson #1: If It Seems Too Good to Be True, It Probably Is

Think realistically: 50 percent returns, risk free? It just doesn't happen—not in the real world. Corporations—even honest ones—are in the business of making money for themselves. The risk-free rate has averaged approximately 5 percent over the last century. When someone like Charles Ponzi offers guaranteed returns of 50 percent, there has to be a catch. Any investment carries a certain amount of risk. The lower the risk, the lower the potential return you can expect from your money. The mere mention of a low-risk, high-return offer should make your ears perk up, not for a chance to invest, but because there may be something dishonest behind the whole deal.

One corollary to this rule of thumb is to keep a sharp eye out for companies that are reporting much better results than their competitors in a sector—or if they appear to have no competitors at all. It's always useful to compare a company's growth rate and margins with those of companies in the same industry. With the exception of patent-protected products and monopolies, the fortunes of an industry's players will generally rise and fall together. When a company seems immune to the troubles of its brethren, beware. Equity Funding continued to report stellar earnings during the bear market of 1969 while every other insurance company was struggling. Ponzi's case was even more outrageous. Ponzi offered his investors 50 percent returns at a time when bank savings accounts were paying just 4 percent. Perhaps more telling: No other company was even trying to engage in the postal coupon trade—because there was no business to be done! It was a scam from the start. If a business is terrific and there are no obvious barriers to entry, competitors will swarm in. If a business is terrific and there are no competitors, beware.

Lesson #2: Beware of Companies Run by Family and Friends

Running even a small company isn't easy. It certainly can't be done alone. A wise chief executive will surround him– or herself with officers and advisors who know the business, who've been around the block, and who will be willing to offer a contradictory viewpoint if they think it's in the company's best interest. The typical rogue, on the other hand, will want to be contradicted as little as possible so they can keep as tight a hold on the business as they can. At Adelphia Communications, John Rigas placed his three sons in key management positions at the company. With a single family firmly in charge of all aspects of the company, there was no one to prevent them from plundering the company for their own gain—which is exactly what happened.

Surrounding themselves with lackeys and "yes-men" is common behavior among rogues: without a strong board to veto dubious business, a CEO can act however he pleases. A board stacked with cronies not only gives a potentially crooked CEO free rein, it also can create conflicts of interest, which increases the likelihood of misconduct by creating competing loyalties. Watch for directors who are also service-providers, for family members in key executive positions, and for former employees who now serve on the board. Disclosure does not cleanse the problems associated with conflicts of interest. It simply alerts investors that there may be trouble down the road.

When conflict spills into a company's deal-making practices, the potential for abuse shoots up. Related-party or too-close-for-comfort transactions can be manipulated to inflate revenue and reduce expenses. For example, Enron boosted earnings by selling assets to special purpose entities which were majority-owned by the company, and where its CFO, Andy Fastow, served as general partner. These asset sales were not genuine exchanges of value, but rather, fabrications that enabled Enron to hit certain earnings targets. The fact that Enron's CFO was general partner of the entities involved was a sure warning sign that something could be amiss.

In the same vein, watch out for bosses who treat company property as their own. Management and directors are compromised when they indulge themselves with corporate goodies such as private jets, luxury apartments, or in the case of former Tyco CEO Dennis Kozlowski, $6,000 shower curtains. This sort of conduct is a sign that the corporate watchdogs are not focused on enhancing and protecting shareholder value.

Lesson #3: Take a Close Look at Who's In Charge

Whether or not a chief executive has surrounded himself with cronies, it's always worth taking a close look at the chief himself. A simple background check often turns up information that could set alarm bells ringing. A quick check of newspaper archives or a fast search of Google.com can turn up all the information, and save you a lot of pain. Look closely at the track record of a company's officers and executives. What you find may surprise you, and just might save you from making a bad investment.

If a guy has had problems in his past, it's a pretty good bet that he will have problems in his future. Rogues don't tend to reform. Charles Ponzi served two prison terms before fleecing Boston's investors, and McKesson & Robbins' Chief Executive Officer—Dr. F. Donald Coster—was actually Philip Musica, a convicted swindler.

By the same token, be careful with companies where the "numbers" guys have undue influence. In general, it's best to avoid companies where accountants control operations and strategy. Accountants and other financial wunderkind often try to massage a business process or procedure so that more revenue can be recognized on paper, whether or not such quick fixes really generate more profits in the long run. Accounting done properly should simply reflect the health and profitability of a company's operations—it should not influence how a company operates. Financial engineering can be useful to ensure that a company is able to access the lowest cost of capital, but basing a business on maximizing accounting profits often can lead real profits to be sacrificed. When strategy is developed by the numbers guys, it's time to cash in. Not surprisingly, the WorldCom, Tyco, and Enron frauds were all committed by financial cowboys.

Lesson #4: Beware of Companies That Go on Buying Binges

One thing we found as we studied the history of corporate fraud is that there is a much higher propensity for fraud at companies that grow by buying other companies than at companies that grow their businesses organically. Merger and acquisition accounting provides corporate executives with numerous tools to inflate and conflate corporate earnings. It is difficult for even the foremost accounting experts to disentangle the financials of a serial acquirer because of the various charges, write-offs, and reserves that can be called into play, not to mention the challenge of intelligently comparing performance to prior periods.

One simple question you can ask is: What does this company do? If the answer includes too many different things at once, it may be a sign that something's wrong. Fraudulent executives often use acquisitions not as a way to build their company, but as a hiding place to park extra cash or to cover up accounts they don't want to be made public. Acquisitions are also frequently used as a panacea to hide problems in a company's core business. It is particularly concerning when a company buys businesses that are outside its area of expertise. Despite statements to contrary, acquisitions of this nature are usually a sign that the core business is in trouble. Enron's expansion into the telecom industry and Charles Ponzi's expansion into real estate are two examples of straying from one's core competency. The holding company for Charles Keating's Lincoln Savings & Loan, for instance, had investments in everything from hotels to junk bonds to smaller companies that had little or nothing to do with the parent's core business of homebuilding and banking. Adelphia, a telecommunications company, owned a National Hockey League team. While investors may like being associated with such properties, an executive who spends lavishly on areas that have nothing to do with the company itself is at least guilty of bad management, and may be guilty of much more.

Lesson #5: Look Twice at Byzantine Business Structures

Though the structure of a business may be complex, it usually can be boiled down to money flowing in one direction and goods and services in the other. Investors should be able to understand the companies they invest in on a similar level. If a business structure is too complex to comprehend even after some study, it may be a sign that there's something to hide. An elaborate web of holding companies and off-balance-sheet partnerships often are a sign of financial gimmickry. They're tough for investors to untangle, and thus good places to hide debt and fabricate revenue. Executives such as Stanley Goldblum, who used his Equity Funding Corporation to manipulate investors in life insurance and mutual funds, often conceal their fraud behind a web of complex business deals designed to be indecipherable to investors and regulators. Enron's special-purpose entities served a similar function, enabling the company to manipulate results and funnel cash to executives. Given the plethora of regulatory hurdles in place demanding full disclosure, rogues often have to resort to financial sleight of hand. Complex organizational structures enable rogues to obscure their fraud behind layers of indecipherable transactions. Ask yourself whether all the complexity is really necessary. If a company's business structure is too knotty to untangle, and if the chief executive can't—or won't—explain it, take it as a sign.

Lesson #6: Pay Attention to Company Accounts

As a forewarned investor, it's your responsibility to look at more than just the value of your portfolio. Publicly reported corporate financial statements hold a wealth of information that can tip off a wary investor to signs of possible fraud. At ZZZZ Best, for instance, Barry Minkow bragged of how explosive his company's growth was, but his balance sheet showed an organization mired in debt. Of course, poor numbers don't crop up only at fraudulent companies, but when they arise at a company that's claiming great successes, it may be a sign that something's wrong.

Investors should examine how aggressive a company's accounting practices are, as there is wide latitude under Generally Accepted Accounting Principles (GAAP). Not surprisingly, the correlation between aggressive accounting practices and fraud is high. The two areas subject to the greatest abuse are revenue recognition practices and capitalizing costs that should be expensed. At Sunbeam, Al Dunlap booked vast sales that under GAAP should not have qualified as income. At WorldCom, whistleblower Cynthia Cooper exposed a full $3.8 billion in capital expenditures that were intentionally misclassified by the company's CFO, Scott Sullivan, so that their real cost could be spread out over several years.

Inventories can also provide clues as to the health of a company. Rising inventories are often a sign that demand may be weakening, and the company may have difficulty hitting its forecasts. Similarly, rising receivables may indicate that the company is inducing customers to make purchases with enticing discounts, credit, and easy cancellation terms—gimmicks known as "channel stuffing" that have the propensity to accelerate customer purchases, but which steal sales from later periods, ultimately hurting the company. As we will see, Al Dunlap was a channel-stuffer extraordinaire.

One important thing to look for in a company's books is cash flow. Where profits are big, cash flow should be as well. The rate of growth of a company's reported earnings should be substantially similar to the rate of growth in its cash flow from operations. Weak cash flow from operations is a sign that bad debts or inventories may be piling up. It is particularly useful to compare the cash flow statements with the reported earnings over a few years, or to compare reported earnings with the amount of taxes paid by the company. Given the incentives that a corporation has to pay less in taxes, companies run by rogues typically will be more honest with Uncle Sam than with Wall Street, reporting poor results to the taxman but good results to investors. By looking at a company's tax profile, investors can see if a company is telling a different story in its tax returns than in its annual report. If it is, something fishy probably went on between the two sets of numbers.

Lesson #7: Listen to the Skeptics

Don't be afraid of bad news. In fact, it may save you a great deal of money. The signs of fraud are often uncovered first by a small number of people who have been watching a company closely. When those people start to make their findings public, they may be the voice of the minority, but they may have important information to share. Even if a stock is still on the rise, don't discount skeptics out of hand, especially if they're people with knowledge of the industry in question. Veteran mining execs were skeptical of Bre-X's "find of the century" from the start. They turned out to be right, and listening to those in the know would have saved a lot of investors a lot of money.

Skeptics can come from a variety of places. One place to look for them is among short sellers, who are betting that a company's stock will decline. When executives blame short sellers for the decline in their stock price, you can be pretty sure that something else is wrong with the business. David Tice of the Prudent Bear fund was blasting Tyco for taking inappropriate restructuring reserves for two years before the misconduct was unmasked by government officials and the media. If a good number of people are skeptical about a single stock out of all the thousands of public companies, investors should take note. Sharks typically attack only when they smell blood in the water, and short-sellers and other skeptics usually don't waste their time unless they too smell blood.

One good place to look for skeptics is within a company itself. Executives do not leave high paying, prestigious jobs when their business is hitting on all cylinders. Don't believe any executive who says he wants to retire to spend more time with his family or "pursue other opportunities." The resignation of Enron CEO Jeff Skilling, seven months after his promotion, was a major red flag. Had they heeded it, investors could have sold Enron at $40 per share rather than waiting until it was a penny stock.

The same goes for the defection of major service providers such as accountants or lawyers. Accountants are paid to provide auditing services and give an unbiased opinion of a company's books. They are also in the business of making money for themselves and their families. They do not resign from a profitable client unless they are extremely uncomfortable with the company's practices. And given the disruption to a company's financial reporting process that results from changing auditors, companies themselves rarely will fire an accounting firm unless the firm is telling it something it doesn't want to hear—and doesn't want investors to find out.

Investors also should keep an eye out for skeptics in government and regulatory agencies. Any kind of probe is generally a sign to head for the exit. The government has limited resources and picks its targets carefully. Such investigations are distracting to management and can hang over a company for months, if not years. A significant amount of value would have been salvaged by investors who sold their shares upon the announcements of government investigations at Enron, WorldCom, Equity Funding, and Adelphia Communications.

Lesson #8: Beware Too Much Focus on Stock Price

Investors should be wary of CEOs who are more interested in a company's stock price than its fundamental business. Al Dunlap, Bernie Ebbers, and Stanley Goldblum were all far more focused on hyping their stocks than on selling their products and services. Enron went so far as to develop numerous financing transactions that depended on its stock staying above a certain price. This created pressure to exceed quarterly earnings estimates at whatever cost.

CEOs infected with excessive optimism are usually guilty of too much focus on the stock price. Every business has strengths and weaknesses, and a failure to address shortcomings indicates a lack of candor, as well as perhaps a CEOs fear of a stock price decline. Evasive executives will consistently blame soft quarters on the weather, worries about war, or anything other than the underlying health of the business. CEOs who overpromise and underdeliver also tend to create internal pressures that can lead to fraudulent behavior. The performance bar is set too high, and executives are compelled to cut corners to "make their numbers."

The same goes for market size. Stock-hyping CEOs tend to overstate the magnitude of their business opportunity. These exaggerations often lead to disappointment, but more disturbingly, they can trigger financial shenanigans to keep the illusion alive. Due diligence is required to understand whether or not a company's financial projections are reasonable, given a realistic assessment of the market. For example, the significant sales gains achieved by Sunbeam under Al Dunlap were possible only if half of America's families decided that they had to buy new barbeques in the middle of the winter. More recently, wildly inflated estimates of growth in Internet and broadband usage—such as that Internet traffic would double every 100 days—led to a glut in fiber optic cable and billions of dollars in shareholder losses at companies such as Global Crossing and Qwest.

With this cheat sheet of danger signs in hand, we begin our journey through the 20th century's most notorious corporate rogues. Through the retelling of these stories of intrigue, investors will quickly see first-hand that the biggest frauds of the past were, by and large, avoidable. To the educated eye, the danger signs were all but screaming at investors. From Charles Ponzi to Enron, Tyco, Sunbeam, and more, the names may change, but the danger signs have not. By studying the frauds of the past, as set forth in this book, you will be better prepared to avoid the rogues of the future.

Chapter 1

If It Seems Too Good to Be True

As the saying goes, there's no such thing as a free lunch. In 2004, investors also learned there's no such thing as a free dessert, when the high-flying donut maker Krispy Kreme was hit with shareholder lawsuits, a federal securities probe, and allegations of padding sales figures. The following year saw yet more trouble, with franchisees charging that the head office was trying to drive them into bankruptcy and the company's stock plummeting to an all-time low.

What happened? And more importantly, how could investors have protected themselves? After going public in 2000 at $5.25 a share, Krispy Kreme's stock shot up to touch $50 in 2003. Everyone from Rosie O'Donnell to the girls on *Sex and the City* were seen munching the richly glazed treats, and the Krispy Kreme craze took hold across the country. Investing in Krispy Kreme looked like a sweet deal. It almost seemed too good to be true.

In fact, it was. In May 2004, the company reported its first-ever quarterly loss. Within three months, the news broke that the Securities and Exchange Commission had opened an investigation into the company's accounting practices. By the end of that year, Krispy Kreme's stock price had fallen to just over $10, and by late 2005, with a new round of lawsuits in the works, you couldn't get $5 a share for stock in what had once been a darling of post dot-com Wall Street. Should investors have known better? Was there any way to see this coming?

It turns out there was. Even back in 2002, before the company ran into public trouble, analysts here and there were sampling Krispy Kreme's stock and finding it none too tasty. For one thing, the company's stock price was priced for perfection. In late 2002, its price-to-earnings ratio was more than 30 percent higher than that of Starbucks, which had been a smashing success since its own IPO. However, Starbucks was a shining exception to the rule that most fad-oriented food chains (such as Boston Chicken) have a built-in expiration date. When the fad runs its course, the chain—and its stock—crashes and burns. Moreover, Krispy Kreme had neither the management team nor the capital to handle its unrealistic and misguided hyper-growth plan. For example, the company's international expansion plans were being undertaken without much of the market testing one would normally expect.

Krispy Kreme told investors what they wanted to hear: the company would be able to grow its earnings and revenues at 20 percent annually for years to come. Against the background of the imploding tech sector, of course, Krispy Kreme's low-tech growth story made the donut maker hugely attractive to unsuspecting investors. Had they looked more closely, however, they would have seen that not only did Krispy Kreme look too good to be true; but that it shared a number of characteristics with what was perhaps the most famous financial fraud of the 20th century.

Charles Ponzi: "Your Money Back If Not Satisfied"

Almost everyone has heard of "Ponzi schemes," but most of us think of them as crude swindles pulled off via chain letters aimed at the elderly or gullible, not something that could be perpetrated by a company constantly in the public eye. But that's exactly what the Italian-born rogue Charles Ponzi accomplished in the early 1920s, despite intense scrutiny from lawyers and analysts and charges of fraud from people within his own company. His business looked too good to be true—and it was. But that didn't stop people from investing with him—and losing millions of dollars in the process.

Born in Italy in 1882, Ponzi set out for America at the age of 21. He wasn't headed for the land of opportunity to strike it rich, though. Rather, he was fleeing his native country after running afoul of Italy's most treacherous criminal organization, the Black Hand. Having amassed enormous gambling debts, Ponzi tried to make good through forgery and theft, which left him on the wrong side of the Italian mafia. His family, suffering disgrace, decided it would be better to cut their losses. They settled his debts and packed the young swindler off to America with $200 to his name—which he proceeded to lose playing bocce ball on the long steamer trip across the Atlantic.

Standing just 5-feet 2-inches tall, Ponzi was a consummate charmer and unflagging optimist. Though his first years in America were marked by short-term stints working in a macaroni factory, a diner, and a grocery store, he remained convinced that good fortune soon would be his. He wrote to his mother religiously with tales of his impending prosperity, promising to send for her as soon as he could.

After three years in Boston, Ponzi was as broke as ever. Seeking a fresh start, he grew a moustache and jumped a train for Montreal, where he sought out a man named Joseph Zarossi, a Boston businessman who was rumored to have made quite a success of his Montreal cigar factory. It was in Montreal that Ponzi would first hit on the ideas that would later catapult him into the spotlight, first as the supposed benefactor of the Italian immigrants of Boston, and later as one of the worst swindlers the New World had ever seen.

In Montreal, fearing Zarossi might unearth his troubled past, Ponzi posed as Carlo Bianchi, scion of the wealthy but fictitious Bianchi clan of Italy. Taken in by Ponzi's charm, Zarossi hired him on the spot.

But the cigar factory wasn't all it was made out to be. It turned out that Zarossi was dodging the loan sharks that were keeping his business afloat, and had hired Ponzi because he hoped the Bianchi family might be able to help him. Ponzi hemmed and hawed, of course, pretending to turn things over in his mind. Finally, he advised Zarossi that the Bianchis wouldn't be able to help him. But Ponzi had a better idea.

Angelo Salviati, a childhood friend of Ponzi's living in Montreal, had come up with a scheme to recast the cigar factory as a bank. By promising superior returns and capitalizing on its ties to the Italian immigrant community, Banco Zarossi could profit from the millions of immigrants who sent money back to Europe each year to help families left behind.

As those wire transfers slowly worked their way across the Atlantic, the bank would place the money in short-term investments and speculate in foreign currencies. The key to Salviati's plan was to hold the money longer than most banks normally did, capitalizing on the delay to collect interest and earn as much money as possible from speculation.

When Banco Zarossi opened for business, the deposits and transfers poured in. But cracks in the facade soon became apparent. Many wire transfers never made it to their intended recipients, and those that did often arrived with chunks of money skimmed off the top. Transfers that could take weeks at competing banks took months at Banco Zarossi. And the illiterate Salviati, it turned out, was also making "loans" to his friends—loans that would never be repaid. Soon enough, Zarossi found himself facing criminal charges—if he survived his infuriated customers and creditors. Swearing his fealty to Zarossi and the bank, Ponzi urged his boss to leave town, promising to take care of his family. But Ponzi was soon in trouble himself, and was sentenced to three years in jail for forging a $400 check. His first scheme in the New World had ended just as all the others had: badly.

Back in the states, Ponzi continued to knock around, spending time in Pensacola, Birmingham, Mobile, Wichita Falls, and the U.S. Penitentiary in Atlanta before returning to Boston. After 10 years, he had little to show for his time in America. In Boston he went to work for an import/export company and then started one of his own, hoping to capitalize on the booming post-World War I economy. Although goods were streaming in and out of Boston Harbor, Ponzi's talents simply didn't run to an honest day's work. With no clients and few promising contacts, his company struggled. An attempt to launch a trade magazine died before it could get off the ground when the Hanover Trust Company not only refused him a loan but suggested he take his piddling savings account elsewhere.

The Securities Exchange Company

The import/export business gave Ponzi a new idea. One of the most popular commodities among immigrants was transoceanic postage. The stamp business, like the wire transfer business, had exploded as the European immigrants pouring into America relied on the mail to stay in touch with their friends and family on the other side of the ocean.

One of the products they used most often was the postal reply coupon sold by the Universal Postal Union, the international body that still coordinates operations between national postal services. A postal reply coupon enclosed with a letter to Europe could be exchanged in any country for stamps at the recipient's local post office, enabling a return letter to be sent at the original sender's expense. While service was slow, it was a reliable and inexpensive way to make sure one's relatives back home kept in touch.

In postal reply coupons, Ponzi saw an arbitrage opportunity he was sure would make him rich. Currency rates were fluctuating wildly at the time, but postage rates stayed relatively stable by comparison. Ponzi's idea was to send a dollar to a partner in Italy, who would convert it to lire, which could be used to buy 66 postal reply coupons. The coupons would then be sent back to America, where each one was convertible into a 5-cent stamp. Thus, a dollar's worth of postal coupons became $3.30 worth of stamps. By selling the stamps to businesses in downtown Boston at a 10 percent discount, Ponzi could almost magically change one dollar into three.

In the autumn of 1919, Ponzi opened the Securities Exchange Company and set about drumming up investors, offering them a return of 50 percent on every dollar invested. (The remaining $1.50 would be used to pay expenses and go into Ponzi's pocket as profits.) With bonds yielding 6 percent and savings accounts paying only 4 percent interest, Ponzi's offer was hard to resist.

Ponzi was a natural salesman, and his pitch was enticing. Invest $100 and you made $150. Reinvest that $150 and you made $225. In six months, you could more than double your money. The checks came rolling in. The Securities Exchange Company took in $870 in December of 1919, $900 in January of 1920, $5,000 in February, $31,000 in March, and an astounding $141,000 in April.

And the returns, as promised, went rolling right back out again. Ponzi made a great show of paying off his early investors in public after only 45 days, counting aloud as he placed huge wads of bills into their waiting hands. The public loved him, and most of his investors handed their money right back to him, to reinvest in what seemed a risk-free, high-return venture. News of easy money soon spread, and Ponzi's investors became his best marketing tool, pulling in many more customers than he could ever have hoped to find alone.

Ponzi celebrated his success with the purchase of a house on five acres in the upscale town of Lexington, known as the "banker's colony." He paid for it with $10,000 in cash and $20,000 in Securities Exchange Company notes, which would mature for $30,000 in 45 days. So great was Ponzi's credibility that his notes were as good as gold. Ponzi's wife, Rose, quit her job and became a society matron. "There has been no small degree of feminine envy coupled with admiration directed toward the unusually pretty wife of the 'postal coupon king,'" reported the Boston Post. The postal coupon queen was chauffeured around town in a new $12,000 Locomobile, quite outdoing the $4,500 Cadillacs preferred by most bankers.

Ponzi had arrived. Throughout the hot summer of 1920, patient investors waited in long lines to give their money to the brilliant Charles Ponzi. The demand was so great that Ponzi opened more than 30 drop-off sites throughout the city and in outlying towns. "Today all Boston is get-rich-quick mad over him," wrote Marguerity Mooers Marshall in the New York Evening World. "Did I say Boston? My mistake. I should have said the entire New England, from Calais, Maine, to Lake Champlain, from the Canadian border to New Jersey." By late summer, Ponzi was taking in over $1 million a week.

There was only one problem: None of the money was being invested in anything at all.

While Ponzi's arbitrage strategy looked sound, he in fact had none of the relationships, know-how, or even the proclivity to put the money he'd taken in to work in such a scheme. Instead, Ponzi's office was simply bursting with cash, with bills stacked on desks and jammed into drawers. The investors who'd been paid their 50 percent returns had been paid from the funds brought in by later investors. As long as the pace of investment continued to accelerate, Ponzi's business was in great shape. Besides, he was simply raking in too much money to lose sleep over details such as how he would actually generate the promised returns.

When he did think of it, Ponzi figured he'd use the cash to buy promising businesses and sell them at a profit to pay back his investors. Plan B was to diplomatically claim his business had failed, and shut it down without paying anyone back. Of course, he could simply have fled back to Europe with the money at any time, but that idea never seemed to have occurred to him. Though it soon became apparent that something would have to be done, Ponzi had an unwavering, almost delusional sense that he could work his way out of any jam. At this point, though, he was no longer a petty thief. He had learned the great lesson of any big-time con artist: To get ahead, you don't try to lift your victim's wallet; instead, you offer him yours.

With Ponzi's office now filled with garbage cans overflowing with cash, he had to find something to do with all the money. The simplest solution was to spread deposits across all the leading banks of Boston, in the process becoming the largest depositor in many of them. In the Hanover Trust Company, the same bank where he'd been told a year earlier to take his account elsewhere, Ponzi held half a million dollars. When Hanover Trust issued new shares, Ponzi managed to take a 25 percent stake in the bank, and demanded an appointment to the Board of Directors. The bank could hardly refuse, fearing both Ponzi and his devoted followers might take their deposits elsewhere.

Ponzi's acquisition binge didn't stop with Hanover. He went on to purchase stakes in other local banks, including Fidelity Trust, South Trust, and Tremont Trust. He bought a building in downtown Boston, and apartments in Winthrop and West End, and bought up the C&R Construction Company, the Napoli Macaroni Factory, and J.R. Poole's Inc, the import/export company where he'd been earning just $3 dollars a day just one year earlier.

Ponzi was now a major player in the Boston financial community, but his rapid rise had disconcerted the establishment. The Tremont Trust, one of Hanover's major competitors, attacked Ponzi with a series of newspaper ads featuring slogans such as "Real Dollars Are Still Made The Old-Fashioned Way—Working And Saving," and "Our Last Monthly Interest Dividend Was 5-1/2% And Was Paid From Our Earned and Collected Income As Are All Our Monthly Dividends." Even when Ponzi tried to buy Tremont's silence by calling the bank's president, Simon Swig, to offer him more deposits, the disparaging ads continued.

The first sign of real trouble came when Ponzi was sued by a man named Joseph Daniels, who claimed to have given Ponzi some $430 in furniture and cash to get the Securities Exchange Company started. Daniels wanted a piece of the action, contending that he was a partner, not a lender. Ponzi pooh-poohed the claim in an interview with the Boston Post. "When I opened, I bought furniture from Daniels; but he never left any money with me for investment," Ponzi told the paper.

While publicity from the Daniels suit only brought Ponzi new investors, the Post article brought him to the attention of Massachusetts bank commissioner Joseph Allen. Although the Securities Exchange Company was outside Allen's jurisdiction, Ponzi's high guaranteed returns left the regulator uneasy. When Allen requested a meeting with Ponzi, Ponzi gave him his usual pitch about the magic of postal coupons and left Allen's office feeling unconcerned. Allen, though, was far from satisfied.

Nor was Allen the only one with growing suspicions, for the secret of Ponzi's scheme was beginning to come to light. The banks where Ponzi parked his cash could not understand why a man whose business was international arbitrage had yet to receive a single foreign draft or wire transfer. As far as they could tell, Ponzi's money was simply sitting in savings accounts drawing 4 percent interest, and yet he was promising 50 percent returns. Where would those returns be coming from? No one had an answer.

Ponzi was broadsided again when Simon Swig, the president of Fremont Trust, demanded Ponzi remove his money from the bank. Ponzi complied, but the battle had begun, and soon he was pulling his deposits out of all the major banks in Boston, and encouraging his loyal investors to follow suit. Ponzi promised $1,000 to the depositor who recruited the most new clients to Hanover. If Ponzi could trigger a banking crisis, he figured, he could buy up their shares on the cheap, and then sell off the assets of his newly acquired banks to pay off the Securities Exchange Company notes.

Deposits began to roll into Hanover Trust, but its Board of Directors was growing nervous, and Commissioner Allen was now scrutinizing the bank's close association with Ponzi. Allen demanded a guarantee from the bank that Ponzi's business dealings would not put other depositors' funds at risk. To satisfy him, Hanover's board required Ponzi to hold $1.5 million at the bank in reserve.

Ponzi was irate. As far as he could tell, the banking establishment was trying to break him. To keep the public on his side, he hired public relations specialist William McMasters, who distributed pamphlets to every depositor in the region hailing Ponzi's achievements and integrity. At the same time, McMasters sought a full accounting of the Securities Exchange Company's finances.

The Collapse

It wasn't just the banking establishment that had its doubts. Richard Grozier, the new city editor of the Boston Post, was skeptical of Ponzi's postal coupon scheme, and took his concerns to Clarence Barron, a titan of Boston society and the father of modern financial journalism. Barron owned the Dow Jones & Co., *The Wall Street Journal*, and the newly launched *Barron's*, which billed itself as "The National Financial Weekly." Barron did some digging and confirmed Grozier's suspicions. The front page of the *Boston Post* blared, "Clarence Barron Questions The Motive Behind Ponzi's Scheme."

According to Barron, while it was hypothetically possible to make money on postal coupons, the strategy just wasn't scalable to the extent Ponzi claimed. An industrious man could make thousands from the business, but not millions. With a simple phone call to the Universal Postal Union, Barron had turned up the fact that there were only a few hundred thousand coupons in circulation at any given time—a far cry from the $10 to 15 million worth of coupons Ponzi claimed to be trading. Moreover, the U.S. Postal Service had announced several weeks before that it would not redeem postal reply coupons in lots larger than ten, which severely limited the ability to convert large numbers of coupons into stamps, as Ponzi would have had to do—if he'd actually been working his own scheme.

The *Boston Post* confirmed that Ponzi had multiple million-dollar accounts at no less than eight different banks in New England. To Barron, the true nature of the Ponzi scheme was clear. "Right under the eyes of our government court officials," he said, "Mr. Ponzi has been paying out U.S. money to one line with deposits made by a succeeding line."

But Ponzi's devoted supporters were hardly shaken, and the *Post* story drew more deposits than ever. When he arrived at his office that morning, Ponzi found a loyal crowd waiting for him. "Three cheers for Ponzi!" they shouted. They were his people, and they were with him.

At the statehouse, however, Massachusetts District Attorney Joseph C. Pelletier was growing concerned, and he demanded an immediate meeting with Ponzi. Once again, Ponzi made his pitch. Pelletier listened patiently as Ponzi explained the intricacies of the postal coupon business and railed against the jealous Boston banking establishment. When he was done, Pelletier wanted to know only one thing: Could Ponzi cover the Securities Exchange Company's notes? Ponzi was indignant. But Pelletier was not convinced. The District Attorney ordered Ponzi to stop accepting new funds immediately, and told him an audit would begin as soon as possible. Pelletier believed Ponzi was a crook, and was not shy about saying so to his face.

News of the audit reached the papers the next day, and suddenly the public reaction was quite different. The lines that wrapped around Ponzi's building were no longer cheering for him; these people wanted their money back. The crowd grew unruly. Four people were hospitalized with injuries.

Ponzi returned money at a furious pace, refunding at least a thousand claims a day. By the end of the week, the Securities Exchange Company had redeemed all but its most recently issued notes, and Ponzi was confident he had taken care of the "disgruntled souls" and would be able to return to business as usual.

But the rickety underpinnings of the Ponzi scheme were beginning to catch up with him. In the six weeks prior to the panic, his most recent round of investors had bought some 30,000 Securities Exchange Company notes, as many as he had issued in the previous six months. And his newest investors had been buying notes in larger denominations than ever. Ponzi would be hit with a tidal wave of redemptions when the latest notes matured.

Remarkably, Ponzi remained unshaken. He fired back at Clarence Barron and the *Boston Post* with a $5 million libel suit. He met with reporters constantly and blamed the attacks on him on racist conspiracies.

Pelletier, meanwhile, was trying to decipher Ponzi's finances from "approximately 40,000 note cards, several bound notebooks, and sundry loose-leaf sheets of paper." In the middle of all this, Ponzi was hit by the *Post* again: "Ponzi Is Hopelessly Insolvent," screamed the headline. The article beneath it detailed his troubles: "Charles Ponzi is unbalanced on one subject—his financial operation. He thinks he is worth millions. He is hopelessly insolvent. He does not have sufficient funds to meet his notes. He has sent no money to Europe, nor received money from Europe recently."

Painfully, the author of the article was none other than Ponzi's own PR man, William McMaster. McMaster questioned Ponzi's ability to do even basic math, and attacked his "gibberish" about postal coupons. While admitting his complicity for having worked for Ponzi, McMaster demanded that Ponzi come clean and pay back his outstanding note holders.

Once again, crowds surged around Ponzi's office, demanding their money. Even so, a loyal contingent continued to back him. Ponzi proclaimed his innocence, and managed to pay back everyone who demanded their money. That soothed the fears of remaining investors, who figured that if Ponzi could pay off claims so easily, perhaps the claims in the Post were incorrect.

Ponzi also continued to maintain his public profile, despite rumors that he'd skipped town. He spoke to reporters regularly and attended numerous social events. Newspapers chronicled his every move, including the theater shows he attended with his wife and mother, whom he'd finally brought to America after 17 years.

But every time Ponzi seemed to be getting a handle on the situation, the *Boston Post* would strike again. The fatal blow came when the paper uncovered Ponzi's former alter ego, Carlo Bianchi, who had done time in a Montreal jail on a forgery conviction. The *Post* ran a cover story juxtaposing a recent picture of Ponzi, complete with painted mustache, with one of Bianchi. Despite the 12-year age difference, the resemblance was unmistakable. Ponzi, of course, had an explanation: he'd been doing secret work for the Italian government and needed a cover.

This time, though, no one bought the line Ponzi was selling. Canadian officials elaborated on "the old game of paying the first fellow with the second fellow's money." Ponzi was on his way to sunk. Hanover's investigation into his affairs turned up a $500,000 check he had written against the $1.5 million certificate of deposit he'd pledged as a reserve to protect the bank. Auditors discovered numerous loans to fictitious people with names like Charles Pizzi—loans secured by notes from the Securities Exchange Company, and which had somehow ended up in the accounts of Ponzi and his secretary, Lucy Meli. And as Bank Commissioner Allen found, not only were Hanover's books filled with bad loans and worthless guarantees, but "practically every employee and most of the directors have funds invested with the Securities Exchange Company." On orders from Allen, the Hanover Trust was shut down.

The results of the District Attorney's audit, meanwhile, weren't pretty. The Securities Exchange Company held $4 million in assets, but owed

$7 million in liabilities. As Ponzi was arraigned on multiple counts of mail and bank fraud, the *Post* struck again: "The Gigantic Ponzi Bubble Has Burst." It was over.

Ponzi's trial drew national attention. His defense attorney, Daniel Coakley, had a reputation as a brilliant lawyer, though one with questionable ethics. William McMasters and Ponzi's wife and mother all testified on his behalf, appealing for leniency in recognition of Ponzi's philanthropy and good heart. Despite their support, Ponzi was sentenced to five years in a federal penitentiary.

Remarkably, many of his former investors continued to support him. And the most loyal group was the poor immigrant class who had suffered the worst losses. Perhaps they identified with this ambitious Italian man who had taken on the Boston establishment. More likely, though, they preferred defending a con artist to admitting they'd been conned. But conned they were. Bankruptcy proceedings left Ponzi's original investors with only 12 cents for every dollar they'd put in. The deal that had seemed too good to be true had turned out to be exactly that.

Lesson #1: If It Seems Too Good to Be True, It Probably Is

While Charles Ponzi was a remarkable salesman with tremendous charisma and an undying faith in his own ability to get ahead, it is astonishing that he was able to pull off a fraud of such magnitude. In retrospect, the warning signs ought to have been obvious to all.

The most important lesson to take away from the story of the Ponzi scheme is that if a deal seems to good to be true, it probably is. Ponzi was offering guaranteed returns of 50 percent. Even setting aside the fact that no return on any investment is guaranteed, the unusually high returns Ponzi was offering should have tipped investors off. Savings accounts, one of the safest investments possible, were paying only 4 percent interest at the time. Ponzi's promised rate of return should at least have indicated a high level of risk in the postal coupon market, and led investors to contribute only speculative capital, not their life's savings.

But even experienced investors can be taken in by companies that look good on the surface. Such was the case with the scandal surrounding Italian foods giant Parmalat, which went broke in December of 2003.

Like the Securities Exchange Company, Parmalat had been a darling of investors based on its unbelievably strong sales and balance sheet. Unfortunately for investors, unbelievable was exactly the right word to describe Parmalat's finances.

The company's meltdown began when it admitted that an offshore account worth nearly $5 billion did not, in fact, exist. Parmalat had been double-billing clients in order to pad its financial statements, and, like the Securities Exchange Company, had been pushing money through fictitious business deals in order to pump up its results. Instead of the healthy balance sheet it claimed to have, the company was in debt for more than $18 billion, eight times more than it had claimed. Until that moment, Parmalat had been an investor's dream, with financial results that looked too good to be true. Unfortunately for investors, that's exactly what they were.

Parmalat's investors ended up in much the same position as Ponzi's: more than 150,000 of them were left holding nearly worthless bonds. Was there any way for them to have been forewarned?

In fact, many of the lessons of the Ponzi scheme apply to modern-day financial meltdowns. Parmalat's financials appeared too good to be true—and they were. But there were also a number of other signs that should have tipped investors off.

The buying binge that Parmalat founder Calisto Tanzi went on throughout the 1990s should have raised more eyebrows than it did. Among his acquisitions were not only foreign food companies but South American soccer teams and other businesses far outside Parmalat's range of expertise. More than 70 years earlier, Ponzi had taken the same tack, buying up far more banks and buildings than his personal share of the Securities Exchange Company's profits should have allowed. In both cases, two important questions should have come to investors' minds: First, did those in charge have the expertise required to manage these new acquisitions? And second, if the core business was going so well, what need was there to branch out in radically new directions?

Tanzi also went on a spending spree, flitting from company to company in a corporate Gulfstream jet and showering money on charities and politicians. Ponzi had done the same, only in early 1920s style. His chauffer-driven, sapphire-blue Locomobile was the most expensive automobile in Boston. He smoked expensive cigars in a diamond-laced holder and carried a gold-handled walking cane. In both cases, the money for those personal luxuries had to come from somewhere; unfortunately, it came from investors.

Tanzi also followed Ponzi's lead by diverting $630 million from Parmalat to a family-owned subsidiary. Ponzi had funneled cash to himself by writing loans to fictitious clients. Parmalat hid its financial shenanigans by creating fictional business relationships with a series of companies that existed in name only. Both bosses tended to treat company property as their own. In fact, it belonged to their shareholders and investors.

Another way clear signs of trouble can be uncovered is by listening closely to what the skeptics have to say. Sometimes they have a point.

Ponzi's nemesis at the Tremont Trust, Simon Swig, was also a competitor with Ponzi's Hanover Trust. Like a modern short-seller who makes bearish comments on a stock, Swig may have had a vested interest in bringing about Ponzi's downfall, but that doesn't mean his accusations weren't correct. Charles Barron, who was not a competitor of Ponzi's, was harder to dismiss. With only a call to the Universal Postal Union, he uncovered the impossibility of Ponzi's scheme. Ponzi's reaction—a libel lawsuit—was telling. Why did he not address the substance of the allegations?

For that matter, why didn't Parmalat? For almost a year before its implosion, rumors were rife that the company might not be in such strapping financial health. Farmers who supplied Parmalat were not getting paid, and analysts had begun to ask why Parmalat didn't just use some of the cash on its purportedly glowing balance sheet to settle its debts.

In fact, some investors did see the signs, and got out early. Those that did got every penny of their money back. But those who chose to ignore the indications of trouble lost nearly everything. All of Ponzi's investors had access to the same information. But only those who chose to look closely at it and to act on what they saw managed to escape with their bank accounts intact.

Follow the Money

Ploys similar to Ponzi's have been used by modern companies to make their financial results appear better than they actually are. In each case, investors could have avoided trouble by asking themselves one simple question: Is this deal too good to be true?

Canadian telecommunications equipment maker Nortel surprised investors in the first quarter of 2003 by reporting a small profit, even in the wake of the dot-com crash that left analysts expecting the company to report a loss for the quarter. Six months later, the company surprised investors again, by announcing that its earnings for not just 2003, but going all the way back to 2000, would have to be restated due to improper accounting practices.

Like Ponzi, Nortel had found a way to create false profits by shifting around money that, in fact, was doing nothing at all. Nortel had ended both 2001 and 2002 with excess reserves that had been set aside for restructuring and other expenses. But instead of simply recording them on its balance sheet, according to investigators, the company accounted for them as profits in the first half of 2003, even though the income that had generated them had already been recorded. As a result, not only did investors look kindly on Nortel shares, but Nortel executives went home with $50 million in bonuses they didn't deserve.

In reality, Nortel had lost money in the first half of 2003. Rather than give an honest accounting of its results, however, the company pointed to cash it had already taken in and called it profit—just as Ponzi had pointed to cash his investors had given him and called that the profits from his nonexistent trade in postal coupons.

All the companies mentioned in this chapter—from Krispy Kreme to Parmalat to Nortel, as well as Charles Ponzi's Securities Exchange Company—looked great to investors eager to believe they had found a way to beat the market. All of them made themselves attractive by offering returns their competitors just couldn't match. But in every case, they outperformed the competition for one simple reason: what they told investors about the state of their business simply wasn't true.

In every case, investors should have been forewarned. Most financial markets provide conditions under which it's difficult to draw very far ahead of most competitors; only a very few companies will be able to do it honestly. If a return on an investment is wildly out of line with other companies in similar situations or sectors, chances are it's because there's something not right at the heart of things. It's not always the case, but the only way to find out what's really going on is to subject such companies to even more intense scrutiny. If the rewards are real, you'll only be more sure of your investment. If not, you might just have headed off disaster.

In the cases mentioned above, a little digging would have saved a lot of investors a lot of heartbreak. But greed often makes us willing to overlook the danger signs in order to reap the promised rewards. The first danger sign to look for is a company that promises those unbelievable rewards. That's a good indication you need to start looking closer. Because if it seems to good to be true, it probably is.

Chapter 2

All in the Family

A company's assets belong to its shareholders. At least, that's how it's supposed to work, in theory. In practice, corrupt company management and directors who are too cozy with the firm may conveniently overlook the fact that company property is not their own. And in some cases, top executives may install friends in important positions in order to make it easier for them to "forget" who the company actually belongs to.

Such was the case at Adelphia Communications Corp., which in the late 1990s was one of the largest cable television providers in the United States. At the height of the dot-com boom, Adelphia was flying high, diversifying into telecommunications services and broadband Internet access. As far as Wall Street was concerned, the company had bright prospects.

Even so, some investors had misgivings, including over the fact that Adelphia's management team consisted mainly of family members of founder and CEO John Rigas. Still,

Adelphia's shares continued their rise as investors poured in, seduced by the high returns the stock was generating at the time.

Unfortunately, many would soon come to regret their decision. In April 2002, the Securities and Exchange Commission opened an investigation into Adelphia's accounting practices, and just over a month later, the Rigas family stepped down, admitting that more than $2 billion of the company's money had been used to finance family loans. A month after that, the company filed for bankruptcy and the investigation widened. In July 2004, John Rigas and his son Timothy, the company's former CFO, were found guilty of 17 counts of bank and securities fraud and of conspiring to loot the company of millions of dollars.

Most corporate bosses respect the division between a company's assets and their own; if there are signs that they haven't, take it as a bright red flag that fraud and self-dealing may be lurking somewhere in the back office. When management and directors indulge themselves with corporate perks—private jets, luxury apartments or, in the famous case of former Tyco CEO Dennis Kozlowski, $6,000 shower curtains—they not only compromise their positions and that of their company, but they put their investor's money at risk as well.

It's supposed to be the corporate watchdogs, comptrollers, and ombudsmen who flag this kind of behavior before it gets out of hand; if they haven't, it may be a sign that some of them are involved as well, or at least that they aren't doing their job of protecting shareholder value. Unfortunately, the kind of inside transactions that made it possible for the Rigases to make off with Adelphia assets aren't always easy to spot. One warning sign, in cases like this, can be found in media reports, which often raise such suspicions long before federal investigators make the scene.

An easier way to spot a company that's at risk for self-dealing is to look at who's running the business in the first place. A reportedly strong CEO or chairman will generally want to have an equally strong management team. If he or she is surrounded by lackeys and "yes-men," it could point to trouble. This is common behavior among corporate rogues: Without a strong board to veto dubious business practices, a corrupt CEO has free rein to do what he pleases with corporate finances.

Even if fraud isn't the intention, the lack of such checks and balances can endanger even the strongest companies. In Adelphia, many investors saw only the fact that the company seemed to be thriving as part of the dot-com boom, then the fastest-growing sector. But even companies that provide services far more basic than Internet access can stumble and fall under a management team that has only its own interests at heart. Broadband is only the latest hot technology to inspire massive corporate pillaging and fraud. Once upon a time, it was electricity itself.

The Electrifying Rise and Shocking Downfall of Samuel Insull

Do it big, Sammy. Make it either a big success or a big failure.

—Thomas Edison to Samuel Insull

For Samuel Insull, the road to hell may have been paved with good intentions, but it was lit by an Edison Tungsten Filament Lamp. While Thomas Edison may have invented the light bulb and harnessed electricity into a useful element of everyday life, it was Insull who would bring this new technology into the homes of America. Along the way, he would build an empire and become an icon in his own right. But he would also invent many of the creative accounting techniques that are routinely used by corporate rogues today. In the end, his willingness to use his company to further his own ends would bring down not only his utility empire, but some 5 million small-time shareholders as well.

Insull's is an inspiring rags-to-riches story—or it would be, were it not followed by a last chapter that returns him to the rags. Born in 1859 to a London dairy farmer, Insull was a driven man from the start. At age 14, despite his father's wishes that he become a minister, Insull took a job as an office boy at a firm of auctioneers. His salary was only five shillings a week (approximately $1.25); more valuable were the skills he was learning: shorthand, stenography, and bookkeeping. Three years later, Insull started working a second job. After a long day at the auction house he would spend four hours with Thomas G. Bowles, the founding editor of *Vanity Fair* magazine. From 8 p.m. to midnight he would take dictation from Bowles, then return home to sleep—but only until four in the morning, when he would awake to transcribe his notes from the night before and deliver them to the printer on his way to work.

Insull's taste for publicity was acquired soon thereafter. Through Bowles, he joined a literary society, soon rising to become its secretary. While in that position, Insull arranged for Phineas T. Barnum to give a lecture to the society on publicity and promotion. Barnum was one of the most well-known promoters in America and founder of *The Greatest Show on Earth*, the circus that had become one of the most popular entertainments in America. Insull was clearly fascinated by how Barnum was able to raise his profile so high so quickly, and the two would cross paths a number of times over the younger man's career.

Insull's association with Edison began in 1879, after he was ousted from his job with the auctioneer in favor of an important client's son. Insull turned to the classified ads and was intrigued by an American banker looking for a London secretary. Insull wrote to offer his services for 30 shillings a week and got the job.

His new employer, Colonel George Gourand, London director of the Mercantile Trust Company of New York, turned out to double as the European representative of Thomas Edison. For Insull, this was a stroke of great luck. He had read accounts of Edison, the 31 year old inventor, in *Scribner's Monthly* magazine, and had even given a lecture about him to the literary society. Edison had become a kind of hero to Insull, and when he discovered Gourand was Edison's man in Europe, Insull was ecstatic.

He worked tirelessly for Gourand, becoming the office stenographer, bookkeeper, and secretary, accompanying Gourand to conferences in London and on the continent, and learning the principles of corporate finance and the intimate details of Edison's European affairs. When Edison's chief engineer, Edward Johnson, visited London that fall, it was Insull who demonstrated the most detailed knowledge of Edison's every asset, transaction, and liability in Europe.

It was also Insull who was most impressed by Edison's genius. During his visit, Johnson was to oversee the installation of Europe's first telephone exchange. But Alexander Graham Bell's Bell Telephone Company had just won a court order preventing Edison from using any technology based on Bell's patents—including a transmitter that was part of Edison's exchange. The exchange looked sunk, but when Johnson and Gourand cabled Edison the news, their boss told them to proceed as planned, and that a replacement for the transmitter would just have to be invented. Within 60 days, Edison had invented and delivered just such a replacement, and the exchange was completed without further delay. Insull, having witnessed at close range Edison's brilliance and commitment, became only more determined to tie his fortunes as closely as possible to those of the American inventor.

To do that, Insull knew he would have to become thoroughly knowledgeable about the technical aspects of Edison's business. With Johnson's engineers in London to install Edison's exchange, Insull took advantage of their expertise. He carried their tool belts, peppered them with questions, and watched closely as they deployed this new and magical technology. When the first small switchboard was installed, Insull acted as its first operator.

By adding technical expertise to his understanding of Edison's financial affairs, Insull was soon one of the most valuable people in Edison's European office. Still, he had yet to meet his idol, nor was Edison even aware of the younger man's existence. To further his aspiration of working directly with the inventor, Insull made himself indispensable to Johnson. Soon enough, with a little prompting from Insull himself, Johnson was working to find Insull a position assisting with Edison's business affairs in America.

It took until January 1881 before Johnson found him a post. But when Edison's private secretary resigned, Insull was chosen as his replacement, and on February 28, after almost two weeks at sea, Insull set foot on American soil for the first time. Later that evening he met Edison himself. As one historian later described it, "Insull looked at Edison, and Edison looked at Insull, and both were disappointed; each said to himself, 'My God! He's so young!'" Insull was only 21, with a slight physique and baby face that made him look more like 16. Edison, though he had already invented the stock ticker, telegraph, mimeograph, phonograph, and transmitter that made the telephone practical—and claimed to have invented electric lighting, electric power, and electric transportation—was just 34.

If Edison had any doubts about his new hire, they were dispelled that same night. The inventor had just received half a million dollars in financial backing for his electrical innovations. But he was in need of far more money in order to build the central station that would allow him to make the technology available on a commercial scale. With only $78,000 in his bank account and stakes in several European businesses, Edison was considering selling his most valuable assets to finance the building of the station himself. Insull, who had been a close student of Edison's European holdings for more than a year, immediately showered Edison with a systematic, concise, and thorough overview of his European assets, along with their approximate worth, potential buyers, and a coordinated strategy for liquidating the portfolio.

Edison was awestruck, and the next day offered Insull $100 a month for his services. Though he had been making close to twice as much money in London, Insull accepted without hesitation, and quickly became indispensable to the older man, opening his mail, writing his checks, and serving as his personal assistant for12 years.

Though he was known as a relentless taskmaster, it seemed that Edison had finally met his match. Although he might be called to work at any hour of the day or night, the rewards, as Insull saw them, were well worth it. Managing Edison's affairs soon brought him into contact with some of the most important and powerful members of American society. Well known actors, politicians, newspaper men, and bankers, as well as heads of foreign governments, were all regular visitors seeking to meet the man who had invented the magical lamp.

Insull had joined Edison at a particularly exciting time. Having invented the electric light bulb, Edison now faced the formidable task of commercializing it, introducing the public to the contraption that would make both the candle and the oil lamp obsolete. But Edison's technology required an enormous, sophisticated, and expensive infrastructure—every component of which would have to be invented from scratch, by Edison himself.

Edison managed to construct the first central power station himself, opening the Pearl Street Station in New York on September 4, 1882. But the problem was money. Bankers were willing to finance isolated power plants designed to service small numbers of buildings, but financing for a central station that would serve an entire community was more than they were willing to risk. By the spring of 1883, over 300 isolated power stations had been built, but Pearl Street remained the sole central station in operation.

Edison saw central stations as crucial to his vision of bringing electric light to everyone, not just to those rich enough to afford an isolated power station. Nor was he one to be deterred by what others thought of his plan. To make his vision a reality, he formed the Thomas A. Edison Construction Department, whose mission it was to sell and build central stations wherever it could. The man he put in charge of it was Samuel Insull.

The 22 year old Insull traveled the country for 18 months, dead set on fulfilling his mandate. Though he faced city governments that were often corrupt or beholden to established gas companies, Insull managed, by the end of 1884, to arrange the construction of almost 20 central power stations. Having studied P.T. Barnum, he was a natural salesman. He also relied occasionally on some not-quite-legal financial arrangements to convince city councilmen to buy into Edison's vision.

Within 10 years, Insull would become one of the most important and powerful men in the fast-growing electricity business. Edison had sent him out into the world with instructions to "Do it big, Sammy. Make it either a big success or a big failure." His plans were to do just that. He had headed up the Edison Machine Works and the Edison General Electric Company, overseen the merger that created General Electric, and moved to become the president of the Chicago Edison Company in 1892, where he would fast gain a near monopoly on power distribution in Chicago. Insull stopped at nothing to buy out his competitors, and soon built the largest power generation facility in the world.

To garner customers, though, Insull instructed his staff to sell power at whatever rates were necessary. With his stream of acquisitions costing him money, he soon found his company starved of cash. To solve his problem, Insull embarked on the first of the creative accounting practices that would eventually cost his investors their capital.

To keep his company afloat, Insull needed to raise $6 million in debt financing. But even with more assurances than usual, Insull's bankers were unable to obtain the necessary funds from Chicago investors. To give lenders an even greater degree of confidence, Insull designed a "depreciation reserve" that would insure that the collateral offered to secure the bonds was adequately maintained. While it wasn't an underhanded practice, it was certainly non-standard. Insull sent his representatives to London with the package and within a week they had sold out the offering.

But $6 million hardly scratched the surface of what Insull had in mind. Insull wanted to bring electricity to every house in Chicago and beyond, a task he figured would cost at least $250 million. When he went to the Chicago Edison Company's board of directors to request approval, he was turned down flat. While the board had no problem with Insull's business strategy, it was difficult for them to accept their company's taking on such a vast sum of debt all at once.

Insull, however, had an idea. Rather than go to his board with a specific number, he would instead ask approval for what he called an "open-ended mortgage," essentially an instrument with *no limit* on its value.

It would be presented to the board as a way to raise a smaller amount of capital more easily; in reality, it was simply an endless promissory note that Insull would eventually borrow more than half a billion dollars against in the course of his career.

The board bought his plan, and Insull was off. He had no fear of debt; in fact, he thrived on it. He knew his companies would never be able to pay off everything they owed, but it didn't matter—they'd simply refinance whenever they needed to so that the entire amount they owed would never come due.

Insull was married in 1898, and his son, Samuel Insull, Jr., was born in 1900. During this period, he acquired a subsidiary, the Commonwealth Electric Company, which would use the newly developed alternating current technology to bring electricity to the areas around Chicago. But to take full advantage of his licenses, Insull needed to effect a merger between them. The accounting methods he would use to do this would push him further toward the gray line between honesty and fraud. Rather than use the conventional "straight-line" method of depreciating assets, which reduces profits bit by bit over a number of years until the capital investment is fully depreciated, Insull chose not to account for any depreciation at all until the asset was retired and then set aside. This allowed him to report higher ongoing profits, and lower capital expenditure needs than was actually the case. The merger of Chicago Edison and Commonwealth Electric into Commonwealth Edison looked great on paper, at least as Insull added it up, even though the combined $45 million company had more debt than equity to its name.

To speed the adoption of his product, Insull also put to use the lessons in public relations he'd gleaned from his acquaintance with P.T. Barnum. More than 15 years before it was required, Insull began publishing annual reports. (Although Insull's read more like marketing materials than financial disclosure documents.) He spoke at numerous civic and community functions, and he trained his employees in public relations as well. He also established one of the first corporate public relations offices, which published a free magazine, *Electric City*, that was distributed to newsstands across Chicago.

Flush with success—and no doubt aware of the goodwill that it would bring him—Insull suddenly developed a generous heart. Like Charles Ponzi, he was the champion of the little guy, doling out a few thousand dollars a year to charitable organizations, but up to $50,000 in small amounts to individuals in need. "I specialize in individual cases," Insull said by way of explanation.

But by now, Insull's combination of ambition, drive, and ego had led him to cross the line. The handouts he made in his own name were not in fact drawn from his own money, despite the fact that he was now worth more than $1.5 million. Instead, they came from the coffers of Chicago Edison. And it would not be the last time he would spend company money as if it had come out of his own pocket.

In fact, the lines between Insull's money and his company's finances soon began to be irreparably blurred. In 1911, Insull established a new corporation, the Public Service Company of Northern Illinois, which would seek to dominate the rural market throughout the state, just as Commonwealth Edison did in and around the city. But because rural electrification had long been considered a fool's task, Insull had trouble raising funds for the company. Instead, he began to finance the Public Service Company based on his own personal credit. His stature in the community let him personally borrow $500,000 at interest rates as low as one-third of what lenders would have required Public Service to pay.

By the beginning of World War I, Public Service had grown into a $50 million enterprise. But as with all of Insull's ventures, it had become difficult to determine where Public Service ended and Insull's other companies began. Public Service's infrastructure was intertwined with Commonwealth Edison's at numerous strategic points, as had been the case between Commonwealth Electric and Chicago Edison. To further bind the companies, Insull put in place a group of managers and advisors whose counsel he respected. This group joined him at each company he managed. The team that headed Public Works was thus indistinguishable from the one heading Commonwealth Edison and the smaller companies Insull controlled.

Insull was now unstoppable. Until founding Public Service, he had either played second fiddle to a brilliant man like Edison, or had been constrained by the collective wisdom of a board of directors. But as Insull's ability to raise funds against his personal credit surpassed that of his companies, neither his board nor anyone else could confine him.

How he would use that power would be determined by a personal tragedy. For five months in 1912, Insull's son was confined to quarantine in the Insull house with scarlet fever. Insull's wife joined him there, despite the risk of catching the highly contagious disease. But Insull himself chose to remain outside the house to run his business affairs, and for five months spoke to his wife and child only through the closed windows of his home.

Samuel Insull, Jr. recovered from the disease, but his wife never recovered from what she saw as a betrayal by her husband. During her time in quarantine she had decided that she could never be as close to Insull again. Insull's marriage, as he knew it, was over. He was 52 years old.

Insull reacted by throwing himself into his work. While he had already built a small empire, he now set out to build an enormous dynasty that he could pass on to the son he knew he had abandoned in his hour of need. He began to expand his business, buying up electricity companies across the nation. His public persona reached new heights. And he began to involve his relatives in the running of his sprawling business empire.

Soon after his son's quarantine, Insull set his sights on the purchase of more than 50 small electric companies throughout the midwest. Despite the fact that his son was only 12 years old at the time, Insull brought him along to discuss the acquisition with his lawyer. The two men, with Samuel Insull, Jr. at their side, set up a holding company to purchase the assets. Insull's brother Martin was brought in to run the resulting entity, the Middle West Utilities Company.

Insull's empire was now in a position ripe for exploitation by a chief executive who was already less than scrupulous in the separation of his public and private finances. Through some creative manipulation of assets between Middle West Utilities and its operating companies, Insull was able to use the credit of some operating companies to raise debt that could then be used by others.

Though he was perhaps well intentioned, the move was Insull's first major step toward the fraud that would eventually take down his empire. In essence, he was stealing from one group of shareholders to give to another. Insull, of course, didn't see it this way. He viewed his business empire as his own private enterprise. He held sole management rights and owned much of the equity in his companies. And as he realized, much of their success was due to his personal involvement and participation. The particular corporate structure—and its attendant legalities—didn't matter to Insull. He saw his empire as a whole and cared only to increase its reach and worth on that basis. If he could do so at the expense of one or two of his operating companies, so be it. Unfortunately, this was not what his investors had bargained for.

With his sense of restraint fading fast, Insull soon found himself diversifying, and he continued to play fast and loose with his company funds. He had Commonwealth Edison guarantee $6 million in debt for the Chicago Elevated Railways Trust to help them effect a gigantic merger. In 1914, when the merger did not come off, Insull's company suddenly had to come up with $6 million with which to purchase 80 percent of the Trust. Now Insull owned another holding company, and controlled not just electricity, but elevated railways in Chicago as well. And when People's Gas, Light and Coke Company came to Insull for help, claiming it had developed a gas engine that could produce electricity more cheaply than Insull's companies, he arranged to become chairman of the board.

World War I turned Insull into an even more prominent success story than he had been before. His efforts to raise money for the war effort, solve labor shortages, and fight high prices of necessary materials like coal turned him into a war hero without his ever having fired a shot. It also left him with a robust public relations machine in place, which he soon turned to his own purposes, creating the first modern investor relations division—one that pushed the idea that support for Insull's utility company was a form of patriotism.

To build further support for his empire, Insull turned his wartime fundraising machine into what was essentially the first retail equity sales operation in America. By selling preferred stock to as many "Mom and Pop" customers as possible, Insull hoped to create what is now known as a "buy-in." If the public owned equity in his companies, he figured, they would be more likely to look kindly on its operations, and to spread that positive image throughout their communities. Insull set out to turn his customers into owners, and his owners into supporters.

His plan worked beautifully, and by the mid-1920s it was hard to find anyone in Chicago who wasn't a huge booster of Insull and his various ventures. His employees certainly loved him. He had begun to shower them with generous benefit packages, including free life insurance, education, medical care, disability compensation, and pensions, and he had purchased a beautiful resort in Wisconsin that employees were able to use at little expense. He had also created employee associations for them, including savings and loans and mutual benefit associations. Few of these things were available to most workers in America at the time. In addition, Insull offered his employees shares at attractive prices, as well as commissions on any stock they were able to sell to family and friends.

What few people knew, though, was that throughout these post-war years, Insull had bankrolled most of these expenses himself. He had largely neglected his business affairs during the war, favoring the war effort itself instead. As a result, his railways were nearly bankrupt, and were relying on Commonwealth Edison for the funds they needed simply to stay afloat. Public Works was scraping by, but had not seen significant profits for some time. Middle West Utilities, meanwhile, was deeply in the red.

To save his empire, Insull doled out his own money as needed. He paid all the salaries at Middle West for a number of years, and he personally borrowed more than $12 million in order to keep the company afloat. He shifted finances from one company to another at will. Finally, as the economy began to rebound in 1923, his empire seemed to have moved out of danger.

Meanwhile, though, Insull lost half a dozen of his closest advisors to old age or illness. At 63, he was now left with a stable of young managers around him, all of whom were either his relatives or people who owed their entire careers to Insull. He was a giant of the industry, with complete control over the boards of directors of all the companies he ran. He was the heart of his empire's financing, and there was no one left alive in his companies who could challenge him. His control was complete—and it would soon lead to disaster.

The year 1923 saw Insull launch another holding company, this one with J.P. Morgan. Known as Midland Utilities, Insull-control entities accounted for 75 percent of the holding company's subsidiaries. Insull promptly turned over the Midland reins to the control of his son, then only 23 years old.

Insull had finally managed to install his son in a position of prominence within his empire. Now he set his sights on amassing the fortune he would eventually pass on to Samuel Jr. In 1927, drained by the war and the corporate financing that had come out of his own pocket, Insull had only $5 million to his name—much less than his success and stature would suggest. And given that his personal credit was still worth more than that of his companies, he considered himself vastly underpaid.

With the complete control he held over his companies, it was easy enough to give himself a raise. To find the money, he would simply shift funds around among his operating companies through shady loans and purchases until extra cash appeared in a holding company. In December

1928, Insull created another holding company to give himself even more flexibility. This one, Insull Utility Investments, or IUI, was meant to "perpetuate the existing management of the Insull group of public utilities," according to a press release. But by this time, Insull alone effectively constituted that management, and if by "perpetuate" the press release actually meant "enrich," well, IUI would eventually become a smashing success.

The scheme got off to a troubled start, though, when Insull's operating companies failed to deliver sound profits in the first quarter of 1929. To overcome their troubling performance, Insull began to shift assets from company to company in order to create the illusion of profits. Because each company was an independent entity, he could sell an asset of one company to another, on credit and at an inflated price, and thereby create a "profit" where none otherwise existed.

But the profits Insull concocted led to other problems. Insull's companies paid generous dividends to their shareholders. Bigger profits meant bigger dividends, but with no actual profits coming in, Insull was forced to pay shareholder dividends out of his operating capital.

Insull's independent auditors were anything but pleased, and they refused to sign off on his books. As they saw it, his corporation should have suffered an operating *loss* in the first quarter of 1929. Eventually, though, they caved to Insull, and he tallied his books using whatever techniques he chose.

Insull took IUI public in 1929 in the midst of the one of the biggest bull markets Wall Street had ever seen. Based on Insull's inflated financials, IUI's shares rose from $12 to over $150 by the spring of that year. "My God, $150 million dollars!" Insull exclaimed to a colleague. "I'm going to buy me an ocean liner!"

Now 70 years old and secure in his legacy (at least for the moment), Insull was finally thinking of retirement. He ran five major companies worth more than $3 billion combined, had more than half a million bondholders and 600,000 shareholders (staggering numbers for the time), and in the weeks after the crash of 1929—which would usher in what we now call the Great Depression—he opened the Chicago Opera House, a project he had spearheaded with the sale of $20 million in stock and bonds. He had achieved his goal of making electricity a mass-market product; he boasted more than four million customers and his companies produced more than one-eighth of the electricity and gas used in the United States.

The stock market crash, though, had reinvigorated Insull's desire to be seen as a man of the people. His new round of philanthropy began with his own employees. Many of them had been encouraged to purchase shares in Insull companies on margin; after the crash they were exposed to margin calls, forced to come up with the money to cover the full amount of their purchases. Perhaps out of concern for his employees or perhaps out of concern for his share price, Insull immediately set about lending his workers the money they'd need to cover the calls.

As word of his charitable nature got out, people from all walks of life came to Insull seeking help. Insull sought to help them all, taking on the debts and responsibilities faced by others as his own. Soon, local businesses were asking Insull for support. By January 1930, he had leveraged his clout, credit, and cash to help hundreds of employees, businesses, and other individuals.

Insull's reputation as a kind and giving leader of the community grew, but as it turned out, it was not Insull's money he was using to help the citizens of Chicago. Instead, he was tapping his company funds. Insull had been through economic downturns before, and reasoned he'd be able to make it through this one without substantial difficulty. To Insull, it didn't look like the depression would last very far into the 1930s, and given what he thought of as the fiscal and operational strength of his companies, his generosity on their behalf endangered nothing.

But this depression was different. And it would soon become much worse. States and municipalities that had overspent during the boom of the 1920s began to face severe financial pressures. By January 1930, Chicago, facing a $50 million deficit, was on the verge of bankruptcy. Understanding that the city's financial troubles threatened the paychecks of thousands of police, firemen, and teachers, Insull did not sit idly by. Instead, he used his company resources to guarantee the city's debts and help cover its expenses.

Insull found opportunities to help wherever he looked. New England's textile and shipbuilding industries had been devastated by the depression. In March, Insull stepped in.

April saw Chicago teetering once again. This time the city actually went to Insull, cap in hand. By popular referendum, a measure was passed seeking Insull's help in bailing out Chicago's transportation system. Insull responded by launching a project that would ultimately require $500 million of financing, all of it secured by Insull's companies and his personal fortune.

Insull also responded to President Hoover's call for American businesses to continue to conduct "business as usual" as a means of pulling the country out of the depression. So Insull made $200 million in capital investments that year, despite an economy that simply couldn't justify spending on such a large scale.

The money for Insull's investments, of course, had to come from somewhere. To fund his expenditures, each of Insull's operating companies, which were already highly leveraged, increased their outstanding debt. Another $90 million in debt was issued by IUI and another Insull holding company, the Corporation Securities Company of Chicago. In total, Insull took on over $200 million in new debt in 1930—the very worst of the Great Depression—and raised another $48 million to enable him to take majority control of his entire collection of companies in order to protect them from takeover schemes.

Miraculously, his company profits appeared to be immune to the depression. As the rest of corporate America withered, Insull's operating companies reported a 15 percent increase in earnings in 1930, and profits hit another all-time high in the first half of 1931. Even in the utility industry, Insull's companies stood out as the only ones that remained financially healthy.

Insull's "profits," however, were accomplished through sleight of hand. Once again, a bit of creative accounting allowed Insull to draw on the reserves he had set aside to offset depreciation, and instead chalk the money up as income. But as he did so, those reserves were fast disappearing. And this time, Wall Street took notice.

As Insull's reserves dried up, analysts and market insiders soon realized that Insull was using the cash to artificially inflate his company profits. Word of his brazen and aggressive accounting techniques soon spread across Wall Street. Many bankers began to question whether Insull had gone mad. Though the laws governing the fiduciary responsibilities of corporate managers would not be passed for four more years, in the form of the Securities Act of 1934, Wall Street was already well aware of what was good practice and what was not. Insull's willingness to use the credit of his companies to support public institutions and other causes seemed anathema to good business.

Wall Street was not too shocked to take advantage of the opportunity, though. Insull was in a vulnerable position. If his shares declined too far, he would eventually be in violation of numerous bond covenants and would be pushed to the brink of default. This would send the stock price further downward—much to the benefit of any short-sellers. Soon enough, banks were aggressively selling Insull's companies short, and profiting as the stock price continued to sink.

Insull learned of the short-selling soon enough, and for a moment seemed to have the problem licked. His primary financial advisor devised a strategy whereby Insull himself would short the stock ahead of the New York bankers, so that the company was hedged against any downward movement. A short experiment yielded $500,000 in profits, but Insull put a stop to it, realizing it would bankrupt all of his employees and the 5 million investors who had put their trust in him. In the end, he was unable to do directly what he had been doing all along through his holding companies: profit through their demise.

The week of September 9, 1931, was Insull's last stand. The market had pushed his stock down precipitously, lopping $150 million off the market capitalization in that week alone. To make matters worse, the economy had finally caught up with him, and his companies' earnings had begun to sag. Soon, Insull and his companies were unable to meet their financial obligations and violated the covenants on their outstanding debt. To stave off bankruptcy, Insull, IUI, and Corporation Securities had to pledge bigger and bigger stakes in Insull's operating companies. Too late, Insull began to realize the extent of his peril. And when his time of need arose, there was no one willing or able to help him. He had stretched his credit to the limit, and the few tricks he had left up his sleeve had no effect. Within six months, he and his businesses were insolvent.

Lesson #2: Beware of Companies Run by Family and Friends

What I did, when I did it, was honest.

—Samuel Insull

Insull's story has caused problems for historians for almost a century. Was he simply scapegoated for a business that, despite his best efforts, succumbed to the Great Depression? Or was he a megalomaniac whose desire for fame, wealth, and acceptance caused him to inflate earnings, misuse corporate funds, and squander the wealth of his shareholders?

Insull fled to Europe in the wake of the collapse of his companies, but was extradited and tried in 1933. On the trip back to America, Insull defended himself to a State Department escort: "What I did, when I did it, was honest; now, through changed conditions, what I did may or may not be called honest. Politics demand, therefore, that I be brought to trial; but what is really being brought to trial is the system I represented."

Under the laws of the day, Samuel Insull was found not guilty.

The establishment of the Securities and Exchange Commission the following year, though, helped settle the question of what the system saw as right and wrong. Measuring Insull's actions against current regulations, it is easy to see where he betrayed his obligations to his shareholders, his employees, and the public trust. But regulations aside, investors of his day, like those of today, could have pinpointed when this good man turned bad by identifying the warning signs.

In Insull's case, as in that of the Rigas family and Adelphia Communications, one of the clearest signs that something might have been amiss was the gradual replacement of a strong cadre of advisors with family members, "yes-men," and other cronies. Insull had climbed to the pinnacle of the business world with the help of strong, proven advisors. Long after he left Thomas Edison's side, Insull surrounded himself with experienced lawyers, accountants, and businessmen. At Chicago Edison, he enjoyed a strong board willing and able to say no when the situation required it. But as Insull's success grew, he turned more and more to family and other insiders to help run his businesses, and began to eschew the advice of experienced men outside his empire. As Insull's public persona grew, it eventually trumped any leverage such advisors could have brought to bear. Insull not only felt he could do as he pleased, but was actually able to.

In any era, that's a potential problem. When John Rigas, head of Adelphia, installed his three sons in key management positions in the company, there was no one to check the family's many excesses—including the use of company funds to build a golf course and buy a National Hockey League team, the Buffalo Sabres. When the Rigases used billions of dollars to finance family loans, no one was there to stop them.

Chief executives can avoid such pitfalls by surrounding themselves with advisors who are not afraid to call a situation as they see it. If the head of a company instead chooses to surround himself with friends and family who are more likely than not to simply nod, investors should take some time to consider whether this is the company in which they want to invest.

One of the main dangers, which both Insull and Adelphia fell prey to, is the temptation to treat company property as one's own. Insull used his company money not just to enrich himself but to help out the less comfortable of Chicago. Tyco CEO Dennis Kozlowski, on the other hand, who was convicted in June 2005 of fraudulently looting his own company of millions of dollars, was not so charitable. He used his shareholder's money not just for that $6,000 shower curtain but for a multi-million dollar Manhattan apartment and a lavish $2.2 million toga party he threw for his wife's birthday.

It is easy to see where a man like Insull could start to lose track of where his funds ended and his companies' began. It was largely the force of his personality and his own personal creditworthiness that had led to the success of his companies. Nevertheless, it is a CEO's responsibility to keep the two realms separate, and wherever there are indications that the two are being mixed, investors should take it as a warning sign, and insist that an unbreakable wall be maintained between the business and personal funds under the control of a CEO.

Setting a Precedent

One of the most remarkable things about the financial improprieties pulled off by Samuel Insull is that companies have been getting away with the same kinds of things for the seven decades since he was exposed. And in each case, the same set of warning signs could have been made out by sharp-eyed investors.

Among the things to look out for is a business that's reaping far better results than its competitors. Insull startled Wall Street by reporting his miraculous profits in 1930 and 1931, while the rest of the country was going bottom-up. But some things a CEO just can't control, no matter how smart or powerful he is. When Insull's companies continued to report record profits in the teeth of the Great Depression while other utilities were struggling to stay afloat, it was a sign that something was amiss. As a rising tide lifts all ships, a receding one usually sinks them all in equal measure. Investors should be wary when the numbers appear to defy the laws of nature. Any business that is not being affected by trends that are sweeping the sector in question, or the economy as a whole, is one that should raise questions.

Insull's profits, in any case, were hard to believe. One sign that they might have been less than solid was the fact that they were always accompanied by cash-flow problems. In a young company that needs a large amount of capital investment to grow, this wouldn't necessarily raise an eyebrow. But Insull's companies were deeply entrenched in the business they had built and were by all accounts wildly profitable. They should not have required ever more debt to finance their operations. The fact that they did should have been a warning sign.

Another thing to watch out for is a complex structure of relationships between subsidiary companies. The holding-company structure that Insull used is one that has always been susceptible to fraud and mismanagement—and remains so today. The financial shenanigans of Enron, for instance, were made possible by the same web of relationships between a parent company and part-owned, independent entities. In both cases, the arrangements put management's interests at odds with that of the shareholders they were responsible to. And in both cases, the shareholders lost.

The shell companies and derivatives schemes that Enron created bears another parallel to Insull's case, in that both companies leaned in part on non-standard accounting practices that were not clearly illegal at the time, but which have now come to be seen as deeply unethical, and in some cases have been made illegal since. In fact, any non-standard accounting practice should be worrying to investors. GAAP, or Generally Accepted Accounting Principles, had not yet been invented in Insull's time. But the degree of his deviance from the norm was quite wide, and investors should have been concerned. As with Enron, Insull's books were so different from those of his peers that an apples-to-apples comparison wasn't possible, and that fact alone should have tipped investors off to the fact that something was wrong.

Insull's critics on Wall Street had a point. Investors should have listened to them and been deeply concerned when Insull became the target of short-sellers. Yet many hung on to the end. By then it was too late. In Insull's case, as with most cases of corporate fraud, the signs could have been made out long before that point. In the end, it's up to investors to decide whether they want to be forewarned.

Chapter 3

Who's in Charge?

The advisors who surround a chief executive can serve as enablers, allowing a company to drift into troubled waters, as Samuel Insull found. But it's no surprise, of course, that the background of the person at the top can be one of the most important factors in the health of a company. A strong and capable CEO who knows his or her business can lead a weak company to profits and new strength. But a CEO who's focused on the wrong aspects of a business, or not focused on the business at all, can lead a strong company into disastrous straits.

The question of who's in charge is also an important one to ask when considering an investment, because many investors will be surprised to find that not all CEOs are exactly who they say they are.

That doesn't necessarily mean there's an active deception going on, just that the person at the top may not be the best person for the job. One of the most basic questions to consider when weighing the pros and cons of investing in a company is whether the CEO is truly knowledgeable about the underlying business of the firm. Companies run by executives with a firm grasp of the fundamentals of an industry are typically safer bets than those run by numbers jockeys, financial cowboys, or investment bankers.

In general, it's best to avoid companies at which bankers or accountants control operations and strategy. A case in point is that of telecom company Global Crossing. Founded in 1997, Global Crossing set out to provide undersea broadband connections that would link financial institutions and consumers all over the world. The company sold itself on the rising demand for Internet services, and investors bought in big time. The company went public in August of 1998 and its stock price more than tripled within eight months, to $64 a share.

Less than three years later, Global Crossing filed for bankruptcy.

What happened? Was there simply not enough business for the company to survive? In the end, it seemed that there was hardly any business at all, and never had been. Instead, Global Crossing had managed to survive as long as it did simply by raising cash through successive rounds of stock sales. When the company went under, it wasn't even clear whether it could actually provide the level of service it advertised.

Had investors taken a closer look at the man who headed up the company, they might have seen the disaster coming. Global Crossing's CEO, Gary Winnick, was not a telecommunications expert, nor a man with particular expertise in the broadband and connectivity sectors. Instead, he had been a junk-bond trader at Drexel Burnham, where Michael Milken pioneered a number of investment banking techniques that ultimately landed him in federal prison.

Winnick dodged a bullet when Drexel imploded, but Global Crossing shareholders would not be as lucky. With the assistance of five different Chief Executive Officers over three years—a danger sign if ever there was one—Winnick provided great incentive for investment banks to recommend his stock. If the share price rose, the investment banks made huge fees, as Winnick raised more capital and pursued numerous acquisitions. The only problem was that Wall Street ignored the health—or lack thereof—of the business itself.

Similar pitfalls can arise whenever too much emphasis is put on share price at the expense of company fundamentals. The person at the helm of a company should be first and foremost concerned with building the business and generating profits. With strong results in place, strong share prices will follow. The opposite is not always true. A strong share price may sound attractive to investors, but without good fundamentals to back it up, it's simply not sustainable.

Too much focus on share price can lead a company to overstate the potential of a business rather than giving an honest account of where things could go, as was the situation with Global Crossing. But in many cases a chief executive who is too focused on pumping up the stock may lead his company to higher stock prices through less than honest means if the fundamentals simply aren't there.

Global Crossing crashed into bankruptcy while Winnick escaped with hundreds of millions of dollars from stock sales. But in his defense, at least he used his real name.

Philip Musica (aka F. Donald Coster, M.D.): Bootlegger or President?

According to *Who's Who* of the 1930s, F. Donald Coster was born in Washington, D.C. in 1884. But finding people who had known the pharmaceutical executive all his life would not have been easy, because the man known as Donald Coster was actually Philip Mariano Fausto Musica. True, he was born in the same year, but to an immigrant family headed by an Italian barber that had settled in Mulberry's Bend, one of the toughest neighborhoods of 19th century Manhattan.

Philip Musica grew up on streets that were "the scenes of many wild fights," where "many a time the ready stiletto ended the lives of men, or the heavy club dashed out the brains," according to Charles Hemstreet's 1889 book, *Nooks and Corners of Old New York.* Although Musica soon would grow into the corruption he saw all around him, his first heroes were not the local *padrones*, forerunners of the mafia, but rather Theodore Roosevelt, the president of the New York Board of Police Commissioners. Roosevelt had recently lost a New York mayoral race and had not yet achieved fame with his Rough Riders at San Juan Hill, but the teenage Musica loved Roosevelt's style and mannerisms, and his high-pitched Harvard voice and refined English.

But formal education bored Musica, who quit school at age 14 and went to work at his father's grocery store. Under Musica's leadership, the store thrived, providing his family with a stable income and financial security.

His techniques, though, were a sign of things to come. Musica trained a younger brother, Arthur, to run the day-to-day operations of the store, while Musica himself moved into the import/export business. By the time he was 24, he had moved to the top of the rough-and-tumble world of New York's docks, eliminating middlemen and importing cheese and other foodstuffs directly from Italy. A. Musica & Son became one of the most successful retailers of fine Italian food in New York, grossing around $500,000 in 1908 and launching Philip Musica into high society. He took to it well, dressing in expensive, custom-made suits and smoking the finest Havana cigars. He dined at the city's best restaurants, dated beautiful women, and swung with the stars of Broadway and the opera.

But the good times were short-lived. In 1909, New York mayor G.B. McClellan instituted a series of anti-corruption measures, including an investigation of the East River waterfront. As the nouveaux riches of the docks, the Musicas stood out, and city officials questioned their speedy ascent through society.

What investigators found was that the secret of their success was bribery. By paying customs officials up to $500 a shipment, the Musicas were able to radically reduce the tariffs they should have been paying on imported cheese, giving them a huge advantage over their competitors. In October of 1909, both Musica and his father, Antonio, were indicated on federal charges of fraud. Musica pled guilty in exchange for having the charges against his father dropped, and was sentenced to a year at the New York State Reformatory at Elmira.

Once out of prison, Musica returned to his family and to the import/export business. This time, though, rather than being chastened by his encounter with the law, Musica expanded his vision. His opportunity came in the form of human hair, which was used in the elaborate coifs and extensions that were popular among women of the period. As the son of a barber, the career move was only natural. What Musica would do with it, though, was something else entirely.

Imported human hair sold for approximately $80 a pound—far more than the 16 cents that a pound of macaroni would bring. Musica built a business of importing and processing hair that would then be sold to wholesalers. His United States Hair Company had operations both at home and overseas, and Musica's long hours meant that money was soon rolling in. He moved his family to a much larger home in the Bay Ridge neighborhood of Brooklyn, and Musica himself maintained a permanent suite at the Knickerbocker Hotel in midtown Manhattan. As socially ambitious as he was financially driven, Musica was soon back to his old life of fine wine, women, and song. But he was well aware that the Musica family fortune was nothing compared to the old money of the Social Register or the spectacular sums men were making on Wall Street. Musica was only in his mid-20s, but already he felt he belonged in the same place. The slow, steady accumulation of riches was not for him.

To speed his ascent, Musica sent his mother to Naples, accompanied by her son Robert and her four daughters, carrying letters of introduction that Musica had forged for her. Armed with the letters, which described her as the representative of a large, global corporation with headquarters in New York, Mama Assunta, as she was known, soon achieved entrée into the top ranks of Neapolitan business and finance. Her ostensible mission was the purchase of long strands of human hair for export to America.

To finance the purchases, she obtained large loans from Italian bankers. As collateral, she provided invoices for hair shipments she had brought to Italy. The crates themselves, however, were filled with worthless sweepings from the floors of barbershops in New York, covered by a thin layer of expensive hair on top. No matter—the bankers bought her story.

After the success of this initial mission, Musica set up satellite offices in major cities around the world—London, Berlin, Hong Kong, St. Petersburg, and Yokohama. He advertised each as the local branch of a major player in the human hair trade. In reality, however, the offices were little more than mail drops for a flow of concocted correspondence about financial transactions that never really existed. In July of 1912, when Musica was 28, the United States Hair Company was incorporated with a capitalization of $2 million, listing as assets $600,000 worth of human hair, most of it held abroad. Musica artfully moved invoices, letters of credit, deposits, withdrawals, and loans around the globe to construct what appeared to be a thriving business. Meanwhile, his fictitious inventory of human hair continued to increase.

Musica's apparent success fed his stature and credibility. In October of 1912, U.S. Hair's shares began trading on the New York Curb Exchange at $2. So popular were Musica and his company that the shares were snatched up by speculators and immediately climbed to $10.

Less than six months later, his tenuous web of lies began to unravel. Two British banks caught wind of the pyramid debts that were being used to inflate the company's business profile, and had refused to honor U.S. Hair drafts totaling $135,000. The Anglo-South American Trust Company, one of the banks that was financing Musica's business, wanted to know why.

Musica put on his best song and dance for the bankers and assured them he would clear up the mistake immediately. But word got out. Shares in the company began to plunge. Musica tried to stem the tide by buying up shares with his own money, but he knew the game would soon be over.

Rather than give up, though, Musica hatched a plan to extract as much money as he could from U.S. Hair before his kingdom crumbled. At the Bank of Manhattan, he sought a $370,000 loan to cover the entire value for what he said were 216 crates of fine human hair that were sitting in his warehouse. While the bank refused to make the entire amount available, they did give him $25,000 in exchange for the collateral, despite the suspicion that already surrounded Musica. The so-called hair merchant was hardly dismayed by the small sum, however, as he had a sheaf of duplicate bills of lading that he used to secure similar amounts from other banks around New York. He extended his takings by purchasing diamonds and jewels on credit from a number of friendly Fifth Avenue boutiques, and he withdrew all the funds from the Musica family's various bank accounts.

If it looked like Musica was getting ready to make off with his ill-gotten gains, that's exactly what was happening. Musica was well aware that his financial dealings were grossly illegal. He had previously purchased a number of international law books, from which he had learned which countries had extradition treaties with the United States, and for which crimes. He had identified Italy and Honduras as possible sanctuaries from prosecution, and had even acquired a steamer, the *Evelyn*, which he registered in Uruguay and intended to use if he needed to flee.

But the *Evelyn* was at sea when he needed her most. A clerk at the Bank of Manhattan noticed that the paperwork for Musica's collateral appeared to have been altered. When representatives of the bank were sent to the piers to inspect the crates of hair, they discovered Musica's ruse of covering worthless barbershop sweepings and old newspapers with a thin layer of valuable hair. The total value of the shipment was less than $250, far short of the $370,000 Musica promised.

Federal deputies raided the offices of the U.S. Hair Company the next morning, but Musica escaped in the nick of time. Though the *Evelyn* was unavailable, he concocted an alternate plan, leading the entire Musica family on a spectacular railroad getaway from Long Island to Washington, D.C. and then on in pairs to Atlanta, Mobile, Alabama, and finally New Orleans. By the time officers reached the Musica estate in Bay Ridge, it had been ransacked. Furniture, paintings, rugs, linens, silverware—everything had been removed. The Musicas were on the run.

And they might have gotten away, had it not been for a private detective named William Burns, hired by the American Bankers Association, who discovered that a bellman at the Knickerbocker Hotel had sold Musica a $12 steamer trunk a week before. Burns tracked the trunk to New Orleans and a passenger ship named the *Heredia*, due to sail for Panama in the next few days. Musica played it cool, posing as a man named William Weeks, but one of his sisters gave the game away. New Orleans police seized all the Musicas' loot, including many thousands in U.S. and Mexican currency, all the diamonds and jewels, and a quarter of a million dollars in insurance policies.

With A. Musica & Son forced into bankruptcy, no less than 78 creditors entered claims, some for more than $135,000. Evidence surfaced that Musica had funneled more than $250,000 to Mama Assunta, who was still in Naples. But she denied the accusation in an Italian court, and the Musica family finances could not be untangled to prove her wrong.

At his trial, Musica pled youth and inexperience, and claimed to have been defrauded by several European firms. "The embarrassment we find ourselves in was due to the failure of three large human hair exporting and importing firms—two in France and one in England," Musica claimed. "We intended remaining away until such time as matters could be adjusted. If I had only had a little more time, everything would have been straightened out and every last creditor would have been paid."

Amazingly, the prosecution bought it. Once again, Musica was allowed to plead guilty while charges against his family were dropped. Musica himself was remanded to the Tombs, New York's historic downtown prison and home of notorious criminals like Dutch Schultz and Abe Landau, to await sentencing.

Even in prison, Musica was able to turn his charm to good effect and profit by playing one side against the other. In the Tombs, he became a stool pigeon for the district attorney's office. But rather than being despised by cops and robbers both, Musica managed to win the respect of both sides of the law. To his fellow prisoners, he was a big-shot con artist who had swindled the leading figures in financial and social circles—he was royalty. To the district attorney, he was a brilliant young businessman who had made a mistake. This time Musica's scheme worked. He was able to put off his sentencing for three years, at which point he received a suspended sentence and was released.

As a reward for his career as a stool pigeon, Musica was hired as a special investigator for the state Attorney General's office. Here again, his methods seemed to fall somewhat short of honesty. In 1919, Musica won a murder conviction against Joseph Cohen, a poultry trucker with a questionable reputation, by convincing a fellow alumnus from the Tombs to sign an affidavit stating that he had heard Cohen hiring killers in an East Harlem saloon. Cohen was eventually let off, and Musica was indicted for soliciting false testimony. Again, he was able to use his charm to avoid being brought to trial; 13 years later, three men rang the doorbell of Cohen's Brooklyn home and fired nine bullets into his body. The assailants were never apprehended, but some believe Musica ordered the hit.

Musica spent much of his time as a special investigator hunting down suspected spies and draft dodgers during World War I. Typically, though, thoughts of personal gain were never far from his mind. William Randolph Hearst's newspapers had given the Musica family sensational treatment during their two family scandals, and Musica had not forgotten. But Hearst had also defended Germany's ruthless sinking of the passenger ship *Lusitania* and the murder of its 1,200 passengers. Musica set out to paint Hearst as a German collaborator, producing affidavits signed by chauffeurs, doormen, and bellboys to the effect that they had seen German Ambassador Von Bernstorff and Bolo Pasha, the top German propagandist in the United States, enter Hearst's Riverside Drive home on several occasions. Musica, of course, was an experienced forger, but Hearst had powerful friends. Senate hearings on wartime espionage dragged Musica's name through the mud. His career with law enforcement was finished.

In 1919, Musica was a 34 year old, twice-jailed swindler, stool pigeon, forger, and discredited investigator in need of a new line of work. He didn't have to look far. The 18th Amendment—better known as Prohibition—had just been passed, and there was plenty of money to be made in booze.

But with two prison terms under his belt, Musica wanted to generate Prohibition-style profits with an air of respectability. So in 1920, Musica took the name of Frank Costa and started the Adelphi Pharmaceutical Manufacturing Company. The company manufactured hair tonic and cosmetics, and Adelphi had a government permit to draw 5,000 gallons of alcohol a month for use in the manufacture of its goods. But instead of reselling the hair tonic, almost all of the company's wholesale clients simply distilled the alcohol out of Adelphi's products, and paid a huge premium for the privilege. Adelphi kept two sets of books: a fictional one showing sales at the normal competitive price, and an actual one with its huge bootlegging margins included.

Adelphi was a success, but Musica's ambitions had grown. He abandoned the company in typical fashion: An anonymous tip to a Treasury agent forced the company to shut down. Musica's partners, with whom his relationship had grown strained, were arrested for bootlegging. No charges were filed against the company's owner, Frank Costa, who had disappeared.

The Birth of Dr. Coster

Frank Costa was no more, but Musica was alive as ever. Flush with cash from the Adelphi scheme, Musica transformed himself into one F. Donald Coster in 1923. Dr. Coster was a native of Washington, D.C. and an alumnus not of the Tombs and the Elmira reformatory, but of the University of Heidelberg, where he had earned both Ph.D. and M.D. degrees.

As Coster, Musica established Girard & Co., another small manufacturer of pharmaceuticals, in Mount Vernon, New York. With his air of upper-class haughtiness, the sophisticated intellectual that was Dr. Coster quickly won the respect of Mount Vernon's leading citizens.

Like Adelphi, Girard sold high alcohol content products to bootleggers, who paid far more for them than the company would have received from the drugstores that were its supposed customers. To conceal its illicit sales, Musica forged invoices to legitimate customers. One of the company's biggest clients was W.W. Smith & Co., a sales agency headed by one of Musica's brothers, who had taken the name George Venard. Though a number of Girard's products competed in the legitimate marketplace, W.W. Smith diverted a substantial volume of the high-proof products to bootleggers.

As another of Musica's brothers who was involved in the scheme would tell investigators years later, "On paper, we sold enough shampoo to wash every head in the world. But 90 percent of it we sold to bootleggers." One of Girard's biggest bootlegging customers was the notorious underworld figure Dutch Schultz, who would convert hundreds of barrels of shampoo into 8-year-old rye or Highlands scotch overnight.

This time, the scheme worked. In its first year in business, Girard & Co. generated approximately $500,000 in revenue. But Musica wanted the company to be recognized as an important and growing enterprise. To build prestige, he decided to hire Price Waterhouse & Co., which he had heard described as "the blue ribbon outside auditors in the country." In December 1924, Price Waterhouse received a letter from the fictional P. Horace Girard requesting an estimate for auditing the company's books and providing advice on bookkeeping. As the letter declared, "We expect to branch out in a different field in the coming year, and we believe that our present system of bookkeeping could be greatly improved." Price Waterhouse accepted the assignment for an annual fee of $550.

Musica knew from his U.S. Hair Company experience that auditors wouldn't normally check warehouses and inventories, but were interested only in reviewing a company's books and supporting documents to make sure the numbers added up. And indeed, Price Waterhouse scrutinized neither Girard's merchandise nor its customers. Even W.W. Smith & Co., which now accounted for more than 10 percent of Girard's business, went unexamined. Despite Musica's fraudulent inflation of receivables, inventories, revenues, and profits, Price Waterhouse attested to the integrity and financial health of the company, and certified that it held assets of $295,000. With this blue-ribbon certification in hand, Musica set out to secure more financing and take his business to the next level.

Musica moved his expanding business to a larger facility in Fairfield, Connecticut, and there secured $400,000 in financing through the sale of preferred stock to Connecticut investors. The deal was handled by Clinton Barnum Seeley, who owned the Bridgeport-City Trust Company. (Seeley might have done well to heed the advice of his grandfather, circus showman P.T. Barnum, who famously declared that "there's a sucker born every minute.") Seeley also had made a personal investment with a loan of $80,000 from his bank, which Musica made sure to pay back within a year. Like Charles Ponzi, Musica understood that there was no better way to take money from people than to first put money in their pockets.

With Musica's bootlegging operation generating enormous profits, Girard was able to pay generous returns to its investors, and Dr. F. Donald Coster soon earned the adulation and respect of the highest reaches of Connecticut business and society. He and his wife Carol lived in an 18-room Italianate mansion on a 7-acre estate, mixed with national politicians, local businessmen, and foreign dignitaries, and looked after Carol's two dozen chows that she kept as show dogs. Dr. Coster's stature soon grew so great that he appeared in *Who's Who in America*. His entry, of course, reflected his talent for fiction. Not only did he falsify his own birth certificate, he also moved the date on his marriage license back five years to conceal Carol's previous divorce, and changed her maiden name to Schieffelin, a socially prominent family in the pharmaceutical industry.

As Girard & Co. grew into the largest bootleg distributor on the east coast, the company came under suspicion. But Musica was always able to put off the skeptics. Bank officers, underwriters, and even federal agents—all were no match for Musica's charm, forgery, and bribery.

But Musica wanted nothing less than to become a major player both in the American pharmaceutical business and on Wall Street. He set his sights on the 90-year old firm of McKesson & Robbins, a large distributor of drugs that had fallen on hard times. Best known for its tooth powder, McKesson had a factory in Brooklyn with 50 employees, and sold products to drugstores throughout the Northeast. Though McKesson's business wasn't what it had been, Musica recognized the value of the sterling national reputation it still enjoyed. In the autumn of 1926, Musica raised $1,650,000 in a stock sale and acquired McKesson & Robbins. He moved the company from Brooklyn to Connecticut and installed his family members—under aliases—in key executive positions.

Soon the company's books were filled with fictional sales of pharmaceutical products to reputable department stores. The larger scale of McKesson's facilities and revenues provided Musica with even better cover for his illicit sale of alcoholic products. Most of this merchandise was channeled through W.W. Smith & Co., which fabricated its own invoices to legitimate customers. Musica's brother Arthur, under the guise of George Vernand, served as the front man for both W.W. Smith & Co. and Manning & Co., the purportedly unaffiliated private bank that Dr. Coster used.

At the same time, Musica used McKesson's legitimate business to pump up its reputation even further. Through legal and political wrangling, he broke monopolies on Chilean iodine, Peruvian quinine, and Bolivian bismuth. His anti-trust crusade generated great publicity and national acclaim for Coster. Based on his success in foreign markets, Musica set up McKesson & Robbins, Ltd., a wholly-owned Canadian subsidiary established to trade in "crude" drugs—raw materials such as saffron from Spain and balsam from Peru that were used to make retail pharmaceuticals. Only Musica and his pseudonymous brother, George Dietrich, had access to the accounts and operations of the Canadian subsidiary.

At the end of 1927, McKesson & Robbins reported profits of $600,000, including robust earnings in the new crude drug division. Dr. Coster's company had investors and directors of unimpeachable social and economic standing. The stock market was booming. It was time to make another run at Wall Street.

This time, Musica set out to expand McKesson's scope further by consolidating hundreds of the nation's regional drug distributors and independent drug stores under one banner. National chains were dominating the business, and small outlets had trouble getting new products and replenishing their inventories. Musica planned a stock swap with independent owners, who would then become salaried vice presidents in the parent company, and be given local autonomy as part of a national distribution network. In 1928, Musica raised $9.7 million through a preferred stock issue, and merged no fewer than 16 regional distributors into McKesson. Julian Thompson, of the respected Wall Street firm Bond & Goodwin, which had helped structure the deal, was brought into the company as treasurer. Together, he and Musica would soon add 50 more distributors and raise an additional $22 million.

Over the next few years, Musica's organization weathered two potential disasters that could have ended everything. The stock market crash of 1929 cost Musica dearly. He spent millions of dollars meeting margin calls and buying up his company's stock, and he pushed his wholesalers to get more McKesson products into the field, even if it meant extending credit to weak retailers. (The company wrote off $3 million in bad debts in 1932 alone.) Musica was also forced to push his fictional accounting operation into overdrive to funnel still more profits from the bootlegging business into the legitimate arm of the operation.

But the legitimate arm of Musica's business was actually doing quite well. So in 1932, when the second near-disaster hit, Musica was prepared. The election of 1932 brought Franklin Delano Roosevelt to the White

House, and subsequently, the end of Prohibition. Musica's bootlegging profits, which were a large part of what kept his operation afloat, might have dried up completely. But in anticipation of the repeal of the 18th Amendment, Coster established a planning board to organize McKesson Spirits, Inc. so that the company would be prepared to sell alcohol the moment it became legal.

Julian Thompson secured valuable supply contracts with European wineries, and the company had a built-in distribution system though its 66 regional wholesalers—not to mention its relationships with the nation's leading bootleggers, many of whom soon became legitimate businessmen in their own right. In the two years following the repeal of Prohibition, McKesson & Robbins' liquor subsidiary generated sales of $22 million. In 1936, the company acquired the assets of Hunter Baltimore Rye Distillery, and in 1937 McKesson's booze business recorded sales of $45 million—all of it legal. Coster had made a seamless transition from outlaw bootlegger to legitimate liquor distributor

An Entire Letter-Writing Plant

By 1937, McKesson & Robbins had grown into one of the largest pharmaceutical companies in the United States, with annual sales of $174 million and a net income of $3.5 million. Dr. F. Donald Coster was a titan, respected for his remarkable business acumen, his stature in high society, and his philanthropic deeds. But although he was a member of the most prestigious clubs in the northeast—including the New York Bankers Club, the Lotos Club, the University Club, and the Brooklawn Club—he rarely showed his face at these places, preferring the relative isolation of cruising down the Long Island Sound in his 123-foot yacht, the *Carolita*, and dropping anchor among the yachts of the Vanderbilts and the Morgans. Musica enjoyed the tranquility of the sea. It was the one place he didn't have to worry about being unmasked. He almost never traveled into New York City and, when he did, he stayed in his hotel room and avoided public places. The Republican National Committee leadership presented him with a telegram declaring that GOP bigwigs would unanimously back him for a run for President in 1940. Coster respectfully declined. He seemed to be on top of the world. But the burden of his past kept him from truly enjoying his enormous success. He lived in fear of being recognized as Philip Musica, the twice-convicted swindler.

Meanwhile, Julian Thompson, Musica's former investment banker, had settled into his job as treasurer of McKesson & Robbins. After a decade with the company, he had made and lost a fortune in the stock market, authored a Broadway hit in his spare time, and assisted Coster in building one of the great success stories of the 1930s. But something wasn't quite right. As treasurer, Thompson had access to all of McKesson's operations—except those of McKesson & Robbins Ltd., the company's Canadian subsidiary dealing in crude drugs, which Musica kept close to his vest.

Thompson began to question the isolated nature of the McKesson Ltd.'s business, which consistently generated the best profit margins in the company and ploughed all of its profits back into the crude drug trade. The unit's inventory and accounts receivables had grown to an astounding $18 million, and Thompson felt that a portion of the subsidiary's profits should be returned to the parent company to reduce outstanding debt. When he brought the idea to his boss, though, he was met with only indignation: "Do you consider it good business to hobble the most thriving division of the company?" Coster demanded.

Thompson knew that Coster was rarely open to a proposal that was not his own, so he took a different tack, discretely raising the issue with several McKesson directors. To avoid a direct challenge to Coster, the board voted to cut the inventories of all divisions by a total of $4 million and use the savings to trim the company's bank debt. The Canadian subsidiary's share of the inventory reduction was to be $1 million. An unhappy Coster accepted the majority decision.

Thompson's eyebrows were raised, though, when Musica saw to it that his attempts to visit the company's Montreal warehouses were thwarted. Thompson had known Dr. Coster for 13 years, from long before he was hired at McKesson, but for the first time he began to worry that something was amiss.

Thompson's suspicions deepened when he learned that Musica had not cut inventory at the Canadian operation, as the board had decided, but had in fact increased it by $1 million. Moreover, Thompson could find no record of insurance for the Canadian inventory. As Musica explained it, W.W. Smith & Co. (the company his brother ran, which had disguised sales to bootleggers as legitimate business) handled all of the business for the Canadian unit, including its insurance. Thompson was skeptical of the arrangement, and Musica blew his top—which

Thompson only took as an indication that his boss might have something to hide.

As Thompson looked more closely, real problems began to come to light. W.W. Smith's annual fee of $150,000, it turned out, was being paid not by the Canadian unit but by the parent company, an arrangement Thompson found alarming. And when he contacted Dun & Bradstreet, the respected business-rating company whose reports on W.W. Smith were provided to Price Waterhouse & Co. during their audits of McKesson, he found that the reports were bald forgeries.

Quietly, Thompson looked into the flow of cash into and out of the crude drug business. While the parent company's records indicated that W.W. Smith had accounts with Chase National Bank and a New York City branch of the Royal Bank of Canada, both of these accounts were small and rarely active. Instead, Manning & Co., another mysterious firm that Thompson had never heard of (also controlled by Musica's brother), appeared to be the main conduit for the funds.

Thompson confronted Dr. Coster over lunch, declaring that he needed to know everything about the crude drug operation. Coster challenged him: "Do you actually believe, Thompson, that there are no assets in our crude drug division?"

"You're too smart not to have assets," Thompson responded. "But I've got to know what they are and where they are. And I want to know why you are stalling me." Coster assured his treasurer that the Canadian company was "entirely healthy," and promised to collect documentation for Thompson in the next few days.

Instead of waiting, though, Thompson went straight to the office building that housed both W.W. Smith and Manning & Co. There he found a two-room suite with only a receptionist and George Vernard (Musica's brother) who reeked of alcohol. Vernard dodged Thompson's question by telling him he took his orders only from the Montreal headquarters. When Thompson left, Vernard called George Dietrich to warn him that McKesson's treasurer was on the scent.

Thompson was closing in on the truth, and the truth did not look pretty. McKesson Ltd., according to its extremely detailed records, traded millions of dollars in crude drugs around the world. The "profits" from the inventories and accounts receivable were fabulous. Coster repeatedly told his Board of Directors that he was stockpiling the drugs in anticipation of better market conditions. But Thompson discovered that the Canadian unit's five warehouses were only small offices that rarely saw much activity. In reality, no drugs were trading hands at all. Musica, with the help of his brothers, who were the only other people to have access to the business of the Canadian unit, had concocted one of the most intricate and well-constructed frauds of all time.

The crude drug division was in fact a complete fabrication. The subsidiary's numerous foreign offices and warehouses were actually just mail drops. Dietrich's job was not to buy and sell crude drugs but to manufacture fake documents to create a fictitious inventory that would fool Price Waterhouse & Co. Purchase orders, records of shipment, factory orders, and sale orders were all generated from nothing, and Dietrich scrupulously saw to it that all of them matched and added up perfectly.

It wouldn't even have taken a visit to the Montreal warehouses to uncover the ruse. To enhance the fiction, Musica would mention casually in board meetings that the company had identified an opportunity in Mexican vanilla beans, or would expound on the demand for Algerian rose-geranium oil, powdered Malayan dragon's blood, or Peruvian balsam. But anyone with even rudimentary knowledge of the crude drug trade could have identified Musica's lies and errors. For example, there were not enough Himalayan musk deer in the world to fill the orders McKesson & Robbins Ltd. placed. The company shipped vanilla beans in tins rather than 200-pound bags. And the amount of procaine or iodoform allegedly stored in the Canadian warehouses represented four years supply for the entire United States. While it is perhaps understandable that such errors were never caught, any observant auditor should have been concerned about shipments that moved merchandise from South America to Australia and China "by truck."

Musica knew his Canadian operation was in danger of being exposed by Thompson, and he moved to defend it, transferring McKesson & Robbins shares from his wife's name to a nonexistent relative, Herbert Dietrich, and engaging two top flight lawyers, Benjamin Slade and Hartford Mayor Thomas J. Spelacy, to help him develop a strategy to block access to the company's records by "conspirators."

When Thompson confronted Musica again at his Connecticut home, the head of McKesson knew the end was near. Musica had George Dietrich remove records, canceled checks, and cash from the company's vaults, and hide two ledgers in an abandoned shack on the McKesson factory grounds. He then proceeded to sell off McKesson & Robbins shares held by various relatives (real and fictional). The denouement had begun.

Days later, on December 6, 1938, a McKesson shareholder named Vincent W. Dennis filed an equity receivership action against McKesson & Robbins. Dennis was corporation counsel for the City of Hartford, but in this case it seemed like he was working for Musica. Dennis had been a shareholder for only a few hours—his filing was part of Musica's plan to tie up McKesson & Robbins' records until the $20 million of fictional inventory could be justified somehow or else completely covered up. A federal judge appointed Musica's lawyers as trustees. The plant was chained shut, bank accounts were frozen, and the remaining records were seized; which was just how Musica had planned it. With his business and its records in receivership, Thompson's investigation would be halted.

Despite the receivership, and a trading halt in McKesson shares, the company's stock did not come in for panic selling, so great was Dr. Coster's stature in financial circles at the time. When McKesson's executive committee asked the Securities and Exchange Commission to launch an investigation, Musica fell back on his reputation. He had his trustees issue a public statement emphasizing that the receivership related to only one of the company's numerous divisions: "The crude drug department of the company is the only department involved. [The investigation] is quite unrelated to the principal business of the company, and there appears to be no question of the company's solvency and continuance in business. All departments, except that involved, have been advised to continue as usual."

But Thompson and the executive committee had other plans, and petitioned the courts for a reorganization of the company under Chapter X of the Chandler Act, which then governed bankruptcies. Federal judge Alfred C. Coxe granted the petition, and appointed a trustee to develop a reorganization plan, manage the business, and protect the company's assets. In deference to the federal court action, the Connecticut receivership was dissolved. Musica no longer had anywhere to hide his fraud.

McKesson & Robbins was the first major corporation to reorganize under Chapter X, and the media and legal profession watched with special attention. The fictionalized accounts soon became front-page news. Price Waterhouse & Co. accountants gave baffled testimony. Ambrose McCall, a Price Waterhouse manager, testified that no one from his firm had ever visited the Canadian warehouses. Instead, McCall said, statements of supplies were checked against records in the Fairfield offices of McKesson & Robbins. A physical audit would have been of little use, in any case: "After all, they could show me a barrel of crude drugs and say it was this or that, and I wouldn't know one from the other."

McCall's partner, Geoffrey Rowbottom, was similarly bewildered: "I can't bring myself to believe that the whole thing is nonexistent," he said. "There must be assets someplace, but where I couldn't tell you. An entire letter-writing plant would have been necessary to transact the alleged sales and to mail statements to or from warehouses concerning stocks of crude drugs on hand, if this had been done fraudulently." Musica's secret was finally out.

Musica and the two brothers who had served as his accomplices were arrested on December 13, 1938, and released on bail. Two days later, his worst nightmare came true.

The publicity the case generated meant Dr. Coster's face had been splashed across newspapers all over the country. That face rang a bell with Henry Unterweiser, an investigator with the New York State Attorney's office since 1920, who recognized Coster as his former colleague, William Johnson. Unterweiser reported his suspicions, and Coster's fingerprints were soon shown to match those of Musica. Inspector James J. Donavan, chief of the Bureau of Criminal Identification, called a midnight press conference on December 15th to announce that Dr. F. Donald Coster, the esteemed business leader and president of the powerful McKesson & Robbins pharmaceutical empire, was actually Philip Musica, a twice-convicted swindler from Little Italy.

The next morning found Musica drunk. The game was over. But the swindler was unwilling to face the music. As U.S. marshals arrived at the Coster estate to arrest him, Musica locked himself in a bathroom in his home, pointed a .38 caliber revolver at his temple, and took his own life.

Lesson #3: Take a Close Look at Who's in Charge

Musica's death triggered one of the most extensive investigations in the history of U.S. law enforcement. Hundreds of agents, accountants, and lawyers worked to untangle the mystery of McKesson & Robbins' finances. Musica had moved more than $135 million through 150 banking and brokerage accounts for 50 different McKesson & Robbins subsidiaries.

And yet, not all of it was fiction. After 16 months, investigators determined that McKesson & Robbins' real earnings had always been sufficient to pay the interest on its debentures, the required dividends on its preferred stock, and a 25 cent dividend on its common stock. Of the company's $150 million in sales, "only $19,000,000 [were falsified] paper sales of crude drugs."

But investors had lost many millions more. Could they have been forewarned? A close look at who was in charge might have tipped them off early that something wasn't right. While it might have been difficult to connect F. Donald Coster to Philip Musica, it would not have been so hard to tell that Coster himself was a recent creation.

Chief executives who masquerade as someone else entirely are, of course, a rarity. But ones with a background similar to Musica's—repeat offenders whose career in fraud began long before their current assignment—can and do appear from time to time. And a close look at an executive's history can give a clue to potential problems, no matter how aggressive a company's public relations clean-up job has been.

Another business leader who managed to sway investors despite a troubled past was Charles Keating, whose Lincoln Savings & Loan ended up costing taxpayers more than $2 billion when it collapsed in 1989. A dozen years earlier Keating had been at the center of shareholder lawsuits and a Securities and Exchange Commission investigation that charged him and his business partners with illegally profiting at the expense of shareholders. The case eventually resulted not in a finding of guilt or innocence, but in a $12 million settlement, paid mostly by Keating's partners, and with Keating agreeing not to violate securities laws or regulations. None of this information was secret, and yet investors chose to ignore it when considering who was in charge at Lincoln.

Philip Musica built an elaborate web of lies around his true identity, but few executives go to such lengths. If a CEO has had brushes with the law in the past, it may be a sign to think twice before leaving your money with the company. Repeat offenders often come back for more.

The irony of the McKesson episode was that Philip Musica actually built a company that was viable on a legitimate basis. The company prospered under receivership, going on to earn $6 million in 1940, far more than Musica's record year of 1937 when the balance sheet was bloated with fictional profits from nonexistent crude drug shipments. 25 years later, Standard & Poors issued a glowing assessment: "McKesson & Robbins has no counterpart in American business, since it is the only company that wholesales drugs, alcoholic beverages, and chemicals on a national scale." The company continues to prosper today—bringing in $50 billion in annual sales—as the McKesson Corporation.

Chapter 4

Look Twice at Byzantine Business Structures

One thing that many of the scams and cons outlined in this book have in common is a business structure that's designed to be impenetrable to the outside eye. The Enron scandal that broke over the American business scene in 2001 was just such a case. Like Samuel Insull's Utility Investments, the executives at Enron employed complex cross-ownership schemes designed to disguise the company's deteriorating financial position, while at the same time enriching themselves.

The mere presence of complicated corporate structures doesn't always mean there's a scam being worked, but investors should be wary as it often makes improper business practices easier to conceal. Such Byzantine structures, whether they reach across numerous companies or simply the internal workings of a single firm, have long been a part of the landscape of fraud. One of the most famous cases, a seminal event in the history of cooking the books, came in the 1960s, with the stratospheric rise of the Equity Funding Corporation of America.

Stanley Goldblum's Unbeatable Stats

The Equity Funding Corporation was the brainchild of Stanley Goldblum, who spent his youth in the 1930s in Pittsburgh's Squirrel Hill district, a predominantly Jewish middle-class neighborhood. By the time Goldblum was in high school, his family had moved to Los Angeles, where the young man excelled in math and science and began what would become a lifelong obsession with bodybuilding. Enlisting in the Army at age 17, Goldblum served in South Korea, but left the service before hostilities began. Back in California, Goldblum married, and enrolled in the University of California at Los Angeles. But two years later he left school to go to work. Tellingly, he would later declare to investors that he was a UCLA graduate.

After leaving school, Goldblum spent a few years trying to find his way in a handful of careers before settling on the insurance business. But the results he saw fell short of his great store of ambition, energy, and intelligence. Still, he was charming enough to ingratiate himself with the right people, and in 1958 Goldblum received a call that would set him on a path to the history books.

The call came from Gordon C. McCormick, a legend in insurance selling circles. McCormick, who had been a top salesman, did everything to excess—including eating, drinking, and smoking cigars. Now he was setting up his own company, and he wanted Goldblum on board.

At the time, the fast-growing mutual fund business was capturing significant market share from the insurance industry. The 3 percent guaranteed returns that insurance policies offered as an investment just couldn't compete with the equity returns of a bull market. But Americans still valued the comfort of protection against untimely death, so McCormick planned to create a new financial product that would combine the returns of mutual funds with the safety of insurance.

In September 1960, McCormick formed the Tongor Corporation, and later changed the name to Equity Funding Corporation of America. Equity Funding was "engaged in the business of coordinating investments in securities and insurance." What it really was doing was leveraging its investors' money in a scheme McCormick hoped would make him rich.

Equity Funding sold mutual fund shares to its investors, and then lent the same investor's money to be used to pay insurance premiums, up to

45 percent of the value of their shares. After 10 years, the shares would be sold to pay off the loan, and the customer would be left with a fully paid life insurance policy. The difference between the value of the shares and the cost of the loan would become profit, allowing investors to acquire insurance and build a nest egg at the same time.

There was only one catch: If the mutual fund rose too slowly (or tanked), it would not be able to cover the interest expense, management fees, commissions, and other costs of the loan. And if the stock market tanked, and the mutual fund didn't hit its targets, the customer still would be liable for repaying the outstanding loan. Of course, this risk was rarely explained to investors.

Equity Funding made money coming and going. It collected commissions on the insurance policies and fees on the loan. The arrangement was a salesman's dream, and Goldblum jumped at the chance when McCormick offered him the position of sales manager and administrator at Equity Funding.

The company grew rapidly by hiring young, aggressive salesmen who were enchanted by the magic of the insurance-mutual fund combination. And given the strong performance of the stock market in the 1960s, it was easy to persuade potential customers of the benefits of mutual funds.

Within a year, Equity Funding became a darling of Wall Street. McCormick established offices in New York, and Goldblum and Ray Platt, the hard-drinking Irishman who helped run the company, established contracts with 56 New York brokerage firms to supply the securities for the mutual fund operation. Soon enough, they'd signed up 1,500 agents to push Equity Funding's product nationwide. The company was a hit. Everyone wanted a piece.

Beneath the surface, though, Equity Funding was already a mess. McCormick had overextended himself financially and didn't have the money to fund the company's fantastic growth. His seat-of-the pants management style resulted in unpaid bills, conflicting financial statements, and numerous profit-participation agreements that would have to be paid one day. Goldblum and Platt were growing concerned—not to mention the fact that McCormick had yet to make good on his promise to give them certificates of ownership in the company.

Goldblum and Platt, along with an Equity Funding manager named Gene Cuthbertson, and Mike Riordan, the superstar salesman who had provided Equity Funding's entrée to Wall Street, finally threatened to sink the company if McCormick didn't split the ownership in Equity Funding equally among the four men. Cornered, McCormick took a different path. He sold the company to his "ungrateful" partners for $55,392.14 in a complex transaction that included the transfer of stock and the retirement of debt. Goldblum, Riordan, Platt, and Cuthbertson each received 23,750 shares of Equity Funding stock.

The company struggled in the early 1960s. Platt's unstable nature cost Equity Funding some key contracts, and his gambling debts, which he attempted to pay off with company stock, finally got him thrown out altogether.

The Securities and Exchange Commission presented another obstacle. In 1962, the SEC ruled that the company's insurance-mutual fund package constituted a security, and would have to be registered under the Securities Act of 1933. Equity Funding's entire business was stalled for 18 months as the company was forced to make its program conform to regulations and then await SEC approval.

But insurance stocks were outstanding performers throughout the early 1960s, and by 1964 Equity Funding's fortunes were on the rise. The company went public in December of that year, offering 100,000 shares at $6 each. Despite its new growth and profitability, though, Equity Funding was eating through huge stacks of cash to pay the large up-front commissions to its salesmen and the financing for its customers' purchase of insurance premiums.

Goldblum and Riordan came up with a solution: They would inflate the company's assets by creating a system of phony loans that would make it look like Equity Funding had more money than it actually did. In the company's very first public filing, it claimed almost $6.7 million in fake loans as assets that would be used to finance insurance premiums for nonexistent customers. To further bolster the bottom line, Goldblum and Riordan also recognized profits from a deal they had yet to make. Thus began the avalanche of lies. In its nine years as a public company, Equity Funding never filed a single truthful financial statement.

Weaving the Web

Backed by its fake assets, the company could now borrow more money and raise cash in the equity markets. Equity Funding was the toast of the town; its stock jumped from $6 to $10. By October 1965, Gene Cuthbertson too had been forced out, and the company was wholly in the control of Riordan as chairman and Goldblum as president. Investors clamored for the stock, eventually pushing it to a high of more than $80 a share over the next five years. Equity Funding, with its win-win product and dynamic sales force, seemed immune to the economic cycles that afflicted other financial services companies. The stock appeared to be a sure thing.

Back in California again, Goldblum took to the high life, divorcing his wife of 17 years and the mother of his two children to marry a younger woman—who just happened to be his first wife's sister-in-law. The newlyweds moved into an elegant Beverly Hills home near Sunset Boulevard; their neighbors were Paul Newman and Joanne Woodward. Expensive Picasso and Chagall lithographs decorated the walls. Goldblum loved the toys of wealth, collecting a Ferrari, two Rolls-Royces, a 35-foot competitive racing yacht, a Honda dirt bike, and a beachfront house in Newport Beach.

Meanwhile, he and Riordan continued to make whatever fictional adjustments were necessary to come up with balance sheets and income statements that would impress Wall Street. Already though, warning signs were starting to show up in discrepancies between Equity Funding's fictional statements and the truthful statements of its business partners. An Equity Funding prospectus of 1966 declared that the company sold $226.3 million of life insurance for Pennsylvania Life—while a prospectus issued by Penn Life showed that Equity Funding had sold only $58.6 million. It was a glaring discrepancy and a sure warning sign—which no one noticed.

Regulators were not so sanguine. Insurance officials in Pennsylvania looked askance at the company's sales practices, as well as at the leverage embedded in its insurance-mutual fund package, and barred the company from selling its product in the Keystone state.

Wall Street, meanwhile, was abuzz with rumors of an Internal Revenue Service investigation. Equity Funding's mutual funds were being sold on behalf of Keystone Custodian Funds, Mike Riordan's brokerage firm. But instead of simply paying commissions to Keystone, Equity Funding directed the company to pay those funds to another company, who subsequently paid three women in the Bahamas for various services. It was unclear exactly what services the women were providing, however, and the IRS, suspecting an elaborate ruse to avoid U.S. taxes, decided that Equity Funding owed the government $34 million in back taxes.

Goldblum and Riordan fought the charges for years. And despite an exhaustive and painstaking audit, the web of companies and transactions that Equity Funding had created proved impenetrable; IRS agents were never able to trace the money back to the two executives. The agency eventually capitulated, reducing Equity Funding's tax obligation to $9 million. Finally, in August 1971, the company settled with the IRS for a mere $165,000. Goldblum declared victory. His financial shenanigans had outfoxed the IRS.

Both the SEC and California regulators had questions for Equity Funding in 1967 as well. But federal regulators, who had received complaints about the company's back-office paperwork problems, decided that Equity Funding was facing the same challenges as the entire securities industry. California regulators were concerned that Equity Funding was "twisting" its customers, convincing them to switch insurers despite the fact that they would lose the value of years of contributions into their original program. When Equity Funding cooked up a disclosure form that would outline risks to its investors, regulators were satisfied. Equity Funding's sales pitch was so good, though, that its customers were happy to take the risk.

Despite its regulatory problems, Equity Funding's stock continued to climb. Goldblum and Riordan now dreamed of transforming the company into a major financial conglomerate. For the moment, though, it was really just an extraordinary marketing operation. To become a true financial services company, Equity Funding would need to own and operate the companies whose products its sales force sold. So in 1967 Equity Funding began an aggressive global acquisition program.

In December 1967, Equity Funding purchased Presidential Life Insurance Company of America, based in Illinois. Goldblum moved the company to California and named Fred Levin as president. Later renamed Equity Funding Life Insurance Company, it would fast become the heart of the company's fraudulent activities, with Levin acting as Goldblum's chief lieutenant in developing and implementing the phony insurance scheme.

The company's next purchase, the Crown Savings & Loan Association, opened the floodgates on its buying spree. Crown came with the Israeli-born Dov Amir, a petroleum engineer initially hired by Equity Funding to develop tax-sheltered oil and gas partnerships. But Goldblum and Riordan directed him to pursue global mineral exploration projects, and before long Equity Funding had made commitments to international consortia exploring for oil in Ecuador, Israel, and Ethiopia, and had formed two subsidiaries—Traserco, Inc. and Equitex Petroleum Corporation—to hold these interests.

Over the next several years, there was nothing that Equity Funding seemed reluctant to buy. The company burned through more than $10 million to acquire everything from a spaghetti factory in Rome to cattle in Madagascar and copper mines in Zambia, and even made plans to build a convention center, hotel, and sports complex in Dakar, Senegal, with the Hyatt Corporation (a project that ultimately fell apart).

Some of Equity Funding's acquisitions were more in keeping with the company's main business. In 1969, Equity Funding bought the domestic assets of mutual fund firm Investor Planning Corporation, or IPC. The operation was vast, with 29 offices and 2,000 salesmen across 21 states. IPC customers had contracted to make regular purchases of mutual funds on a monthly or quarterly basis, and as part of the acquisition, Goldblum and Riordan made sure Equity Funding would receive the sales commission on those purchases in future.

But even though IPC was part of Equity Funding's core business, it also was part of its officers' fraudulent schemes. Goldblum calculated the commissions that the acquisition would generate over subsequent years and recognized *all of this projected income* in fiscal year 1969. Whether that money would actually materialize, of course, was open to debate, as customers were free to terminate their contracts at any time. So, to reduce Equity Funding's risk profile, Goldblum and chief financial officer Sam Lowell sold the rights to the future commissions for $13.5 million to a Panamanian company known as Compania de Estudios y Asuntos, purportedly owned by the law firm of Pavia & Harcourt.

Estudios, however, was in reality owned by Equity Funding. The down payment for the commission rights flowed from Equity Funding through a series of domestic and offshore banks and back to Equity Funding in the end. A fictional transaction was created to offset the income, and the sham transactions did their job: Equity Funding looked so good on paper that it was able to raise $40 million in debt in 1969 to provide working capital and finance further acquisitions. A year later,

Equity Funding would make the big leagues with a listing on the New York Stock Exchange.

Mike Riordan never lived to ring the bell at the NYSE, though. In January 1969, at the age of 41 and on the edge of an early retirement, Los Angeles saw the wettest month the city had known in 80 years. The torrential rains sent a mudslide crashing through Riordan's Brentwood home, trapping him inside. He did not make it out alive.

Sticking It to the Shareholders

With Riordan gone, Goldblum was the undisputed captain of the ship, and he relished every minute of it. When a research analyst asked Goldblum what he would do if a board member opposed him, Goldblum declared: "Get a new director." Equity Funding moved into a skyscraper in Century City, and Goldblum installed Fred Levin and Sam Lowell as his chief lieutenants. Goldblum compensated them handsomely, with $250,000 salaries and $1,000 monthly expense accounts. They flew first class, stayed at the best hotels, and hired limousines wherever they went.

The atmosphere at Equity Funding was freewheeling and energetic. It was a hip place to work, and as one of the most dynamic financial conglomerates of its day, attracted scores of bright young graduates. Not surprisingly, the conduct of the ethically-challenged CEO set the tone for the rest of the organization. It was common practice for executives to bill the same business dinner to three different Equity Funding subsidiaries. Shortly after his arrival, Lowell discovered a loan to Equity Funding that had been delinquent for five years—because Goldblum had kept it out of the collections department of the shell company that had made the loan (which was, of course, fictitious). When Lowell challenged the loan, Goldblum challenged Lowell: "Sam, you've got two choices. You can leave or you can help me clear this up." So Lowell created another shell company, juggled some numbers, and got the loan off the books.

The atmosphere seemed to encourage scams even on the part of Equity Funding's employees, including one that ultimately would inspire the company's biggest fraud, when Fred Levin discovered that one of his middle managers was fabricating insurance policies and including them in a group of policies that were being sold to a reinsurance company.

Insurance companies raise cash and reduce risk by selling blocks of insurance policies to reinsurance companies. The reinsurer receives a projected stream of premium payments and assumes the underwriting risk for the policies. Levin's employee took advantage of the arrangement by receiving sales commissions on the faked policies—and by periodically killing off the fictional policyholders to collect their death benefit! Some of the cash was used to pay the premiums on the other faked policies, while the rest went into the manager's pocket.

Rather than being fired or even reprimanded, though, the crooked employee was emulated. Over the next three years, Equity Funding manufactured up to 56,000 fake life insurance policies for sale to several leading reinsurers. The company simply provided the reinsurer with a listing of the names of policyholders and their account numbers. Because reinsurance business was done on a "good faith" basis, no due diligence was conducted. And with no sales commission being paid to any sales agents, Equity Funding generated an 80 to 90 percent profit margin on the policies.

To perpetuate the fiction, of course, policyholders had to die at a rate comparable to the actuarial death rate. And in order to avoid the red flag that would have popped up if too many policyholders failed to renew their insurance, Equity Funding had to pay the premiums on a subset of the fake policies of those policyholders who had "survived." The company also had to generate a phony loan for each phony policy, because its customers were supposedly borrowing against mutual fund shares to pay their premiums. Ultimately, more than half of the $117 million in loan assets on Equity Funding's balance sheet would turn out to be bogus.

When Equity Funding needed to produce an actual policy for one of its fictional policyholders to show to an auditor, the work fell to the "Maple Street Gang," so called because of their meeting place at 341 North Maple Drive in Beverly Hills, the heart of the company's counterfeiting operation. While mid-level executives had conducted the early forgeries, the company eventually hired a dozen young women in their late teens and early 20s to create fictional policies and policyholders. The women spent most of their time lounging, gossiping, smoking marijuana, and napping. But every other week or so, a middle manager named Bill Symonds would lead them in an all-night forging session. The Maple Street Gang would copy the personal information from Xeroxed original insurance policies, leaving out only the names. Equity Funding executives later added fictitious names to create the new policies.

The Maple Street operation was so successful that in 1970 Equity Funding posted "earnings" of $11 million while the rest of the insurance industry was losing money. In fact, if the fake policies had been excluded, the company would have posted a $7 million loss. In 1972, Equity Funding reported earnings of $27 million when it actually had lost $400,000. Gross sales for 1972 were an astounding $2.5 billion, with the Maple Street office contributing $800 million of the total.

The End of the Manufacturing Party

In 1971, Equity Funding promised Wall Street another big year. But by mid-November, the company had sold only $375 million in insurance, versus the prior year's concocted figure of $370 million. So Fred Levin stopped circulating weekly sales reports and started plugging big blocks of phony business into the general ledger. By year's end, Equity Funding's super salesmen had "written" $826 million in business. Levin could not suppress a nervous laugh when he announced the results internally.

To those who had seen the interim sales figures, it was obvious that the annual results just weren't possible. There was no way Equity Funding's team could have sold more in the last six weeks of the year than they had in the prior 46. The fourth-quarter report the company filed with regulators offered a clue to its financial shenanigans. Revenue from securities sales commissions jumped from $3.2 million in the second quarter to $5.3 million in the fourth quarter. But expenses had stayed flat, at $1.2 million. To make figures like that, Equity Funding's sales force would have had to be selling insurance without getting paid for their services.

There was also talk around the office that the company was transferring to reinsurers the free policies it offered employees for one year. If true, the practice would stick reinsurers with sizable losses, because most if not all of the employees were unlikely to renew the free insurance. Essentially, Equity Funding was selling an asset of no real value in order to pump up its financial statements even further.

Despite the growing internal concerns, Wall Street, by and large, continued to be wowed by Equity Funding. Research analysts at leading firms such as Lehman Brothers, Standard & Poors, Burnham & Co., Wertheim & Co., and Adams, Harkness & Hill recommended the stock. Adams, Harkness & Hill's report included some insightful observations:

"Equity's management has made itself so available to analysts that it did not seem to do anything else....There are always negative rumors floating around about Equity Funding, but we have not been able to substantiate any of the rumors. Despite these reservations, we recommend purchase of the stock."

The love affair was not unanimous, however. A handful of analysts were uncomfortable with the lack of management depth and the complexity of the company's structure. Goldblum had a reputation for being arrogant and intolerant. A report from the well-respected Argosy Group took a contrary view: "Accounting practices are seen by most as complicated and by some as suspect or creative....Equity Funding is perceived as a go-go company rather than as a fiduciary institution." Goldblum lost no sleep over the Argosy report. He knew that all he had to do was keep putting up the numbers.

At the company, meanwhile, at least one top executive was starting to cry foul. Pat Hopper, a vice president in Equity Funding's Bankers Life subsidiary in New Jersey, had been asked by Fred Levin to transfer assets from Bankers Life to the parent company in Los Angeles, to open a $3 million demand-deposit account in New York, and to invest Bankers Life funds through an Equity Funding company in the Bahamas. Increasingly troubled by the constant shuffling of funds from one subsidiary to another, Hopper managed to fend off the request for several months before he'd had enough and resigned from the company.

Meanwhile, Fred Levin was growing increasingly concerned that the company would soon face an exhaustive audit by one of the many regulatory agencies responsible for the insurance and financial services industries. What worried Levin most was the $25.3 million in bonds on the books of Equity Funding Life Insurance. The company previously had reported that it owned a portfolio of high-quality bonds from companies like Dow Chemical, General Mills, and Texaco—every one of which amounted to nothing more than a phony bookkeeping entry.

To take care of the problem, Fred Levin commissioned yet another forgery, directing Robert Ochoa, the 28-year-old manager of Equity Funding's print shop, to create $100 million in counterfeit bonds that would appease any regulators concerned with the company's financial wherewithal. In the end, though, the faked bonds couldn't even pass muster with Levin.

The early 1970s saw Equity Funding dodge another bullet when William Mercado, the head of the company's data processing unit, was fired for insubordination. Mercado went straight to the SEC, claiming Equity Funding had exaggerated its 1970 assets by at least $8 million, and that he could prove it. The SEC investigated the accusations by interviewing CFO Sam Lowell and two other company employees—who assured the regulator that no, there was nothing out of order about the company's figures. In a move that would later prove a great embarrassment to the SEC, the agency went away satisfied.

But Equity Funding would not be so lucky in the case of Ron Secrist, a clean-cut 27-year-old assistant vice president at Equity Funding Life who was laid off as part of a cost-cutting effort. Before the Maple Street office was up and running, Secrist had participated in a "manufacturing party" at which he and other employees had created phony insurance files that would be used to dupe auditors. Angry and bitter over being fired, Secrist took his story to Ray Dirks, a well-regarded research analyst at Delafields, Childs, who had garnered acclaim by scuttling the merger of ITT and Hartford Fire Insurance with a skeptical and insightful analysis of Hartford's balance sheet.

Secrist explained Equity Funding's entire scheme to Dirks, outlining how the company was able to convince reinsurers to buy so much business by offering 90 percent of second-year premiums, funds that were then paid by the creation of ever more phony policies—just as Charles Ponzi had paid off his early investors by recruiting an ever greater flow of later ones.

As Dirks looked more closely, he became more convinced that something was amiss. A 1972 financial statement from the company seemed to indicate that Equity Funding had used a bit of creative accounting to shift investment profits away from policyholders and into the pockets of shareholders.

As Dirks continued his investigation, Secrist pointed him to Pat Hopper, the former Bankers Life VP, and Frank Majerus, a former comptroller for Equity Funding Life. Hopper related his experience protecting Bankers Life's assets, and Majerus told Dirks that he had altered Equity Funding Life's accounts receivable ledger at Levin's request. Both men outlined the various rumors that had circulated through the company—of the policy factory, of secret computer files, and of the printing of forged securities in the basement office. Their stories convinced Dirks that something was very wrong at Equity Funding, and that anyone invested in its stock should get out now. Dirk passed his concerns along to his institutional clients that held Equity Funding shares and soon enough the institutions began to dump large blocks of the stock.

At about the same time, two examiners from the Illinois Insurance Department, having heard unsettling reports about Equity Funding, descended on its offices there to conduct a surprise audit. Fred Levin, looking for information about the Illinois audit, turned to an acquaintance at the California insurance department, where he learned to his dismay that Maury Rouble, a veteran California insurance examiner, was also conducting an independent investigation. Rouble had a reputation as one of the toughest and most knowledgeable investigators in the country. His involvement indicated that the California regulators were very concerned.

What Rouble couldn't understand was how Equity Funding's business could continue to grow when its lapse rates were falling. The lapse rate—the measurement of policy renewals—normally rises in proportion to the growth in new policy sales. Rouble brought his concerns to the company's chief actuary, Art Lewis, but received no satisfactory explanation.

By now, Goldblum and Levin were well aware they were in trouble, and had even installed electronic bugs and wiretaps in the hopes of eavesdropping on the various investigations. Equity Funding was becoming the Watergate of Wall Street.

Rumors of fraud drove the company's stock down from $27 to $20 on heavy volume, and Goldblum defended the company in a press release, stating "there have been no adverse developments in the company's operations which would account for the market activity in [Equity Funding Corporation of America] stock." But the price kept dropping.

In 1973, Dirks passed the Equity Funding story along to a friend at the Wall Street Journal, who forwarded it to Edward Blundell, the paper's Los Angeles bureau chief. Blundell conducted an independent investigation of Equity Funding, and contacted the SEC to check on Dirks's allegations. At about the same time, SEC regulators in New York had informed the commission's Los Angeles office of the rumors of fraud that had been flooding Wall Street. Gerald Boltz, head of the SEC's Los

Angeles office, interviewed Dirks, Majerus, Hopper, and Blundell, and asked for affidavits from Equity Funding's top executives addressing the rumors of fraud. Given the activity in the company's stock, the SEC finally decided to halt trading in Equity Funding shares. The last trade on the New York Stock Exchange took place at $14.375.

Soon after that, the Goldblum era drew to a close. Regulators and auditors had by now assembled the various pieces of the massive fraud. It was clear now that the company's financial statements had been falsified since well before the onset of the reinsurance scheme. The volume of phony assets and fictitious policies was mind-boggling. The SEC's Boltz demanded that Goldblum, Lowell, Levin, and several other executives resign. The commission would put the company into receivership if its demands weren't met.

An all-day Equity Funding board meeting was called to discuss the SECs demands. Amazingly, Goldblum remained unrepentant, refusing to answer his board's questions about the regulators' concerns. Like the SEC, the company's board soon was convinced that Goldblum should leave. After a feeble and unsuccessful attempt to secure a lucrative severance package, Goldblum finally handed over his resignation.

Lesson #4: Look Twice at Byzantine Business Structures

On November 1, 1973, in a 105-count indictment, a federal grand jury charged 22 men in connection with the Equity Funding scandal. The charges included securities fraud, mail fraud, bank fraud, filing false documents with the SEC, interstate transportation of counterfeit securities and other securities obtained by fraud, and electronic eavesdropping. As U.S. Attorney William D. Keller put it, "This type of crime is epidemic in this community, as the individual feels shielded by the complexity of the enterprise."

Once the SEC began to understand the true nature of Equity Funding's business, it filed a civil lawsuit and charged the company with massive fraud. Days later, the company's banking consortium seized its $8 million account. Telephone service was shut off, doors were locked by landlords, the sales force had nothing to sell, and the company could not meet its payroll. It was finally forced to file for protection under Chapter X of the Federal Bankruptcy Act. On October 8, 1974, though he had been defiant to the end, Stanley Goldblum stunned a Los Angeles courtroom by pleading guilty to five criminal charges. He served four years in prison.

For investors, the revelations came too late, but they need not have. From the very beginning, warning signs were present that should have tipped off investors to the fact that what Equity Funding was offering was in fact too good to be true. Chief among them was the fact that what Equity Funding claimed was a simple business of reinvesting mutual fund shares in life insurance was backed by a complex and indecipherable business structure that was comprehensible by no one but the company's principals. Even Equity Funding's basic product—the insurance-mutual fund hybrid—was more complex than those of most of its competitors. At the very least this was a strange, expensive, and risky way to purchase insurance, and should have made investors take a closer look. Other companies did offer the same product, but none other than Equity Funding had found any meaningful success with it—another warning sign that investors should have heeded.

The company's buying binges not only helped add to the Byzantine structure that helped hide the fraud, but were a sure indication that perhaps something more than simple insurance sales was going on. Besides the basic question of why Equity Funding was spending money on cattle ranches, copper mines, and a spaghetti factory—especially in far-flung places such as Zambia—there was the fact that the company's numerous acquisitions only added to the complexity of its corporate and capital structure, making it nearly impossible for anyone but Equity Funding executives to understand what was going on behind the numbers.

Other Lessons of the Equity Funding Corporation of America

Though the company's incomprehensible structure was the biggest red flag, wary investors might have been given pause by several other aspects of Equity Funding's business. Among them was the fact that, despite its stratospheric profits, the company was constantly raising money in the capital markets. But where earnings are strong, cash flow should follow. The fact that Equity Funding constantly seemed to be strapped for cash should have been a warning sign.

Financial oversight was another area in which things appeared to be less than sterling. Among the people at the company whose job it was to provide oversight, there was in fact not much impartiality. While Goldblum refrained from placing family members in positions of responsibility, very few of the company's board members could have been characterized as "independent." The top financial executives at Equity Funding, including the company's treasurer and CFO, previously worked as the company's auditors, giving them ties to auditing firms that could well have created conflicts. And Equity Funding's outside auditors, in any case, sometimes seemed to be a bit too close to Goldblum. For the first few years it was a publicly traded company, Equity Funding's auditor was a small, barely known firm. When that company was acquired by a more established accounting firm, Goldblum insisted that the same men continue to audit his company.

A quick background check might have turned up more suspicious information. In 1967, the company had been implicated in a bribery scandal in which an officer of one of Equity Funding's insurance partners had pled guilty to two counts of bribery and one of conspiracy. According to Minnesota's Department of Commerce, the officer "paid said bribes with the implied approval of Stanley Goldblum," who later reimbursed him for his expenses using Equity Funding cash. The episode would arise again in 1971, when Equity Funding acquired Banker's National Life of New Jersey. Because of the bribery case, approval of part of that acquisition was still pending at the time of Equity Funding's collapse, a fact that should have made investors look twice at the company.

And in Equity Funding's case, investors could have been warned off merely by listening to the skeptics. A number of research reports, both positive and negative ones, made reference to the pervasive gossip about the company's aggressive accounting. At the very least, persistent rumors are indicative of heightened risk, and should prompt investors to reconsider their holdings. Regulatory problems are also a clear sign that something shady may be going on. The company had been suspended from doing business in Minnesota, forced into an anti-twisting agreement in California, and banned in Pennsylvania. The IRS investigated the company twice, and the SEC three times. Even though the SEC gave the company a clean bill of health in two of its investigations, these recurring encounters highlighted a company with a clear bias toward pushing the envelope.

To find the skeptics, investors don't need to be in Wall Street's inner circles. A *Forbes* magazine profile of Goldblum proved prescient: "That's the thing about the Stanley Goldblums of the world: They refuse to believe that luck plays a major part in their success. They tend to attribute it all to their own brains and energy. Which is why they move ahead so fast. And which is why they sometimes fall on their faces when things start going wrong. Frankly, we don't know how the Goldblum saga is going to end, but we do know that Goldblum can't stop with what he's got now."

Chapter 5

Beware the Buying Binge

Most Americans investing in the markets today remember the Savings & Loan crisis of the late 1980s. The scandal that was sparked by the collapse of a single local lending institution brought down senators, regulators, and businessmen; left shareholders and bondholders hanging onto tens of billions of dollars in worthless paper; and ultimately wound up costing American taxpayers some $800 billion to clean up the mess.

But few people realize that warning signs had been evident long before the destruction and deceit began. A fundamentally flawed regulatory system had set the stage for the S&L crisis: The debts of the recently deregulated savings & loans were backed by a U.S. government guarantee. Secure in that knowledge, lenders were free with their money, and evaluated neither credit risk nor what plans the borrowers had for the cash. Instead, both borrowers and lenders knew that when S&Ls needed to repay their loans, they could borrow new money to repay both capital and interest. Government regulators had unwittingly created conditions ripe for a scheme like the one Charles Ponzi had worked almost a century before. Debt piled upon debt until hundreds of billions of dollars were at stake. By the time regulators realized that many of America's S&Ls were little more than sophisticated pyramid schemes, it was too late.

The regulatory system governing the S&L industry was fertile ground for rogues. Dozens of S&L operators took advantage of the easy money, but none abused it more flagrantly than Charles Keating. Keating, a flamboyant, deal-making lawyer who already had built a successful homebuilding company called American Continental Corporation used the California-based Lincoln Savings & Loan as the beachhead for his financial operations. Lincoln enabled Keating to gain access to an unprecedented amount of capital at the abnormally low interest rates extended to government-backed institutions. Keating then invested the borrowed capital into incredibly risky ventures ranging from a custom-built hotel in Phoenix to junk bonds issued by his friend Michael Milken. When bets went bad, Keating simply hid behind Lincoln's government backing and doubled down, hoping for the one big winner that would wipe out Lincoln's escalating debt load.

But the big winner never came. And if investors had only looked closely, they might have seen that one of the biggest losers of all time had arrived.

The First Rise and Fall

Charles Keating, Jr. was a compulsive dealmaker from the start. Born in 1923 to a staunchly Catholic family in Cincinnati, Keating and his brother William were forced to take a series of odd jobs to support their family after their father was stricken with Parkinson's disease. Though he had a promising future as a swimmer, the University of Cincinnati hardly held his attention, and he left school halfway through his freshman year to become a Navy fighter pilot. Four years later, when Keating's military service ended, he managed to convince the University of Cincinnati to offer him another scholarship. Keating rewarded the school by bringing home a National Collegiate Swimming Championship and a gold medal from the Pan Am Games, and took away a law degree in return.

Keating's legal practice took in whatever cases were available. Rather than specialize in one area of the law, Keating thrived on charting his own course and making his own rules. For several years, he pursued any deal where there was money to be made—although his enthusiasm was not always met with success. In addition to his legal work, Keating sold life insurance, ran a fruit stand, and even worked as a Roto-Rooter man for a spell. But his varied experiences helped him hone his skills as a salesman, a dealmaker, and a risk-taking entrepreneur.

His legal work soon led him to the man who would become his mentor and business partner for the next decade and a half: businessman Carl Lindner, Jr. Keating had represented a supermarket company that Lindner bought, and the two men developed mutual respect throughout the negotiations. Soon, Keating was working almost exclusively on Lindner's behalf. Within a year, Lindner bought three small savings and loan associations and began to build his company, American Financial Corporation (AFC), into a small empire. Keating would spend more than 16 years working as Lindner's right hand man as the CFO of AFC, and developed a number of financial tactics he would later use to defraud his own investors at Lincoln Savings & Loan.

With Keating at his side, Lindner set out to build AFC into a "financial department store" that would serve the needs of investors large and small. Lindner and the young lawyer from Cincinnati were a bold and fearless team. Under their stewardship, AFC pushed limits and challenged traditional boundaries. By the time they took AFC public, Keating had helped Lindner create more than 50 subsidiary companies, as well as an endless number of subsidiaries to those subsidiaries. As would become a trademark of a Keating business (and as with previous fraudsters such as Samuel Insull), all of AFC's subsidiaries wheeled and dealed with one another so frequently and in such a complex manner that Keating was the only person able to make sense of the chaos.

To raise more money to support AFC's ever-expanding range of companies, AFC issued financial instruments constantly: new warrants, preferred stock, debentures, and so on. The company was swimming in a "whirligig of debts interlaced through the maze of subsidiaries," recalled one stock analyst, who concluded that he had "never come across a company that has had so much strange paper on its books."

Soon, AFC was issuing more paper than any other corporation in the United States. But Lindner and Keating weren't interested in raising capital through equity offerings that would dilute their ownership interest. To create the cash flow they needed to support their aggressive expansion,

AFC turned to the debt markets. With each deal, the company's debt load increased. The cash flow generated by money-making subsidiaries, however, was never used to pay down debt. Instead, it was used to invest in further growth—and to tack on additional debt. As a result, though AFC's earnings increased steadily between 1960 and 1972, the company's debt load became heavier still, and AFC was eternally strapped for cash.

The 1960s and 1970s saw Keating build a reputation as a moral crusader. Keating's chosen cause was anti-pornography; he was a rousing speaker, linking the spread of lewd publications with the deterioration of society's morals and values. Keating urged people to rise up against pornography, and often brought along adult magazines and films as props, displaying their lewdest elements in his campaign for supporters.

Audiences reacted strongly to Keating's rallying cry, and he was soon enjoying the attention and acceptance he had been unable to find as a younger man. In addition to his work at AFC, Keating began traveling the country to spread his word, and he found himself testifying about pornography before Congress—where he memorably attempted to read graphic excerpts from a magazine in order to demonstrate its filth.

Keating's campaign won him many friends in Washington (including politicians who would go on to become S&L regulators), but it also made him a number of enemies, not the least of which was Larry Flynt, publisher of Penthouse. The animosity between the two was intense and personal. When Keating's daughter fell prey to a gang of rapists, Keating, among others, refused to believe she had been a random victim, and contended that Flynt had hired the thugs. When Flynt was shot by an unidentified gunman in 1978, paralyzing him from the waist down, many speculated that Keating was more than just an innocent bystander. When asked about Flynt's shooting, Keating simply stated that the publisher "got what he deserved."

Keating's anti-pornography crusade did little to hurt his business success. From 1960 to 1972, AFC's earnings were on a tear, jumping an average of 28 percent per year, far faster than many of the company's competitors. But the dramatic growth was puzzling. For one thing, AFC's products—financial instruments such as annuities and mortgages—were sold by dozens of other financial services companies. And AFC's competitors often had better access to capital and stronger balance sheets. Many of AFC's most formidable competitors had fallen victim to the turbulent markets of the late sixties and early seventies, yet AFC seemed immune.

AFC finally succumbed in 1975, when America's housing market began to slump. Profits shrank from $25 million in 1974 to $9 million in 1975, and the dividend the company paid collapsed from $1.43 to $0.22. Shareholders who had come to count on AFC's large annual distribution were unnerved.

With the sudden downturn in AFC's fortunes, the financial arrangements between AFC and Keating came under scrutiny by shareholders and analysts alike. Even with profits falling, AFC paid Keating a substantial bonus in 1975 for his work on the sale of the *Cincinnati Enquirer*. But Karl Eller, the man who bought the Enquirer, had spent six intense months negotiating the transaction with AFC, yet claimed never to have dealt with Keating. Later the same year, AFC agreed to pay Keating $700,000 for warrants that were essentially worthless. Moreover, by August 1976, AFC and its subsidiaries had made over $625,000 in unsecured loans to Keating, who was not shy about using them to finance his lifestyle and pad his wallet.

Keating focused on supporting AFC's sagging stock price by having the company lend insiders and other investors money that was then used to buy AFC stock. Keating's own nonprofit, anti-pornography charity invested more than $200,000 of its reserves in AFC to prop up its share prices, and AFC loaned company insiders between $5 and $10 million from 1972 to 1975 to be used to purchase AFC shares. Such loans shot up to $14 million in 1976 as the markets slumped. When one insider sought to borrow around $500,000 to purchase AFC stock, Keating insisted on a loan of over three times as much, in order to insure the stock price was sufficiently supported.

Manipulating AFC's stock worked so well that Lindner and Keating soon expanded their horizons. To get top dollar for the 650,000 shares of Time Warner stock they held, Keating hired three different brokers to make trades on the floor of the New York Stock Exchange on March 21, 1975. The first two brokers were to buy a combined 40,000 shares, driving the price from $13 to $14. When the price hit $14, the third broker was instructed to dump a total of 690,000 shares.

Keating's plan was executed to perfection, netting almost half a million dollars in profits—but it also drew the attention of regulators. Investors had already begun filing lawsuits against the pair in 1976, alleging that Lindner and Keating were running AFC for their personal gain instead of on behalf of shareholders. Soon, the Securities and Exchange

Commission joined the fray, issuing a laundry list of charges against both men. The government accused Keating of using "devices, schemes and articles to defraud" and making "untrue statements of material facts" in order to perpetrate "fraud and deceit upon purchasers and sellers of securities of AFC." Keating's relationship with both AFC and Lindner was finished in short order. On August 4, 1976, Keating resigned from AFC in disgrace. Settlement of the shareholder lawsuits were paid mostly from Lindner's pocket.

Keating Goes West

The empire that Keating and Lindner had worked so hard to build had crumbled around Keating's ears. Keating was devastated. With his reputation in shambles, Keating's last job at AFC was to structure his own severance package. In addition to a forgiveness of his debts to the company and a standard stipend, Keating gave himself control over a virtually worthless subsidiary of AFC, a homebuilder that Keating would rename American Continental Corporation, or ACC.

But after years of headlines proclaiming his various successes, Keating was now nearly irrelevant. When Keating moved to Phoenix, the *Cincinnati Post* hardly noticed.

Although Keating arrived in Phoenix embarrassed, angry, and determined to start a new life, he also arrived without the baggage of the Ohio scandal. Keating once again was an unknown. In Phoenix, there was no history, only opportunity.

The instrument Keating would use to capitalize on that opportunity was American Continental Corporation, the AFC subsidiary he had taken control of as part of his severance package. In fact, the techniques Keating had used to give himself ownership of the company on his way out the door of AFC had themselves required a little sleight of hand, as he acquired ACC from AFC through a complex structure of guarantees, write-offs, and concessions without spending a dime of his own. By this time Keating was a practiced hand at obfuscating the real ends and means of his financial transactions. Getting control of ACC was the easy part. Getting its finances in order was tougher.

On the surface, ACC had been a homebuilder. But it had had a more important function as a subsidiary of AFC—serving as a black hole for many of AFC's accounting shenanigans. Whenever Keating had a loan or other questionable transaction he wanted to hide, he sent it to ACC, a small subsidiary with looser reporting requirements than other AFC companies. As a result, ACC's finances were in shambles; a quick look at the company's balance sheet would have set off alarms for even the most inexperienced investor. By January 1, 1978, ACC had assets of $510,000 and debts of over $110 million, a debt-to-equity ratio of 216-to-1, dreadful in even the most capital-intensive of industries.

Rather than liquidate the company, which would have gained him next to nothing, Keating decided to roll the dice, hoping to turn the homebuilder into an AFC-like financing company that would underwrite loans, sell mortgage-backed bonds, issue insurance policies, and enter whatever other line of business looked like it could make him money. If he could build ACC into an empire, perhaps one even greater than AFC, he might finally receive the public acclaim that had been taken from him in Ohio.

Keating began courting loyal employees with whom he had worked at AFC, and identifying properties and assets that he could sell off to bring ACC onto more secure financial footing. Soon enough, ACC's homebuilding business was actually doing well. New home developments in the western U.S., driven by the maturation of the baby-boomers, were in high demand. Keating began building houses as quickly as he could finance them. By 1982, ACC was completing eight new homes a day. In 1983, Keating's company had been responsible for almost 20,000 new homes. But Keating did not stop at putting up the houses. He also expanded into other "complementary" industries, such as mortgage lending and debt financing. In a few short years, Keating had turned ACC into a thriving company that was about to turn a profit.

As he revived ACC, Keating surrounded himself with loyalists. He made his children's former babysitter a senior manager. He hired his son, Charles Keating III—a college dropout then working as a busboy—as another executive. Keating himself was personally responsible for the hiring and the firing of every single person at ACC, and he demanded total dedication from them. Keating's employees didn't just take on a job—they took on a lifestyle. They entered a world controlled by Keating.

Keating's control over the lives of his employees wasn't just megalomania. He had learned from his days at AFC that rotating employees through different jobs would solidify his control over the financial workings of the company. Few employees stayed in one position long enough to understand the complex workings of ACC's books—making Keating the only person who really knew how to piece together the flow of money through the organization.

Soon, with ACC generating free cash flow, Keating was back to his old tricks. As before, he treated the company treasury as his own. By 1983 he had loaned himself $2.5 million in corporate funds. When he needed extra money, ACC was only too happy to buy back his shares at artificially inflated prices.

ACC was emerging as a profitable enterprise—but much of its "profit" was the result of unreasonably aggressive accounting, including booking as profit any outstanding interest owed, despite the possibility of default or changing interest rates. In 1981, ACC lost $2.6 million from its housing business. But after capitalizing the interest from its lending business, the company reported $3.7 million in net income. By 1983, ACC was reporting over $19 million in net profit. Of course, Keating could also make profits disappear when the need arose. Through similar accounting practices, ACC had built up a capital loss carry-forward of more than $120 million, which Keating used to shield the company from corporate taxes altogether for a number of years.

But even with ACC running smoothly, Keating wanted more. His opportunity came in 1982, when President Ronald Reagan signed into law a bill that deregulated the savings and loan industry. Shortly thereafter, the California legislature passed a bill that gave even more freedom to California-chartered S&L organizations. Here, Keating saw his opening. He would transform ACC into a merchant bank, enabling him to make direct investments in real estate projects and assume a profit-sharing position alongside his current borrowers. Through ACC, Keating would build an empire, not just homes.

California Frontiers

The deregulation of the S&L industry at both the national and state levels was just what Keating had been waiting for. The effect of the laws was to allow California S&Ls to invest their deposits however they saw fit. The new laws also reduced the percentage of overall deposits that the government required banks to hold in reserve as cash for return to customers. Meanwhile, all deposits were insured by the federal government—effectively giving S&Ls free rein to do what they liked with the money of their depositors.

In September 1983, Keating arranged for junk-bond king Michael Milken to finance the $51 million purchase of Lincoln Savings & Loan, a company that had a market capitalization of just $34 million. But with over a billion dollars worth of federally guaranteed deposits and other assets, the price was irrelevant to Keating: he now had access to all the capital he needed to finance his merchant-banking aspirations—or any other business he wanted to go into, for that matter. The game was on.

Deregulation meant there was no limit to the type of investments Lincoln S&L could make. In the first year Keating owned Lincoln, he virtually eliminated what had been its core business: home loans. Instead, Keating invested over $600 million in junk bonds with his friend Milken. He gave financier Ivan Boesky a check for $100 million to invest with no strings attached. He bought billions of dollars in raw land, built a businessman's hotel, played the gold and silver markets, and planned a $300 million resort in Phoenix.

Access to capital was no longer a problem. When Keating wanted more money to invest, he called up a broker and bought federally insured short-term deposits from other banks and S&Ls. Known as "hot money," the deposits became Lincoln assets, which Keating sought to invest in ventures whose returns would outpace the interest payments that were due on them. Within a year, Keating had bought so much hot money that he had doubled Lincoln's assets, from $1.2 billion to $2.5 billion. Over the course of the four years he spent at Lincoln's helm, Keating would buy over $5 billion worth of such deposits. When Keating's investments failed to make the necessary returns, he simply bought more deposits to cover the short-term interest payments. To finance his purchases, Keating sold more than $250 million of Milken's junk bonds to investors, representing them as being backed by Lincoln deposits and thus federally insured (though they were not). Keating had discovered his very own Ponzi scheme, only he had the federal government behind him to make his offerings look even better.

To avoid the scrutiny that had sunk him in Ohio, Keating sought to insulate himself from Lincoln. Although Lincoln was a wholly owned subsidiary of ACC, which Keating owned, he refused to have any official role or title at Lincoln, nor was he a member of the board. In practice, though, it was clear that he was firmly in control. Charles Keating was Lincoln Savings & Loan, and the stock market loved him.

Regulators were not so sure. In only a year, Keating had transformed Lincoln from a savings and loan with no ability to make investments on its own into a financial behemoth with its fingers in all sorts of speculative ventures. But S&Ls all over the country were undergoing similar transformations, although on a smaller scale, as entrepreneurs figured out the same things about deregulation that Keating had. In fact, the industry had grown so fast that regulators were starting to have second thoughts. In late 1984, the amount of hot money being purchased by the newly deregulated savings and loans—Lincoln among them—and being used to finance direct investments in speculative enterprises began to concern chief S&L regulator Ed Gray.

Once a spokesperson for the S&L industry, Gray had been a champion of deregulation. Now, responsible for the industry's oversight, Gray recognized the vulnerabilities and deficiencies of the new system. Gray knew that, left unchecked, the industry was heading for disaster—and that the federal government would be left holding the bag. A whopping $800 billion in funds was being invested by the S&Ls—while the government had only $2 billion set aside to secure such investments. To head off a catastrophe, Gray designed a series of new regulations that would let S&Ls allocate no more than 10 percent of their funds to direct equity investments, and proposed that Congress immediately set policies aimed at protecting deposits by steering S&Ls toward making debt investments instead. He also began to look more closely at the dealings of a number of S&Ls—including Lincoln Savings & Loan.

Keating, whose business was based on just the kind of direct equity investments Gray was trying to clamp down on, was furious. Since childhood, rules and regulations had been nothing more than unjustified impediments to him. He had purchased Lincoln specifically to avoid such rules. He was not about to succumb to the whims of the bureaucrats.

Keating leveraged his reputation as a businessman and anti-pornography crusader to strengthen his political relationships, and started parceling out some of his profits to a few key legislators. To Congressman (and soon to be Senator) John McCain of Arizona he donated some $110,000. Senator Dennis DeConcini of Arizona received $40,000. Senator Don Riegle of Michigan took in over $150,000. Senator John Glenn of Ohio was given more than $225,000. And a million dollars went to California Senator Alan Cranston. Keating's relationships with these key politicos went beyond the financial. In informal meetings, he shared memories of piloting fighter jets with John Glenn, and connected with John McCain on issues of morality and values. McCain and Keating began spending family vacations at Keating's summer house. By 1986,

Keating had built a cadre of sympathetic politicians who were willing to take up arms for his cause. The Senators—who would later be known as the "Keating five"—went directly to Ed Gray, and they strongly urged him to back off from his aggressive regulatory scheme and his investigations of Lincoln. Gray heard their message loud and clear, but refused to yield.

For a stamp of approval, Keating went to one of the most influential and politically savvy economists in Washington, and hired Alan Greenspan (later Chairman of the Federal Reserve Board) to look over Lincoln's finances. For a $40,000 fee, Greenspan told all who would listen that Lincoln was a financially secure institution, and that the biggest threat to the company was not Charles Keating, but federal regulators and government intervention.

But Keating knew that political maneuvering was unpredictable and could take time to yields real results. In the meantime, he had a business to run. With his lawyers and accountants by his side, Keating committed himself to find a legal way around Gray's regulations.

The Final Collapse

While others were ringing in 1985, Keating was hard at work. New Year's Eve marked the end of the fiscal year, the last chance to get the affairs of Keating's companies in order. His plan to circumvent the new government regulations started out simply enough. Keating arranged for a subsidiary of Lincoln named Crescent Hotel Group (CHG) to buy the Pontchartrain Hotel, a 422-unit building in Michigan, for $19.5 million. Keating then formed the Hotel Pontchartrain L.P. (HPLP), which was owned and operated exclusively by Keating, his family, and senior executives of ACC. HPLP then bought the hotel from CHG for $38 million.

But there was a catch: HPLP didn't have $38 million. So Keating, as he had in the past, orchestrated a series of loans, agreements, and transactions to facilitate the purchase. First, Lincoln loaned the $38 million to a subsidiary, Lincoln Commercial Properties (LCP) in the form of two separate notes. LCP, in turn, loaned the money to CHG. HPLP then assumed the liability for these notes from CHG, in return for ownership of the hotel. Keating now owned the hotel—a direct investment—and Lincoln was able to skirt federal regulations preventing such deals because the money was tallied as an inter-company loan.

But Keating went further. In October 1985, HPLP refinanced $8 million of its debt through new notes from Credit Lyonnais. In January 1986, CHG began making monthly advances to HPLP of almost $1 million—advances that were bankrolled by Lincoln, via a $20 million loan to one of its subsidiaries, which ultimately had passed the loan through to CHG.

In order to justify the mounting debt that was secured against only the Pontchartrain Hotel, it was important that the hotel be appraised well above its $38 million purchase price. When an initial appraisal came back at $37 million, Keating instructed one of his top executives to try again. Soon thereafter, a new appraisal valued the hotel at $44.4 million. Keating, as always, took care of his loyal crew. The two ACC employees who had located the more flexible appraiser were justly rewarded: One received a new swimming pool, the other a new Porsche.

HPLP consistently fell short of registering the operating cash flow necessary to pay all of its debts, but Keating was always one step ahead, continually shifting money to HPLP from one of ACC's 54 subsidiaries. A pleasant side effect of this scheme was that Keating and the other owners of the limited partnerships were able to capture massive operating-tax losses each year—almost $9.5 million over a three-year period. Nor did the scheme damage ACC's earnings; becauseHPLP's debt was held by ACC subsidiaries, Keating just restructured its notes so that they never came due.

Even Keating's own accountants were unable to keep track of his transactions. In Keating's world, corporations were like pieces in a shell game—their every move was designed to obscure the true purpose of his actions. No one in any of the companies objected to his plans. Keating selected their boards from among his most loyal employees. He shuffled directors from one board to the next so frequently that some boards turned over several times in a year. In all his empire of more than 50 companies, Keating was the only seat of institutional memory.

Keating believed himself to be a revolutionary, creating a business driven by debt. To Keating, cash flow was what made everything work. He called his operation an "accounting-driven company." In simpler times, business had been about making something at a certain cost and selling it for more. Keating pooh-poohed such primitive companies as "economically driven." To him, the traditional business world was doomed; the key to the new world was cash flow. Rather than look to an income statement to measure the profitability of his various companies, Keating looked to his accountants, who could help structure transactions so that profits would grow no matter what a company was buying and selling. To Keating's eye, profits generated by a pencil were as valuable as those that manifested themselves as cash in the bank. Many observers agreed. After ACC's profits blazed forward at a 60 percent compounded annual rate from 1970 to 1985, *Forbes* magazine celebrated the company as the fastest growing firm in the nation.

Charles Keating was on top of the world again—and up to his old tricks, as well. Between 1984 and 1988, Keating's family received $34 million dollars in salaries and bonuses for their "work" on behalf of ACC. He donated tens of millions of dollars each to Mother Theresa and Reverend Father Bruce Ritter, and enjoyed the positive publicity that came from his charity. But as with Insull, Keating's income tax statements showed that the money came directly from company coffers, not his own. The same held true for the money Keating donated to politicians. John McCain, Dennis DeConcini, and Alan Cranston received millions, all from company funds. Keating also spent upwards of $35 million maintaining three corporate jets and a helicopter for his travels. He hired nine pilots and an assistant to fly the three planes, so that the planes could be at his disposal at any time. Keating was even known to send the helicopter to pick him up a hamburger and shake from his favorite restaurant—all paid for from the company piggy bank.

In the mid-1980s, as he was living large, Keating decided it was time to shed ACC's housing division—the core unit around which his entire shadowy complex of companies had originally been built. Not only did he find the homebuilding business dull, it did not fit into his vision of a financial empire. Plus, it drained cash flow that Keating could use to generate profits at Lincoln.

Keating knew that the sale, along with the staggering volume and complexity of his investments and transactions, would draw the attention of even the most inexperienced auditor. He also understood that with his dubious past at AFC, the government already was suspicious of his activities. But Keating was confident that neither the SEC, nor the IRS, nor any other regulatory body had the resources to track all his activities and find their way to the heart of his fraud. In 1984, there were only 700 S&L examiners to keep track of the entire savings and loan industry of more than 3,000 companies. Each examiner was paid between $14,000 and $25,000, and about a quarter left their jobs each year. Lincoln Savings

& Loan, by contrast, had at its disposal dozens of CPAs, 54 clandestine subsidiaries, an army of obstructionist lawyers earning a total of $10 million a year in legal fees, billions of dollars in assets and investments, and an obsessively ambitious mind capable of orchestrating some of the most complex transactions ever.

What Keating underestimated was the will and perseverance of a regulator scorned. As head of the S&L oversight board, Ed Gray brought an almost religious passion to the task of auditing Lincoln. In 1985, Gray hired a shrewd, experienced bank regulator named Mike Patriarcha and set off one of the longest, most in-depth federal investigations in history. For almost three years, the Federal Home Loan Bank Board, or FHLBB, pored over Lincoln's accounts, untangling complex transactions and sidestepping the ethical flexibility of the hoards of lawyers working for Lincoln. Their task was further complicated by the fact that Keating often seemed to be one step ahead of them—he had, in fact, bugged their hotel room in order to have a better idea of what they were after, and how he might be able to circumvent their task.

In May of 1987, Patriarcha recommended that Lincoln be placed in conservatorship. The company was a disaster waiting to happen, according to Patriarcha, a castle built out of fantasy profits atop a foundation of lies. But still, regulators did nothing. Patriarcha's old boss, Ed Gray, had been ousted over his refusal to yield to political pressures. Patriarcha's report was buried—only to turn up in July in the pages of *Regardie's*, a Washington business and political magazine, under the byline of a little-known independent reporter named Michael Binstein.

Binstein's story told all: internal details of the Lincoln audit, the scores of subsidiaries, real-estate deals done without even a credit check, inflated appraisals, the junk bond sales, and excessive corporate spending. Everything that looked real and upstanding was shown to be a shameful farce.

Furious, Keating denied the allegations in the story as distortions, misinterpretations, and lies, but he also took defensive action. Soon after the story was published, he shifted the legal home of Lincoln from California to Seattle by engineering a merger with a small Seattle-based S&L. Lincoln was no longer under the jurisdiction of the San Francisco office of the FHLBB. To be sure he was safe, Keating contacted Danny Wall, who had replaced Ed Gray, and sought to strike a deal. Of course, Keating contacted his politician friends as well, including Senators

Cranston and DeConcini. Wall, not wanting to suffer Ed Gray's fate, did everything Keating asked and more. In an unprecedented move, the FHLBB agreed to a Memorandum of Understanding giving Lincoln a clean slate and forgiving the company for any past transactions that might have violated regulations. Keating had skated by. But he would not escape the next blow.

In September, Keating's accountants at Arthur Young began to pose a problem. His long-time accountant Jack Atchison recently left the firm and the new lead accountant, Janice Vincent, was unable to reconcile some of Keating's transactions with Generally Accepted Accounting Principles. "Lady," Keating told her, "you have just lost the job." Keating simply replaced Arthur Young with another firm, Touche Ross.

Although the federal regulators had given Keating a clean slate, they did not go away. In September, regulators ordered Keating to stop selling ACC junk-bonds out of its Lincoln branch offices because of accusations that Lincoln had consistently misrepresented the bonds as federally insured investments. Another report in the ongoing government audit was due in December. Meanwhile, Lincoln's investment portfolio had not been performing well; bad debts began to accrue. There was no telling what information might come out in the audit. Finally, Keating had enough. It was time to get out.

Keating began a frenzied search to find a buyer for Lincoln. He found a group of investors willing to take the S&L for $50 million—about what Keating had paid four years earlier. But government regulators had to approve the buyers before any deal could go through. Unfortunately, Keating's investors simply didn't pass muster and the proposed merger was rejected by the regulators.

Keating desperately needed an exit strategy. Around the end of the year, a fire broke out in the Los Angeles office of the California State Banking Department, where all of the Lincoln files were kept. The fire was deemed arson, though the culprit was never discovered. The loss of the files was a dramatic setback to the investigation—but the December audit report came out on time.

It was worse than Keating had imagined. For a second time, the auditors found that Lincoln was on the verge of default and in violation of scores of regulations. Worse, regulators now ordered Lincoln to stop shifting its hot money to its parent company, ACC. This had been the backbone of Keating's strategy; his lifeblood was now cut off. How was he to continue servicing his debts and generating cash flow without the freedom to shift money throughout his complex organizational structure?

ACC's shares reacted with a sharp thud. The price sank to $4.50 on the news, and rumors began to circulate that Keating was desperately shopping for a buyer but could find no acceptable takers. He was desperate for capital. ACC issued $50 million in junk-bonds through Milken's firm to meet its short-term needs. Keating waded into the global currency markets to try to make some extra money, but his spin of the wheel only backfired and he found himself in a progressively deeper hole, losing $11 million in one month alone.

By February of 1989, Keating was on the cusp of failure, and short sellers were pushing the stock price down further on rumors of ACC's impending demise. In March, regulators ordered Lincoln to come up with even more cash with which to increase its reserves, and they began taking steps to seize the company.

Keating again turned to his political friends, managing to convince Senators Cranston and DeConcini it would be disastrous if Lincoln were seized. ACC, cut off from its source of free money, would be forced into bankruptcy, he told them, and the investors who had bought the $200 million in junk bonds that ACC had outstanding would be left holding worthless paper.

But Cranston and DeConcini were unable to persuade regulators not to move, and on April 14, 1989, the FHLBB seized control of Lincoln. A week later, ACC declared bankruptcy and both its debt and its equity became worthless.

By this time, regulators were acutely aware of what a house of cards Keating had built around Lincoln. They immediately moved to liquidate the S&Ls risky investments and salvage what they could. When the sale of Lincoln's assets was completed, they found that the company's debts exceeded its remaining cash by more than $2 billion.

When asked whether his massive donations to the politicians known as the Keating Five had swayed any of them to support his business, Keating answered, "I want to say in the most forceful way I can, I certainly hope so." They could not help him now. In California, Keating received a 10-year sentence for his transgressions. In federal court, he was hit with a 93-count indictment. After refusing to mount a defense, he was convicted of securities fraud, looting the S&L, and bilking investors of $200 million. He was sentenced to over 100 years in jail. But after serving only four years, Keating's lawyers were able to get the charges against him thrown out on a technicality. Keating eventually settled all matters with the government by pleading guilty to four felony counts in a deal that enabled him to avoid any additional jail time. The punishment hardly seemed to fit the crime: American taxpayers ultimately lost $3.4 billion due to the Lincoln Savings & Loan fiasco, and confidence in America's regulatory and banking system was dealt a staggering blow.

Lesson #5: Beware of Companies That Go on Buying Binges

Similar to many of the rogues examined within these pages, Charles Keating always insisted that the collapse of his company was due not to his fraudulent, reckless management and investment style, but rather to interference from government and regulators. "Never have so many taxpayers and institutions suffered so much from so few," was his response to questions of blame.

But as the dust settled around the S&L crisis, it became clear that Keating himself had hardly suffered at all. In fact, he retained assets of more than $30 million, while the stock and bonds in his businesses became virtually worthless. As with other schemes, investors who held on until the very end wound up with nothing but bad memories. Those who recognized the numerous warning signs were, in most cases, able to escape relatively unscathed.

Though Charles Keating fooled the public, investors, and regulators on any number of levels, one thing that might have tipped people off that something was amiss was Keating's unprecedented buying binges. As soon as he had unfettered access to capital through the misuse of the "hot money," Keating started buying up everything in sight, making investments in everything from hotels to junk-bonds to subsidiary companies that seemed to have little to do with his core businesses of homebuilding and banking. Such ravenous acquisitions can be a warning sign in several ways. Though Keating's main goal was not to obfuscate poor results through acquisition accounting, such number crunching in the wake of a merger or buyout can help put a shine on accounts that are actually in poor health.

So-called "spring loading" can be used to artificially boost the growth, profitability, and cash flow of an acquired company by making the company's financials look worse during the final quarters of its existence as an independent company. Tyco was the master of this technique, fudging numbers during these "stub" periods just prior to the closing of an acquisition. Executives at Raychem, an electronics manufacturer acquired by Tyco in 1998, have testified that they were ordered to accelerate the payment of expenses, hold back the posting of payments until after the acquisition closed, and overstate reserves. While a Tyco spokesman emphatically defended the company's accounting practices, those maneuvers artificially inflated Raychem's contribution to Tyco's bottom line.

In Keating's case, the jumble of companies he ended up with ultimately had a similar effect. The corporate "shells" he threw up helped to deceive regulators and investors, and bury his tracks through the sheer volume of transactions he created. Runaway acquisitions can be a sign that such accounting shenanigans lurk beneath the surface of what looks like a good investment. But Keating's sprees also left his companies mired in debt, and neck-deep in businesses—such as hotel management—that neither Keating nor any of his employees knew anything about.

Other Lessons of the Lincoln Savings & Loan Scandal

In Lincoln's case, investors could have been tipped off by any number of warning signs. A close look at who was in charge of the company would have revealed that when Charles Keating moved to Phoenix to take control of ACC, he still was facing SEC charges of fraud and misappropriation of corporate funds. Keating ultimately pled guilty to the charges in court, but continued to maintain his innocence in public, claiming that his plea was the only way to get overzealous prosecutors off his back. Investors bought the excuse.

Unlike Ponzi, Keating's past was no secret. But investors seemed blinded by his deep religious conviction and his lofty political connections. At a minimum, investors should have insisted on full and complete transparency and a strong independent management team or board of directors. Instead they fell prey to Keating's charm and subsidized his foray into the exact same business—financial services—in which he had defrauded the public in another city. Any CEO with a questionable past should raise immediate alarm bells among investors, who should demand increased safeguards for any future activities if they are to stay with the company.

Investors looking at ACC and Lincoln also should have been concerned by the complex web of corporate entities that sprang up around the companies. Like Samuel Insull a century earlier, Keating used his subsidiaries to hide his company's poor capital structure, failing financial health and nefarious activities. Complex corporate structures that are necessary for operational reasons are one thing; in this case, though, the primary justification for such a shadowy corporate architecture was that it enabled Keating to raise capital more easily. Investors should be concerned whenever a CEO believes that hiding a company's financial situation is better than allowing potential investors and lenders to clearly understand and evaluate all of a company's dealings. If a company can raise money only by obscuring the inner workings of an organization, watch out. When lenders who truly understand the inner workings of an organization won't part with their cash, investors shouldn't either.

Keating also fell into the same pattern as Samuel Insull when he began hiring family and friends to help run his companies—or at least to draw paychecks. A chief executive who populates his or her payroll with "yes-men" and cronies is unlikely to be looking out for the best interests of the stockholder. Keating's son was hired on a $1 million salary to take on a senior management position at the company; weeks earlier, he had been working as a busboy. Was this really the most qualified executive Keating could find? Investors should be wary of a CEO who pays unqualified relatives or friends outrageous amounts, and gives them responsibilities that exceeds their talents or abilities.

Of course, it hardly mattered to Keating that no employees at Lincoln had the skills necessary to manage aggressive investment portfolios. He would not have trusted professional investors anyway, as they would have only impeded his total control. As it was, every decision ran through Keating. He rarely slept. He rarely ate. And he did not have time for niceties. His life was a blur; time was his biggest challenge. Keating also had a tough time drawing the line between the personal and the professional, another warning sign. To him, it was all one.

Aside from the management benefits delegation can have on an enterprise, investors should be concerned when a CEO seeks to control all company information. CEOs who hide transactions from their own employees are not likely to be open and honest with investors. CEOs who demand total allegiance are probably doing so to insure that employees will keep quiet when their conscience might demand otherwise. With Keating treating his company's actions as though they were state secrets, investors should have wondered what he was trying to hide.

Keating confused personal matters with business in the area of corporate accounts as well. Keating was widely heralded for his generosity to Mother Theresa, to the Catholic Church, and to civic organizations throughout the world. Keating also contributed mightily to politicians in his quest to curry favor for his business. But all of these donations added up to far more than his $2 million annual salary could possibly have afforded. In addition, he kept a fleet of airplanes and helicopters at his disposal to run personal errands as trivial as picking up a burger. There was no question that Keating was using business money for personal expenses. He had pleaded guilty already to similar conduct at AFC. Investors had no reason to expect his conduct would be different at his new company.

The nonstandard accounting methodology Keating used—particularly his decision to "capitalize" the interest due on outstanding loans—should also have been a clear sign something was wrong. If a financial institution cannot show strong results using the same accounting principles as any other, it's a good bet that's because the results are not as strong as management would have you believe.

At a minimum, if a CEO believes that an alternate way of viewing revenues or profitability is more accurate, investors should demand that he demonstrate why. If the industry in question has not yet moved en masse toward the new accounting techniques, investors should demand that CEOs report results in the same way that competitors report them. Had Keating been forced to report numbers without capitalizing interest, investors would immediately have been aware that Lincoln was taking on huge risks, and that a liquidity crunch threatened the company's viability.

Keating considered himself a revolutionary. He espoused a new kind of accounting-driven business and was openly unconcerned with the level of cash in the coffers of his companies. All that mattered to him was how much profit showed up in their annual reports. To him, booking earnings, not making money, was the key to a successful business, so he hired an army of accountants and financiers to tweak, adjust, and structure each transaction to enable him to book the most earnings possible. Without Keating's army of number-crunchers, his business would not have looked like such a good investment. But accountants should document earnings, not create them. A CEO who places such an emphasis on accounting tricks and who openly dismisses traditional economics should himself be dismissed by investors.

Even at the end, investors could have saved themselves pain simply by listening to the skeptics. When Michael Binstein's article appeared, cataloguing the excesses and lack of investment discipline at Lincoln, Keating was furious. He dismissed the accusations out of hand and called the article a pack of lies. But Keating did not directly address any of the reported misconduct. Had Binstein's accusations been false, Keating could easily have produced documentation outlining Lincoln's due diligence procedures. He didn't. Binstein's allegations about the substantial amounts invested in junk bonds could have been defeated by providing a simple letter from an accountant certifying otherwise. Keating instead simply brushed the allegations aside. Investors should have brushed Keating aside and invested instead with a CEO willing to address legitimate concerns head on.

Chapter 6

Pay Attention to Company Accounts

As investors have discovered painfully over the last 10 years, the accounting entries a company makes in its ledgers and statements are not always an accurate representation of the relative health of the business. Although wide latitude is allowed under Generally Accepted Accounting Principles (GAAP), accounting practices are sometimes used to cover up poor results, to make mediocre results look better, or even to hide massive fraud—as we've seen in several examples. Not surprisingly, the correlation between aggressive accounting practices and fraud is high. Fortunately, a sharp-eyed investor can learn to spot the danger signs that indicate there may be more (or less) to a company's financial results than first meets the eye.

The two areas subject to the greatest abuse are the ways in which companies record their revenues, and how they account for costs that should be recorded as expenses.

Revenue recognition is, on the surface, a simple matter. You sell products or services and receive money in return.

But unscrupulous managers can find very creative ways of inflating those figures. For instance, if a vendor has agreed to provide significant services in the future to a customer buying its product, that money should not be recognized as revenue. But where multi-year service contracts are involved, or things like follow-on equipment sales or no-fault returns, there's a lot of wiggle room that a creative accounting department can use to convince themselves that the money coming in should, in fact, be accounted for as sales. The result is that a company's profit-and-loss statement may be pumped up with money that is not actually flowing toward the bottom line.

Fiddling with how costs are capitalized can also make a company's earnings look stronger than they actually are. Normally, capital expenditures—money that's spent on equipment that's necessary to a company's ongoing business—should be amortized over the useful life of an asset, so that the cost of acquiring and maintaining the equipment is distributed over a number of years. Ordinary expenses, on the other hand, are charged against earnings in a single year, which can sometimes sharply reduce a company's profits. To avoid this, unscrupulous managers will sometimes record ordinary expenses as capital investments, boosting profits by spreading the cost over a number of years, even though they're supposed to be recorded in a single quarter. At WorldCom, a staggering $3.8 billion in expenses were intentionally misclassified by CFO Scott Sullivan as capital investments rather than one-time expenses in order to make the company's business look better than it really was. Canadian telecom giant Nortel, once the largest company on the Toronto Stock Exchange, combined a number of such underhanded practices, booking sales in the wrong year and shifting expenses around to make one year look worse so the next year would look better. The scandal eventually led to a massive shake-up of the company's board and executive offices, leaving Nortel little more than a shell of its former self.

Fortunately for investors, many of these fraudulent practices produce warning signs that can be spotted with a close look at company accounts. One correlation to look for is between earnings and cash flow. In general, earnings and cash flow should grow at similar rates. Weak cash flow from operations is a sign that bad debts or inventories may be piling up. When weak cash flow is accompanied by strong earnings over a number of years, it's possible that something less than honest is going on to produce such a profile.

Another area to look at is taxes. A highly profitable company should be paying a commensurate amount of tax to Uncle Sam. High profits accompanied by low taxes can be another clue that something shady is going on; either the profits are not as strong as is being reported to the public, or the tax burden is being artificially—and fraudulently—reduced.

While any one of these practices can create a hole in a company's accounts that is being filled by fraud, truly ambitious fraudsters have been known to build an entire company around such vacuous structures, essentially constructing company accounts from top to bottom out of nothing but air and lies. One such ambitious young man was Barry Minkow, whose carpet cleaning and restoration company, ZZZZ Best, became one of the hottest stocks on NASDAQ in the mid-1980s, when Minkow was barely out of his teens. By the time he was 22 years old he would end up in prison.

Crooked From the Start

Barry Minkow was born on March 22, 1966, in Los Angeles. Though his childhood home was a 1950s ranch-style house in the San Fernando Valley with a swimming pool and central air conditioning, the Minkows were frequently under financial stress, and often found themselves borrowing money from family and friends to get by. Barry's father, Robert, held a variety of jobs, from real-estate sales to property management to working as a night watchman. His mother, Carole, made cold calls for a carpet-cleaning company to make ends meet.

Minkow's childhood was troubled. A disruptive schoolboy, he was sent to a military academy where he fared no better than he had in public school. Back in a public high school, Minkow seemed more interested in weight-lifting than in studying, and at the Valley Gym he met Tom Padgett, a 30 year old self-proclaimed white separatist who would play a significant role in Minkow's story.

From the start, Minkow sought the shortcut to success in whatever he was doing. At the Valley Gym he quickly started using anabolic steroids, which made his volatile personality harder to control. And when at the age of 12 he began helping his mother make cold calls for Same-Day Carpet Care, he quickly realized that the secret to the business was not carpet cleaning at all, but sales. Cold callers pounded the phones throughout the day, hoping to convince people that their dirty carpets needed professional cleaning. Ridiculously low prices were quoted, only to disappear once the cleaner arrived. To save money, stain-proof coating was sprayed only in high-traffic areas, if at all, rather than throughout the house as advertised. Minkow quickly picked up on just how many corners were being cut, and realized the industry was a potential gold mine.

To extract the rich ore, Minkow started his own business, borrowing $1,600 from one of his gym buddies, Dan Krowpman, in exchange for 50 percent of the profits. He used the cash to buy a carpet shampooer, a steam-cleaning machine, and cleaning chemicals, and set up shop in the family garage, dubbing his enterprise ZZZZ Best. Minkow's mother, his first employee, made sales calls while Minkow was in school, and Minkow went out and cleaned carpets in the afternoon. Soon he was paying classmates $150 a week to go door-to-door with a sales script Minkow had prepared.

Minkow talked to anyone who would listen about his business—meanwhile failing accounting class in 11th grade. The fact was, Minkow was a lousy businessman. He could barely afford his payroll and the tiny office he rented. His competition was intense and he had no real business plan. Almost from the beginning, ZZZZ Best was bleeding money, and Chip Arrington, the struggling, uneducated carpet cleaner Minkow had installed as chief operating officer, could do nothing to stem the losses.

To keep his business from going under, Minkow saw no alternative but to get creative. An early trick was to claim that his equipment had been stolen from his parents' home, getting Krowpman to give him money that would supposedly go to buy new equipment. Minkow borrowed and stole from his grandmother, and constantly bounced checks to vendors and employees. Four lawsuits in five months were brought against him for bouncing checks. When confronted, Minkow eventually paid up.

But even in high school, Minkow was able to turn his youth, and the exaggerated hard-luck story he told about his family, to his advantage. Bob Turnbow, the manager of the West Valley Bank, where Minkow kept an account, stuck by him through the lawsuits, the flood of bad checks, and a constantly overdrawn account.

Minkow's friend Tom Padgett also helped out. A claims adjuster for Allstate Insurance, Padgett referred carpet repair jobs to ZZZZ Best in return for kickbacks. When a customer refused to sign the form Minkow needed to get paid, Minkow simply forged the signature.

But the kited checks and forged signatures were hardly enough to pay ZZZZ Best's bills. Minkow used the stolen equipment ploy on his insurance company—a total of seven times in 12 months. He also borrowed thousands of dollars in cash from Padgett, and swiped several Allstate bank drafts from Padgett's car, depositing them in his own overdrawn West Valley Bank account, a move that eventually cost Padgett his job.

Despite the fact that he could hardly keep his business afloat, even by underhanded means, Minkow hired Jeri Carr, a fledgling public relations agent, to promote the company's image. Carr did good work, and before long, Minkow was being featured on radio programs and receiving a commendation from Los Angeles mayor Tom Bradley.

But the real story was not so happy. Besides being a poor businessman, Minkow also was lousy at cleaning carpets. When he was sued in 1984 for destroying a pair of Oriental rugs, he refused to compensate the owner and eventually spent a night in jail. As usual, when finally confronted with his crimes, Minkow had little choice but to pay up.

Over the next couple of years, Minkow spent a good deal of his time in court, being sued by vendors for failing to pay his bills or by the government for failing to pay his payroll taxes. He stole $13,000 worth of money orders from a liquor store, and then settled out of court when he was sued. Utilities companies constantly threatened to cut him off, and he finally resorted to placing an ad in the L.A. Times pleading for cash, which resulted in a $30,000 loan at usurious rates.

Growing the Business

The fact was, Barry Minkow's business was never based on cleaning carpets, which he was not good at anyway, but simply on raising money any way he could—something else he didn't seem particularly well-suited for, at first. But soon enough, he began to expand his operations. In 1984, at the age of 18, he made the jump from kiting checks to credit card fraud when ZZZZ Best opened a merchant account at West Valley Bank; Minkow promptly began forging charge slips using customer credit card numbers, which were deposited to the account like cash. Minkow knew he would soon be found out, but he didn't seem to care. When a credit card processing company inquired about the numerous disputed charges originating with ZZZZ Best, Minkow blamed crooked former employees for the theft. West Valley was forced to shut down the company's merchant account.

West Valley's Bob Turnbow, meanwhile, had moved on to Valley State Bank, and Minkow followed him there. ZZZZ Best had entered the restoration business, Minkow said, and was working on a $3 million project in Arroyo Grande. Turnbow was impressed, but the project, of course, was fictitious—the small town of Arroyo Grande had no buildings over three stories tall, let alone one that would have cost $3 million for the kind of restoration work ZZZZ Best claimed to be doing. Minkow offered Turnbow the opportunity to make a $15,000 loan to help with the completion of a $61,000 restoration project in downtown Los Angeles, even producing a phony work order from State Farm Insurance and a fictionalized personal financial statement showing Minkow's net worth at $228,548. Turnbow approved the loan.

Tom Padgett, now an automobile claims adjuster with Travelers Insurance, helped with this new line of deception. For $100 a week, Padgett happily told inquisitive bankers that Travelers was indeed providing ZZZZ Best with restoration projects. Padgett also made Travelers stationery available to Minkow, which he used to concoct work orders for phony restoration jobs.

Minkow's operation headed down more crooked road when he was referred to Jack Catain for a carpet repair job. The 55 year old Catain was at the time a notorious Southern California mobster who, in addition to loan sharking, racketeering, extortion, and money laundering, had run afoul of the Securities and Exchange Commission for defrauding investors and manipulating the stock of a publicly traded building supply company. Minkow quickly fell under Catain's spell, and sought his help raising money for ZZZZ Best.

Catain helped Minkow secure a $25,000 loan—which came in a brown paper bag filled with cash. He also introduced the young "entrepreneur" to a number of divorcees and older single women—including aging beauties such as Elaine Orland, singer Tony Orlando's former wife—who were looking for both investments and attention. Minkow showered the women with attention and respect, and they loved him.

The women loved his business too, impressed by the illusory trappings of ZZZZ Best's success and the letters from Travelers certifying the company's restoration jobs. What Minkow wanted, though, was their money, and to get it he promised them astronomical returns, ranging from 1 percent to 5 percent a week. And the women bought it, initially making small investments with Minkow but eventually increasing their stakes to a combined $1 million and more. Like Charles Ponzi, Minkow at first paid interest as promised and always offered his investors their money back. He held regular meetings at which he spoke of upcoming restoration jobs—including one in Sacramento worth $7 million, far more than any reasonable restoration job could possibly have cost—and provided fictional financial projections and architectural plans for the job, though he claimed the insurance company would protest when investors asked to visit the site.

Catain also introduced Minkow to Mark Morze, a former UCLA linebacker who joined ZZZZ Best's dysfunctional management team in 1985. Though Morze had filed for personal bankruptcy after his health club business had collapsed, he was a wizard at churning out falsified financial statements and tax returns. Armed with Morze's false statements and the Travelers seal of approval from Padgett, Minkow was able to raise money from a number of Los Angeles banks. He eventually convinced Padgett to leave Travelers and set up a company called Interstate Appraisal Services, which provided ZZZZ Best with phony restoration contracts in exchange for having Minkow pay the company's expenses. The ruse worked beautifully. For a time, he was riding high.

When law enforcement agents did come to call, it was not to inquire about ZZZZ Best but about Jack Catain. The FBI had heard that Catain had loaned the company money at loan-shark rates. Minkow denied he had borrowed from the mobster, and spoke of him only in glowing tones.

At about the same time, Catain had begun to grow suspicious about ZZZZ Best's operations; Minkow had told him the same story he'd told everyone else. Minkow, as well, had grown less and less impressed with Catain. Tired of funneling money to him, Minkow stopped payment on three checks worth a total of $350,000. When the FBI came for another visit in November 1985, this time with a subpoena for any checks of records pertaining to Catain, Minkow claimed he was being extorted by the mobster. Minkow hired Bobby Victor, another mobster, to provide protection for himself and Padgett, and heard nothing more from Catain for the moment.

Still only 19 years old, Minkow was careening from gangster to gangster—but it was a path that would eventually lead to his company going public. Bobby Victor introduced Minkow to two ex-cons, Richie Schulman and Maurice Rind, and together the three men established B&M Insurance Services Inc. to provide financing for the restoration projects ZZZZ Best ostensibly was working on, and to collect payments from insurance companies. Victor lent the company $250,000 and Schulman put up $90,000. B&M made money for its owners, but Minkow continued to be strapped for cash. To solve the problem, Schulman and Rind decided to take Minkow's company public.

Rind's plan was to merge ZZZZ Best into a shell company that was already publicly traded by means of a reverse merger in which the shell company could buy ZZZZ Best, but ZZZZ Best would end up with overwhelming ownership and control of the combined entity. The process would make ZZZZ Best into a public company without the expensive and time-consuming process of a traditional initial public offering. Perhaps more importantly, it would also avoid the exacting disclosures and due diligence that would have been necessary in an IPO.

Rind identified Morningstar Investments, Inc., a Utah-incorporated shell with no capital and no business, as a likely candidate, and had ZZZZ Best reincorporated in Nevada, a state with no income taxes and loose corporate oversight laws. The plan was slowed down by Jack Catain, who filed a lawsuit for breach of contract and fraud against Minkow in the Los Angeles Superior Court. But when Minkow agreed to a settlement of $650,000 before interest and fees, Catain went away and the merger was allowed to proceed. In January 1986, the ZZZZ Best gang gathered in Las Vegas to close the merger. Minkow, who was not yet old enough to gamble, became chairman and chief executive officer of the new company, still called ZZZZ Best, and gained ownership of 75 percent of the company's 15 million common shares. Victor, Schulman, and Rind acquired 1 million shares for $15,000, which they later sold through a front company known as Brooklyn Enterprises for a whopping sum of more than $6.1 million.

Going Pro

Although ZZZZ Best was now a public company, it remained as thirsty for cash as it had ever been. To get his hands on more money, Minkow tried out new fraudulent schemes, this time in equipment lease financing. He cut a deal with a company known as Fiduciary Funding

Corporation, convincing them to lend him $100,000 to buy 20 Triple-Vac Dual Pump Waterheated Steamcleaners—a piece of equipment that didn't actually exist. He went on to borrow money from several other leasing companies for the same equipment. Ken Pavia and David McHugh, Fiduciary Funding's principals, were so enamored of Minkow that they were moved to invest in several of ZZZZ Best's restoration jobs, including the fictional $7 million job in Sacramento. Fiduciary Funding put $250,000 into that project, receiving a promise of 100 percent return plus principal within 90 days. When the time came, of course, Pavia and McHugh chose not to take their money back; instead they doubled down, reinvesting their "profits" with ZZZZ Best.

The new debt meant that the company was now saddled with stiff monthly payments. But Minkow's strategy of creating business and assets from thin air, he found, could be used to address this problem as well. To generate additional cash, Minkow started selling the company's fictional receivables. But when the company handling the receivables grew suspicious, going so far as to verify that ZZZZ Best had no contracts with Travelers, Minkow had no choice but to pay up. Once again, he was able to buy his way out of trouble. When Maurice Rind put Minkow in touch with JLB Equities of New Jersey, a lender of last resort known for short-term loans at high rates of interest, Minkow borrowed and repaid a $1 million loan at 24 percent interest, then secured a $2.1 million credit line, more than half of which he drew down immediately. When Minkow missed a payment, JLB cancelled the credit line. Minkow's escapes were growing narrower and narrower.

ZZZZ Best was a public company and its stock had risen to $4 a share, but it still traded in over-the-counter "pink sheets" rather than on an exchange. To cash in on his shares, Minkow needed ZZZZ Best to qualify for a NASDAQ listing. But NASDAQ's listing requirements included a minimum net worth, audited financial statements, and up-to-date filings with the Securities and Exchange Commission—none of which ZZZZ Best could produce easily. So Minkow set about cooking them up.

To meet the net worth requirement, Maurice Rind bought 22 used electric generators for $580,000 and days later sold them to ZZZZ Best for $1.1 million. Making up his own accounting rules, Minkow recorded the new assets as being worth $2 million. Four of them were never even delivered to the company. An outside auditor, George Greenspan, a sole practitioner from New Jersey, gave ZZZZ Best a clean bill of health based on phone calls to Bob Victor and Tom Padgett. But Minkow still needed more cash.

To help move ZZZZ Best up into the next bracket of publicly traded companies, Richard Charbit, the company's new financial consultant, put Minkow together with Randy Pace, the chairman of New York-based bucket shop Rooney, Pace—a firm that had been censured by the SEC in 1983, even after Pace had been suspended for two months in 1981. Rooney, Pace was the perfect fit for ZZZZ Best. The firm had a history of raising money for fast-growing, highly speculative, and sometimes questionable companies. When Minkow found Rooney, Pace, the firm was actually under investigation once again by the SEC.

Pace took a shine to Minkow—who said he needed $8 million because he was planning to open two new carpet-cleaning outlets every month—and was also hungry for the fat fee he knew his struggling brokerage would garner for handling the stock sale. But to raise the kind of money Minkow was talking about in the public markets, ZZZZ Best would have to put a newly professional shine on its operation. Rooney, Pace's Faith Griffin, who was handling the stock sale, demanded that Minkow hire new lawyers and a "Big Eight" accounting firm to look at his books. Mark Moskowitz, ZZZZ Best's primary lawyer at Hughes, Hubbard & Reed, bought Minkow's line completely, even buying 25,000 shares for his own account.

Minkow's relationship with Faith Griffin was not so smooth. Griffin was infuriated to see that ZZZZ Best's numbers seemed to have little to do with the business Minkow described. And Minkow, who by this time had gained a certain amount of regard as a successful young entrepreneur, was angry with Griffin for forcing him to turn down an appearance on Johnny Carson's *Tonight Show* because that company was in the "quiet period" that precedes public stock offerings.

Griffin was also concerned about the collection of flunkies that made up ZZZZ Best's management, and insisted that Minkow hire an in-house controller—he found another sycophant—and that the company run major decisions by its board of directors. Minkow was only too happy to comply; ZZZZ Best's board consisted of Minkow's early backer Dan Krowpman, his girlfriend's father (his former weight-lifting instructor), the company's landlord, and a ZZZZ Best telephone salesperson.

Ernst & Whinney, the company's new auditors, would need to see every document related to ZZZZ Best's finances before the stock offering could go forward. Minkow handled this by having Mark Morze, the accounting wizard who had joined the company's management team early on, create phony invoices for restoration projects and forge nearly two full years worth of detailed bank statements. To answer questions about Padgett's Interstate Appraisal Services, which did not appear in Dun & Bradstreet's listing of companies, Morze simply provided a falsified letter on Valley National Bank stationery attesting to the company's financial health. To Ernst & Whinney, and to the rest of the world, ZZZZ Best looked like a thriving enterprise.

But before they would sign off on the stock offering, Faith Griffin and Larry Gray, the Ernst & Whinney partner in charge of the ZZZZ Best account, demanded that someone on their team actually visit a restoration project. Minkow stalled for as long as he could, but the accountants wouldn't budge. Finally, Minkow sent Tom Padgett and Mark Roddy, an ex-con friend, to find a building in Sacramento that could conceivably harbor a $7 million restoration job.

Padgett and Roddy met with building managers at 300 Capital Mall in Sacramento and professed an interest in leasing a considerable amount of space in the building. They leased and furnished an office, and turned it into Assured Property Management, a completely fictional company which was supposedly overseeing the restoration project. On the office wall, a map hung covered with pins identifying numerous other projects ostensibly under Assured Property's supervision.

Minkow explained that his insurance company had demanded a weekend visit. In truth, he figured he and his friends would have a better chance to pull off the scam when fewer people were around. On the day of the visit, Roddy slipped $50 bills to security staff at 300 Capital Mall and Padgett hung ZZZZ Best signs at strategic points throughout the building. When Gray and a lawyer from ZZZZ Best's new securities firm arrived, Padgett gave them each company identification badges with their pictures on them. The accountant and the lawyer spent a total of 20 minutes in the building; they bought the ruse completely.

On October 29, 1986, ZZZZ Best filed a registration statement with the SEC for a secondary offering of stock underwritten by Rooney, Pace. Notwithstanding the work done by an experienced, skilled, and honest group of bankers, lawyers, and accountants, the document filed with the SEC was amongst the most fraudulent filings in the history of U.S. securities regulation. The operating statement was fantasy, assets were vastly overstated, and the shady backgrounds of Minkow's team members largely omitted. According to the document, revenue had skyrocketed from $575,117 in fiscal year 1984 to $1.84 million in 1985. Profits had soared at even more astronomical rates, from $152,192 in 1984 to $1.24 million in 1985. Most impressively, in the single quarter ending July 31, 1986, revenue was an amazing $5.4 million with profits of $1.83 million.

The prospectus acknowledged $6.2 million in short-term borrowings and $1 million in long-term debt (the actual amounts were much higher), and disclosed Minkow's dealings with Jack Catain, as well as warning that the company was entirely dependent on its 20-year-old CEO. But none of this mattered to investors. Rooney, Pace sent Minkow on a nine-day roadshow across the country. His performance was amazing. He offered to fix a torn carpet in a conference room, provided quotes to shampoo an entire office suite, and estimated square footage with precision at a glance. Brokers and investors were wowed by what appeared to be a comprehensive knowledge of securities laws and market psychology on Minkow's part. The trip was a huge success. Rooney, Pace sold 1.1 million shares for gross proceeds of $13.2 million, more than $11.5 million of which went to Minkow and ZZZZ Best.

As usual, the money did not last long. Some $1.5 million went to investors in an earlier private placement, and another $5.5 million went to pay off various debts. Minkow took $1 million for himself, and immediately set about raising even more cash. Trading on the ZZZZ Best's new credibility, he opened a $7 million credit line with Union Bank and a $3 million line with First Interstate. He immediately drew down both facilities.

Now Minkow was living large. He was on a roll. He had a $130,000 Ferrari, a mansion with a huge Z on the bottom of its swimming pool, and a company softball team for which he paid loud, supportive fans $100 each. Los Angeles Mayor Tom Bradley declared November 8, 1986, Barry Minkow Day. As a highly visible figure, Minkow began to draw a certain amount of skeptical coverage, but most of his press was favorable. The Association of Collegiate Entrepreneurs ranked him as the most successful of 100 young entrepreneurs. *Newsweek*, *American Banker*, and *Inc.* magazine all ran flattering profiles.

ZZZZ Best's stock shot up, rising 331 percent in the first quarter of 1987 to peak at $18.375 on April 6, giving Minkow a net worth on paper of $109 million. The company claimed to have 13 carpet-cleaning offices at the time of the stock sale, and promised to open 10 more in the coming year, but in reality the business side of the operation was losing money hand over fist. The fact was, Minkow had never really been concerned with the carpet-cleaning business in the first place; all he was interested in was the money.

With his business struggling and his stock flying, Minkow turned to acquisitions to bail him out. The first deal he tried, however, didn't work out as planned. Minkow offered $10 million to take over A-1 Carpet Cleaning, an extremely attractive price that Rod Paulson, A-1's owner, was happy to accept. But Minkow insisted that the sale be booked at only $5 million, with the other $5 million to be handed over in a briefcase filled with unmarked bills. Concerned about the shadiness of the deal, Paulson turned him down.

Meanwhile, the house of cards that Minkow and his cronies had built was costing him money. When the Ernst & Whinney accountant working to complete the company's 1986 audit asked to visit a large restoration job in San Diego (which didn't actually exist), Minkow sent Padgett and Roddy to stage another fake. This time it cost the company $1 million, but again it had the desired effect.

Minkow's next takeover target was the KeyServ Group, which cleaned carpets for department stores under the Sears, Roebuck & Co. name. Though the business wasn't particularly profitable, KeyServ's deal with Sears covered 43 top U.S. markets and generated approximately $70 million in sales. But profits could be made to appear, Minkow figured, so he hired Michael Milken's Drexel Burnham to raise $40 million for the acquisition through a private placement of junk bonds. To Minkow, this was the light at the end of the tunnel. He would own the Sears seal of approval, pay off his debts, and finally get out of the fictional restoration business.

As Drexel began the due diligence on the deal, Minkow appeared on the *Oprah Winfrey Show* for a segment on young entrepreneurs. The performance was vintage Minkow. "Life is a movie," he explained. "You're the actor, you're the director, and you're the writer. And if you don't like the way your life is going, you'd better change the script, because it's your life and you have complete control over it." When another guest,

Neil Balter, founder of the California Closet Company, disagreed, Minkow retorted, "Excuse me, Neil, your sales were $17 million. Mine are $50 million. End of story."

Lifting the Carpet on ZZZZ Best

On May 18, 1987, the Wall Street Journal ran a story about ZZZZ Best's announcement of a $13.8 million restoration contract from Assured Property Management and Interstate Appraisal in Dallas. The Journal story was duly favorable, but some in the carpet-cleaning industry were less impressed. As the president of one Texas firm would later explain in an interview, "A $14 million contract would be the biggest contract ever. That we wouldn't know about a deal like that in our backyard would seem incredible. We monitor that day and night. That's our business."

Others had already started asking questions behind the scenes. Norman Rothberg, an accountant at Padgett's Interstate Appraisal, had learned that his bosses were actively deceiving the company's lawyers and accountants. He brought his concerns to Ernst & Whinney, asking for $25,000 in return for the information. Ernst & Whinney looked into the allegations briefly, but Rothberg's desperate demeanor led them to dismiss him as a credible source.

Meanwhile, the SEC had received a tip from one of Jack Catain's old associates to the effect that ZZZZ Best and its CEO were involved in a stock manipulation scheme. Rose Schindler, an SEC attorney, promptly "blue-sheeted" ZZZZ Best, sending SEC questionnaires (on blue paper) to the market makers in ZZZZ Best stock, requiring them to provide information on the buyer and seller of the stock for every transaction.

Public trouble began with a *Los Angeles Times* article of May 22, 1987, which carried a headline that blared, "Behind 'Whiz Kid' Is A Trail Of False Credit-Card Billings." Reporter Daniel Akst had been looking into credit-card fraud and had stumbled onto ZZZZ Best's fraudulent charges. His article painted ZZZZ Best as an empty fraud. The stock plunged from $15.375 to $11.125. With Drexel's due diligence on the KeyServ acquisition not yet complete, the timing could not have been worse.

When *Barron's* and *The Wall Street Journal* picked up the story, both pointed out that Minkow was blaming subcontractors for the false charges—despite the fact that ZZZZ Best's prospectus specifically stated that the company didn't use them. By the third day after the credit card story broke, ZZZZ Best's stock had plunged to $6.75. Lawyers and accountants from both ZZZZ Best and Drexel Burnham demanded to know what was really going on.

To try to mitigate the damage, Minkow turned to one of his favorite strategies: lies. A May 28th press release put ZZZZ Best's fiscal year net income at $5 million, versus less than a million the year before. The release announced "record preliminary results" and reported that an independent investigation of the credit card problems had exonerated management. Minkow claimed to have a $25 million backlog of insurance restoration business and projected "substantial growth" in sales and profits for the coming fiscal year.

The entire press release, of course, was a lie. Ernst & Whinney were outraged that the numbers had been released without their consent. At Ernst & Whinney's insistence, a ZZZZ Best board meeting was convened the next day. Unable to satisfy the concerns of new directors and the company's accounting firm, Minkow reluctantly agreed to an independent inquiry that would hopefully clear the air.

Drexel Burnham's lawyers had also begun investigating the allegations of credit card fraud, and were convinced that Minkow was lying. When Minkow told the Los Angeles Times that an independent investigation conducted by Drexel had cleared management of any wrongdoing (another lie), Drexel pulled the plug. The next day Ernst & Whinney resigned as ZZZZ Best's accountants.

And the day after that, ZZZZ Best received a subpoena from the SEC for documents relating to Interstate Appraisal, among other matters. Over the following week, two separate class-action shareholder lawsuits were filed against the company. The stock drifted downward, and the short sellers began to circle.

It was not turning into a good summer for Barry Minkow. His response was to grab as much as he could before his company fell apart completely. Sensing the end was near, Minkow withdrew $3.4 million from ZZZZ Best's account at Lincoln National Bank in Encino, California, borrowed $600,000 from Fiduciary Funding's Ken Pavia, and margined his ZZZZ Best shares for $1,775,000 from Prudential Bache. He even borrowed $1 million from one of his directors. And on July 2, he resigned. ZZZZ Best's stock flopped further to $1.125.

Gradually, all the sordid facts came to light. At a July 2 board meeting, shellshocked directors were informed that the company had only $68,000 in the bank. Chief financial officer Bruce Andersen had learned only hours earlier that the insurance restoration jobs were fakes. There was some $200,000 of revenue coming in each week, but there were $350,000 in expenses going out. The company filed for bankruptcy, and filed a lawsuit against Minkow, Morze, Padgett, and Interstate Appraisal. Shares in ZZZZ Best were trading for less than a dollar.

In January of 1988, Minkow and 10 accomplices were charged with a host of federal charges. Despite his attorney's advice, Minkow refused to accept a plea agreement. After a 16-week trial, Minkow was sentenced to 25 years behind bars. He served seven and a half.

Lesson #6: Pay Attention to Company Accounts

Barry Minkow was particularly skilled at manipulating the public perception of himself and his company in order to build credibility for a business that was fraudulent from top to bottom. The renown he gained simply from being a successful young entrepreneur was enough to garner him relationships with respected Wall Street firms, which then lent him more credibility. On that reputation—and little else—Minkow was able to carry his money-losing business from his father's garage to the list of best-performing NASDAQ stocks. Had investors looked beyond the hot air, though, they might have seen signs early on that Minkow's bubble would burst.

They might have started with the company's accounts, looking for some of the warning signs described at the beginning of this chapter. A close examination of the company's balance sheet and income statement would have raised more questions than it answered. ZZZZ Best's cash flow, for one thing, was never even a shadow of what it should have been, had the company actually been booking as much business as reported. If profits were so strong, why was the company constantly so deeply in debt? Another tip-off might have been found in the bloated level of receivables ZZZZ Best constantly claimed. Sharply rising receivables may indicate that a company is inducing customers to make purchases by using discounts, credit, or easy cancellation terms that could seriously weaken profits—or that the purchases are entirely fictional in the first place, as was often the case at ZZZZ Best.

Some of the problems with ZZZZ Best's company accounts could have been discerned by conducting a thorough background check on the company. Companies that start crooked tend to stay crooked, and ZZZZ Best certainly was no exception. The credit card fraud was there for all to see right from the start. Minkow's relationship with the mobster Jack Catain should also have raised some red flags. Minkow and ZZZZ Best had been named in numerous lawsuits, accused of bouncing checks, defrauding customers, and breaching any number of contracts. While the dollar amounts in the various lawsuits were small, the volume of problems should have indicated that something was not right. In addition, the company had been dropped by a number of banks, and had a terrible reputation in its local banking community.

Other Lessons From ZZZZ Best

Like many fraudulent businesses, what Barry Minkow was promising his investors sounded too good to be true. And in fact, as in many other cases, it was just that. Like Charles Ponzi, Minkow promised his early investors outsized returns, ranging from 1 percent to 5 percent a week, or 68 percent to 1,164 percent on an annualized basis. He claimed the tremendous profitability of restoration jobs made it possible to offer such high interest rates. But there is no business on the planet that can operate profitably with such a high cost of capital.

In any case, all investors would have had to do was look to ZZZZ Best's competitors to get a sense of how profitable such jobs really were. Carpet cleaning is a highly competitive, low-margin business with almost no barriers to entry. There were no other companies in the field generating similar financial results, and to Minkow's competitors it was clear from the start that the company's purported growth and profitability were improbable, if not impossible. Minkow made the ridiculous claim of 50 percent margins on his restoration projects, despite the fact that the industry average was just 8 percent.

A close look at ZZZZ Best's management team should have set off warning bells as well. Minkow and his cronies were arguably the biggest collection of goofballs ever to run a public company. Most 21 year olds can hardly balance their checkbooks, let alone run a multi-million dollar public company. Minkow's youth and inexperience might have been acceptable if he had surrounded himself with top-notch advisors, but he did nothing of the sort. Chief Operating Officer Chip Arrington was a 26-year-old carpet cleaner without a college education. Senior Vice President Mark Morze was an accountant and former health club owner who had filed for personal bankruptcy before joining the company. Tom Padgett at least had a master's degree, but he was also a self-proclaimed white separatist who appeared on a cable television show called *Race and Reason* with former Ku Klux Klan leader Tom Metzger. ZZZZ Best's board of directors was similarly rife with conflicts and inexperience.

Anyone who stayed with ZZZZ Best beyond all this received a final warning from both the press and the company's own insiders. When respected publications such as *Barron's* and the *Los Angeles Times* print damning allegations about a company, it's usually because they've collected evidence to support the charges. And the resignations of Drexel Burnham and Ernst & Whinney, two firms that were very respected on Wall Street at the time, should have been the final straw. The announcement of a change of auditor—never a good thing—included the revelation that the board was conducting an independent investigation of the company. While the stock dropped on these announcements, investors still had plenty of time to extract considerable value from their positions, if only they had sold.

Barry Minkow knew how to kite checks, defraud credit card companies, and raise money, but he had no idea how to run a business. After a while, he did not even try. ZZZZ Best was a Ponzi scheme predicated upon raising increasing amounts of cash in order to stay ahead of the noose. An amazingly charismatic businessman, Minkow was also manipulative and pathological. When his empire crashed, it ruined the lives, careers, and reputations of dozens of people, as well as the investments of thousands more. In the words of Stuart D. Wechsler, one of the lawyers responsible for recouping ZZZZ Best investor losses, "It's astounding that a fellow who's hardly shaving could cause a financial debacle of this kind." One of Minkow's federal prosecutors described him as a "natural predator." Shame on him. But shame on us for letting him get away with it when the signs were clear to see.

Chapter 7

Listen to the Skeptics

As any smart investor knows, it pays to listen to what other people have to say about the companies in which you hold stock. Whether the person speaking is a company executive, a member of the media, an investment analyst, or a government regulator—and no matter whether you agree with them or not—it's helpful to know what the opinions are, from all sides.

By paying close attention to the skeptics, a savvy investor often can spot signs of possible fraud that will allow him or her to get out before much damage is done. Three groups of people in particular often come up with valuable insights: short-sellers, company insiders, and government officials.

When executives blame short-sellers for a decline in share price, it's a pretty good sign that something else is wrong with the business. The stock of huge conglomerate Tyco International had been riding high coming into 2002, beginning the year at just under $60 a share. But by the end of January, the shares had been pushed down to half that by what analysts were calling the "Enron ripple," after the collapse of the energy company. Tyco execs blamed the decline on "an environment where people are intensely skeptical of corporate America," and called the drop in share price "unjustified." But just three and a half years later, those same execs were sentenced to prison terms of eight years and more for plundering the company.

Wall Street had taken the skeptical view as well. David Tice of the Prudent Bear Fund had been blasting Tyco for taking inappropriate restructuring reserves for almost two years before the misconduct was unmasked by government officials and the media. The fact is, investors should take note any time a significant number of short-sellers or other skeptics begins to form. Given the vast number of public companies (a total of more than 6,000 on the NYSE and NASDAQ alone), finding a critical mass of short-sellers and other skeptics focused on a single stock is often a sign of real problems. Why risk it?

An even more valuable resource to watch can be company insiders. Executives do not leave prestigious, high-paying jobs when they know their business is hitting on all cylinders. Enron CEO Jeffrey Skilling resigned his post only seven months after being promoted. Had investors taken this as a red flag, as they should have, they could have sold Enron at $40 a share instead of waiting until it was a penny stock.

The same goes for the defection of major service providers such as corporate accountants and lawyers. An auditing firm has to be extremely uncomfortable with a company's financial practices before they will refuse to work with a client, and the significant disruption to a company's reporting process when it changes auditors makes most companies very reluctant to do so. If it's the company that has terminated the relationship, it's a pretty good bet that there's something wrong at the company, not with the auditor. Watch changes in this area closely, as they are a sure sign that something may be wrong. An auditor's resignation should be treated like a government investigation, as there is usually one on the way.

When skeptics do start to crop up in government, it's time to get out. Any kind of government probe is generally a signal to head for the exits. Government regulators pick their targets carefully; they have neither the money nor the time to chase down every idle rumor. While one is always innocent until proven guilty, investors should be a cynical bunch, and remember that where there's smoke, there's usually fire.

One case in which vigilant investors would have been able to get out before the conflagration took hold was that of the Canadian mining company Bre-X. Bre-X would have made even King Midas jealous. In the mid-1990s, the company stumbled on what it called one of the largest gold deposits in the world—perhaps the largest. Its stock, which had traded around 30 cents a share before its Indonesian discovery, climbed to more than $300, as institutional investors and individuals alike clamored for the chance to participate in the strike. But there was only one problem: the strike wasn't real. Less than five years later, Bre-X would be delisted from the Toronto Stock Exchange. By the time it was all over, one man lost his life, and investors had lost billions of dollars.

Going for the Gold

Bre-X was headed by a chain-smoking stock promoter named David Walsh. Walsh, born in August of 1945, had grown up in Montreal, Quebec, in the middle-class, English-speaking Westmount district, where he and his family were deemed too Irish, too loud, and too fond of alcohol.

Walsh struggled as a student, but fared better in his father's trade as a stockbroker, dropping out of high school before his 18th birthday to hawk securities. By the mid-1970s, he had built a successful brokerage practice at Midland Doherty, a respected Canadian investment bank, and enjoyed a six-figure income.

But almost as soon as Walsh began to enjoy the good life and build a family, his business began to suffer. Canada's language wars were heating up, and Anglophones were migrating en masse to other parts of Canada. Walsh's business, which catered primarily to English-speakers, suffered. In 1982, he moved his family and business to Calgary and joined Midland's local office.

His timing was terrible. Prime Minister Pierre Trudeau's burdensome energy policy was crippling Calgary's economy. Interest rates and unemployment shot higher, making it difficult for Walsh to rebuild his customer base. Midland cut his pay to a mere $2,500 a month, citing low productivity. After only a year in the Calgary office, Walsh left, suing the firm for breach of contract as he departed. The parties ultimately settled the case out of court.

In 1983, Walsh changed direction, founding a junior exploration company called Bresea to purchase claims on unexplored land in the hopes of discovering gold, diamonds, or other valuable resources. Most such claims are as worthless as a lottery ticket, but one lucky discovery can bring riches. That's just what Walsh was hoping for, but the next 10 years would bring him no such luck.

Walsh's fortunes seemed to slip almost from the moment he founded Bresea. None of the claims the company purchased paid off, and Walsh's income often came less from the company and more from speculating in the stock market, rarely holding a security for more than a week. His wife's $20,000 annual secretary's salary was often the only thing supporting the family. Capital for exploration dried up overnight after the stock market crash of 1987. To raise capital, Walsh managed to get Bresea listed on the Montreal exchange, but investors proved to have little appetite for his two-bit collection of claims.

In 1988, Walsh wiped the slate clean and founded a new company, Bre-X Minerals, of which Walsh served as chairman, CEO, and president. The company's initial board of directors included Walsh, his wife Jeannette, and his lawyer, Joel King. Walsh owned shares in the company directly, as well as through Bresea, which acted as a holding company.

But Bre-X did little better than Bresea, and Walsh continued to make more money in the stock market—though his trading was so aggressive that his broker sued him and won after Walsh took advantage of an accounting oversight. By June 1992, Walsh was on the brink of personal bankruptcy and his family was piling up debt. With Bre-X shares trading at around 27 cents, it hardly looked like the company would save him.

Casting around for ways out, Walsh remembered a man named John Felderhof, a Dutch geologist Walsh had hired briefly in 1983 to do some exploration work in Indonesia. None of Walsh's North American ventures had panned out, but Indonesia, at least for a moment, had looked promising. In early 1993, out of ideas, Walsh contacted Felderhof again.

Felderhof was at the time working in Indonesia with a Filipino geologist named Michael de Guzman. De Guzman claimed that a little-known mine called Busang, on the Atan River in Kalimantan, had a potentially rich deposit of gold—despite the fact that half a dozen other mining groups, including all the major Australian players, had previously rejected the site.

For Felderhof, Walsh's call was a godsend. Felderhof knew he would never be able to sell Busang even to a small Australian concern, and he and de Guzman both were just scraping by. Felderhof agreed to assemble a property profile for Walsh, and the two met in Jakarta toward the end of April. For Walsh, it was a do-or-die moment; he had to borrow money to make the trip. Back home, bill collectors were showing up at the door of his house on a regular basis.

Perhaps because of his financial stresses, Walsh accepted Felderhof and de Guzman's claims at more or less face value. The geologists provided documentation on their surveys, but not as much as Western companies would normally require. Kevin Waddell, the consulting geologist Walsh had brought along to review Felderhof's finding, figured that was just because they did things differently in Indonesia. Over the next few weeks, Walsh negotiated a deal to purchase Busang's central claim, paying $100 for an option to buy 80 percent of Busang for $80,000.

The valuation made Bre-X, at least on the surface, look like it had gotten a steal of a deal. "Junior" gold companies, those that normally sell their finds to larger concerns, often trade at valuations of about $50 per ounce of estimated gold. Walsh's deal would have had him paying the equivalent of about $0.08 an ounce, based on de Guzman's "conservative" estimate of 1.3 million ounces of gold. Of course, Walsh's price probably said more about de Guzman's shoddy work than anything else. And there was another catch: All ownership in Busang was based on a grant from the Indonesian government, known as a contract of work, or "CoW," that would be up for renewal in less than six months. Walsh, however, paid no heed to such details.

With Felderhof running the exploration and de Guzman as chief geologist, Walsh turned to the task of raising funds with which to explore the property. He first approached Bre-X's existing shareholders, releasing de Guzman's projections stating the potential for 1 million minable ounces at Busang. What they didn't release was the "40 percent minability confidence factor" de Guzman had hung on his report. Nor did they make public the underwhelming results from the assay holes on which de Guzman had based his projections. Still, Walsh and Felderhof estimated that the after-tax cash flow from Busang would be something like $10 million. All this without drilling a single hole.

Walsh raised the funds to exercise the Busang option by July, but it took several months to raise additional funds to set up the team and operations necessary to begin drilling at Busang. Finally, in October 1993, drilling began, but time and money were tight. Felderhof and de Guzman knew that if the first few holes did not turn up any gold, the project would run out of money and they would be back on the street.

The first two holes the team drilled came up empty. But with the third hole, the Bre-X team began to produce remarkable results, and holes 4 through 9 all turned up discoveries of mineralized gold. De Guzman also decided to re-drill hole 2, and, surprisingly, the results indicated a considerable quantity of gold. As the company began to release the news in December 1993 and early 1994, Bre-X began to receive favorable attention from Canadian stock analysts. Its stock rose to $0.75 a share, and Walsh was able to raise the additional capital necessary to continue the drilling.

There was only one thing wrong with Bre-X's results: they were completely fabricated. Feeling the pressure to produce, Felderhof and de Guzman had added sprinkles of gold particles to the samples they'd obtained from the holes—a practice known as salting that is normally easily detected. But the Bre-X team also brought on board Jerome Alo, a metallurgist who knew how to salt samples with sophistication. Alo brought in a small team of other metallurgists to help with the work, and soon enough, Bre-X's results were turning heads.

As Walsh raised more money, the operation settled into a groove. Walsh oversaw the company's financial affairs from Calgary as Felderhof oversaw drilling and exploration from an office in Jakarta. Almost the only interaction the two offices had was when Walsh would send money to Felderhof to continue the operation.

Soon enough, Bre-X began to see inquiries from larger mining companies that would potentially be able to provide the funding Walsh felt he needed. Though early negotiations with Barrick Gold, one of the world's largest gold-mining companies, eventually fell through, news of the interest pushed Bre-X's share price past $1. With his new profile, Walsh began shopping the Busang mine to other companies. Two more companies, Teck Corporation and Newmont Mining, also showed interest but ultimately passed.

Another mining company that visited the site, Placer Dome, had a reaction that, given later events, proved to be prescient. When Lawrie Reinertson, president of Placer Dome's Placer Pacific unit, visited the site, he came away skeptical of both the project and the team Walsh had assembled. Specifically, Reinertson became suspicious when he learned that such a young, struggling company as Bre-X was paying to have a metallurgist at the property. To Reinertson, having a metallurgist on staff at a junior mining company was like having a cubic zirconium expert working for a diamond producer; there are few benefits unless something unsavory is taking place.

In fact, Jerry Alo had previously been fingered in a salting scam in the Philippines. An executive at the Filipino company Benguet Mining had encountered Alo twice on previous projects, and both times had suspected him of tampering with results. The experience was enough to convince Benguet not to invest in Bre-X and Busang.

All the major mining companies Walsh contacted ultimately passed on Bre-X, and the company's stock slipped back to 59 cents a share, but Walsh wasn't ready to give up. Soon, Bre-X got its break. Ted Carter, a stock speculator who wrote an investment newsletter, *Carter's Choice*, which was considered one of the best of its type in North America, took an interest in Bre-X. According to Carter, if Felderhof delivered on his projections, Bre-X had the potential to climb to $10. Carter told his subscribers that the deal was too compelling to ignore.

Things started looking even better that spring, when Walsh was able to convince Dr. Paul Kavanagh, head of exploration at Barrick Gold, to join the company's board. Kavanagh, who had been impressed on his initial visit to the Busang site, was an icon in the mining industry. He had led one of the largest and most respected operations in the industry. When he joined the Bre-X board, the entire mining establishment was surprised. Kavanagh brought Bre-X the respectability the company so badly needed. Investors took notice.

Less than six months later, Bre-X released the results of six more holes. The results were staggering. The exploration had surfaced a large gold deposit and unearthed two new target areas on the property. Busang was becoming a huge embarrassment to those who had previously explored the territory and failed to discover anything worthwhile.

Of course, the startling results all stemmed from calculated salting. From hole 3 onward, the Bre-X team fudged the samples with ever greater sophistication. Particularly eye-raising were the results from the redrilled hole 2, now known as 2A. Whereas the initial drilling had found two small, mineralized intersections, hole 2A found the intersections to be much longer and richer. In April 2004, de Guzman's internal progress report to Felderhof blustered that the find "fully justifies the stage-two deep-drilling program." Remarkably, de Guzman had found this deposit—large enough to easily justify further exploration—just when Bre-X's financing was running out.

By now, investment banks were ready to get in on the act. Robert van Doorn, a mining analyst at Loewen, Ondaatje, McCutcheon (LOM), a well-respected Canadian investment banking firm, put a buy recommendation on Bre-X in March, describing the company as "a small hunter in elephant country." Bre-X had already passed $2 by then, and van Doorn set a 12-month price target of $4 a share. In early May, LOM led a new round of financing that raised $4.5 million.

But van Doorn's report contained an interesting footnote that did not go unnoticed by expert readers. The gold recovered in the Busang testing was coarse-grained, van Doorn pointed out. For the Busang mine, this was notable, because coarse-grained gold is not typically found in glacial deposits like the ones at Busang, but in placer deposits like those found in other parts of the world. But with the growing momentum behind Bre-X, no one seemed to care enough to make a fuss over the inconsistency. Soon enough, Walsh had gained important new allies in the financial community. John Embry, who managed mutual funds for the Royal Bank of Canada and who was known not to be bullish on mining stocks, looked favorably on Bre-X, and American mutual fund Scudder bought into the company as well, introducing Bre-X to the vast U.S. market.

"The biggest gold mine in Indonesia"

Soon after releasing the startling results of its new drilling, Bre-X changed the process it used to analyze core samples, switching from "fire assay testing," the industry standard, to a cyanide leach method, an unproven technology—and one that wouldn't necessarily turn up evidence of salting. The company also stopped retaining half of each sample for future testing, a practice that normally allows later analysts to verify test results. Although this dramatic departure from standard operating procedures should have raised eyebrows, the buzz surrounding Bre-X was by this time so great that analysts and investors were inclined to overlook the change. Soon, more analysts were issuing buys on Bre-X, setting similar price targets to the $4 van Doorn had cited.

In September, Bre-X reported the results of 31 new holes that were even better than what had come before. One newsletter writer noted that if such results bore out, Busang would be "the biggest gold mine in Indonesia." By the end of 1994 the stock was trading at nearly $3.00 a share.

In February of 1995, Bre-X sought to increase its credibility by commissioning an independent resource calculation for the project. The company hired geologist Roger Pooley for the job, but since it was no longer splitting its core samples for future testing, Pooley could only rely on the results given to him by the company. Within a month, he issued his findings, estimating the site had 1 million "proven" ounces that could be mined.

Around the same time, Bre-X expanded its operations into two other regions of the Busang property that de Guzman had previously reported might harbor similar deposits. Walsh purchased claims on Busang II and Busang III, and de Guzman, now eager to come up with some real finds to make up for the salting at Busang I, set about further exploration. Soon enough, he was trumpeting substantial exposures of rocks containing high levels of fractured sulphides, often a good indication of a high potential gold deposit. De Guzman mapped a whopping 5.4 kilometers of attractive rock structures, and the mere size and geological characteristics of the southeast Busang zone transformed the property. Busang was no longer just a good-sized discovery—it now had the potential to dwarf all other gold deposits in Indonesia and perhaps the world.

When news of the discovery reached Walsh, he was jubilant, and set out for Kalimantan. To the surprise of all, the rotund exec strapped on his hiking boots and made the long trek to the southeastern region in withering heat to view the rock fragments in the creek bed. The market was just as thrilled. Analysts, eager to believe that Busang was the real thing, neither questioned the discovery nor issued words of warning. There was no stopping Bre-X now.

The stock picked up momentum in April 1995 on the heels of the discovery, when Busang released the results of the first two holes drilled at Busang II and III. The sites showed "significant mineralization," according to the company's reports. And Busang II, the southeastern region of the site, was particularly good news, as Felderhof told analysts, because Bre-X owned 90 percent of the claim there, rather than the 80 percent it owned at Busang I.

Ownership of claims in Indonesia, though, is a complicated thing. Among other regulations, each claim must be partially owned by a local company, and operators have a strict duty to share information and benefits with their joint-venture partners.

Bre-X, though, circumvented both of these rules. Busang I was co-owned with a company known as PT WAM, which itself was owned by Jusuf Merukh, a key figure in Indonesian mining circles. At Busang II, though, Bre-X joined forces with a different Indonesian company, PT Askatindo Aarya Mineral, to explore the area. Excluding PT WAM was a huge mistake. The Contracts of Work issued by the Indonesian government provide a tenuous license that could be easily revoked by the government. A dispute with a well connected local figure such as Merkuh would risk jeopardizing Bre-X's entire ownership interest in Busang.

But none of this filtered back to Walsh, or if it did, he ignored it. Instead, his optimism grew almost to the point of arrogance. Stock speculator Ted Carter, who wrote *Carter's Choice*, noticed that Bre-X executives had gone from being cautious about Busang I having even 3 million ounces to being glib about the site potentially containing 20 or 30 million.

Carter noticed something else he found strange and disturbing: The results from the southeast region (Busang II) were actually from drilling locations in the central region (Busang I). Mis-characterizing the location of the holes was akin to padding the results coming out of the southeast zone. Drilling in Busang II had also become less methodical, with new holes spaced widely apart, making it difficult for analysts to identify inconsistencies and aberrations in the data. Bre-X's exploration tactics meant the public was completely reliant on reports issued by Bre-X when it came to making judgments about what actually lay beneath the ground of Busang. When Carter brought his concerns forward, Walsh just laughed.

In fact, Bre-X had devised a system of reporting that was virtually immune to outside scrutiny. No core samples were kept on hand for the retesting of results. Its drilling pattern didn't lend itself to statistical studies. And it used a sampling method that was nonstandard and therefore not well understood by analysts. Furthermore, those analysts, competitors, and investors who actually made a visit to Busang were kept under stringent supervision whenever they were on the site.

Walsh took advantage of the favorable atmosphere to raise more cash in May, hiring LOM and several Canadian investment banks to raise $7.5 million in another round of financing, selling shares at $3.75 each. In June, Bre-X reported that Pooley had updated his independent resource calculation to 2.3 million ounces. Simultaneously, the company reported that a "visual analysis of four completed holes indicates considerably more materialization than originally anticipated." Walsh told shareholders he was confident that Bre-X would be able to prove at least 3 million ounces in Busang I and 6 to 8 million ounces by later that year. Bre-X shares hit $6 on the news, and by July were trading at twice that. As 1995 progressed, Walsh and Felderhof talked up Busang II more and more aggressively, and the stock, in turn, shot higher.

By now, Walsh actually was turning away the offers he had sought when the operation had just been getting off the ground. The Teck Corporation had taken a renewed interest in Busang, but Walsh knew that any deal would inevitably bring thorough due diligence that might uncover the fraud. Besides, the stock was soaring. By October it was trading at $18 a share. When Bre-X reported results from seven more holes in the southeastern zone, the Jakarta office made sure to mix a little bad news in with the good so as not to raise eyebrows. Five of the seven holes had produced impressive results, the report said. The stock was soon trading at $29 a share.

October turned Bre-X from what had been merely an exciting story into a phenomenon. Late that month, the widely respected Canadian firm PT Kilborn released a new independent evaluation—again based on numbers provided by Bre-X. But Kilborn projected that more than 2.75 million ounces of gold existed at Busang. Felderhof also reported three more holes, drilled away from existing deposits, that also yielded spectacular results. The new numbers raised the specter that the Busang deposit could be far larger and more valuable than anyone had previously imagined. Bre-X was flying high, and everyone was talking about the find of the century.

All That Glitters

Bre-X's rise was not without its bumps in the road. When the Calgary Sun asked Ted Carter for his opinion on the stock, Carter said he felt it was "way ahead of itself." Bre-X plummeted to $36 the next day. But it rose again when another firm, Yorkton Securities, initiated coverage with a buy recommendation and a six-month price target of $75.

Already, though, questions were beginning to surface in Bre-X's publicly available reports. Tucked away in the notes to its consolidated financial statements in its 1995 annual report were disclosures that raised two major questions about Bre-X's ownership of Busang. The fact was that the company's Contract of Work applications had yet to receive approval from the Indonesian government. In addition, the share transfer from PT WAM that was supposed to have taken place in 1993 for $80,100, giving Bre-X an 80 percent stake in Busang I, had not been formally completed. It turned out that Felderhof, never one to focus on administrative details, had forgotten to complete the simple task of registering the change of ownership with the government.

These disclosures posed enormous risks to the venture, yet garnered little attention from investors. What did raise eyebrows, though, was PT Kilborn's "prefeasability study," released in early 1996, which indicated that the gold being tested was far more coarse-grained than the gold observed in de Guzman's original samples from 1992. No explanation was offered for the discrepancy. The report also indicated that more than 85 percent of the gold deposits could be extracted by a simple "gravity test"—meaning that almost all the gold in the core samples was simply falling off the rock without need for processing, an amount unheard of in any gold-mining context. Typically, no more than 40 percent of gold can be extracted through such a simple procedure. When skeptics queried Bre-X about the results, Felderhof brushed them aside, claiming Busang was "one of a kind in the world." As he noted, "we can't be giving away all our secrets."

By February 1996, Felderhof had upped his estimates of Busang's potential to 30 million ounces of "readily attainable" gold. The stock continued to climb with each new find, and each time it rose, it leaped by more than the value of the new find would seem to justify. Bre-X had become a speculator's stock. Analyst Paul Esquivel at McDermid St. Lawrence Securities cautioned that Bre-X was "obviously overpriced, and people are getting over-exuberant." But, blinded by one amazing discovery after another, investors paid no heed to such warnings. Bre-X did its best to keep the fire burning, apparently targeting unsophisticated investors with reports that spoke broadly of implied resources, not proven reserves with corresponding confidence factors.

While investors might have been fooled, professionals in the mining industry knew better. Placer Pacific's Lawrie Reinertson was having a hard time believing Bre-X's numbers. Michael Gray, a vice-president at American mining company Phelps Dodge, was also skeptical, commenting that Bre-X didn't split their core samples for future testing. Dale Hendricks, another mining veteran, was astounded. Splitting core samples was such a fundamental precept of the industry that it was simply assumed that Bre-X was following suit. John Levings, one of the men who first drilled the Busang region back in 1989 was convinced that Bre-X actually had found nothing at all.

But no one seemed to care about science and practices. Walsh dismissed his skeptics as bitter at having missed out. It would not be the first time, he noted, that an exploration had hit a mother lode on a site that had previously been thought to be barren.

By March 1996, Bre-X had surged to more than $100 a share, and analysts were tripping over each other to raise their price targets. One analyst put his six-month projection at $210 per share, and was looking for Bre-X stock to triple over the next five years. In March, the stock reached $170 and was showing no sign of letting up. At an informal shareholder's meeting the same month, Walsh and Felderhof gave investors the red meat they craved. "We are confident we have a resource of 30 million ounces of gold, and we would not disagree with an estimate made by an Indonesian mining director who publicly described the resources as being 40 million ounces," Walsh boasted.

Peter Kenney, of Canada's *Financial Post*, covered the meeting. But instead of a uniformly glowing story, he noted Bre-X's unusual assaying methodology, suggesting that this could point to fraud. His story alarmed many investors who had not been aware of this, and the stock fell to a mere $132 per share.

By May, though, Bre-X was trading for more than $200. In April, the company reported it had proved up 25 million ounces of gold. Six days later, it's shares were listed on the Toronto stock exchange. A 10-for-1 stock split put shares around $20 each, making it easier for even more new investors to get in. With each analyst visit to Busang, projections of how much gold the site might contain kept rising. One analyst called it one of the largest, lowest-cost mines in the world. Bre-X stock traded up to $27 a share.

Under the Surface

Meanwhile, all was not well in Indonesia. Unbeknownst to analysts and investors, Bre-X's ownership of Busang was in real legal danger. Jusuf Merukh of PT WAM felt that he'd been cheated out of a partnership in Busang II and III, and he was making a stink about it in government circles. And Busang's former owner, William McLucas, was circling the operation as well. Felderhof had never registered the change of ownership with the Indonesian government, and had not even received the actual shares of stock. McLucas realized that he was in a strong position to demand concessions.

Walsh knew he could not keep the ownership disputes a secret much longer, but a more pressing problem presented itself: Bre-X had attracted so much attention and investment by that point that there was nothing left to do but start extracting the 25 million ounces it claimed to have proved. Unfortunately, they simply didn't exist. Clearly, it was time to get out of the game.

Over the next six months, Walsh and his cronies did just that, unloading approximately $175 million in Bre-X stock on an unsuspecting public. Walsh himself sold almost $30 million he owned directly, and more than $100 million he owned through Bresea, the holding company. Public relations exec Stephen McAnulty sold $6 million, and Felderhof bailed out of $53.5 million worth of shares. Insider sales also proliferated in Jakarta, as De Guzman and his associates cashed out, ultimately selling more than $8 million in stock during 1996.

To try to put the ownership disputes behind it, Bre-X agreed to pay McLucas $5.6 million as "additional consideration" to complete the previously agreed transfer. The deal eventually came to light, but investors by that time were so fixated on the southeast zone that an extra $5 million or so made little difference to them.

Bre-X sought to cash in on American investors by obtaining a listing on the NASDAQ exchange. But the move only further incensed Merukh, who pressed the Indonesian government for action. Indonesian officials themselves were by now unsatisfied with their arrangement with Bre-X, and had begun to wonder why the only party to benefit from this huge discovery in Indonesia was a small Canadian mining company.

The problems manifested themselves in the increasing trouble Bre-X had in getting its permits approved. Then, on August 15, 1996, Bre-X found itself on the verge of losing all rights to Busang, when its permit to mine the southeastern region was cancelled by Kuntoro Mangkusubroto, director-general of the Indonesian ministry of mines.

The company mentioned neither its permit problems nor its dispute with Merukh in any public statements, but on October 4, the story broke. The Canadian newspaper *The Globe and Mail* ran an article exposing Bre-X's cancelled permit and quoting Merukh himself, who was now demanding 40 percent of the entire Busang mine, plus punitive damages. Walsh dismissed the claims as "false and misleading," and denied that the Busang stake was materially at risk—but at the same time, the company admitted it had met with Merukh to "seek a resolution by negotiation."

Walsh knew Bre-X couldn't stave off disaster alone, so he set about enlisting an ally in the form of a major mining company. In a news release, Walsh said Bre-X would "pursue all available opportunities" in finding a corporate partner. He also sought to build the company's political clout in Indonesia by giving PT Panutan Duta, a company owned by Sigit Harjojudanto, President Suharto's eldest son, a 10 percent interest in the revenues from Busang.

Meanwhile, Bre-X had garnered stiff competition. In early November, Barrick Gold announced that it had formed a coalition to pursue an interest in Busang. One of its coalition partners was the Citra Group, an Indonesian construction company controlled by Suharto's eldest daughter, Siti Hardyanti Rukmana. Unfortunately for Bre-X, Sigit carried far less weight with his father than Siti did. Barrick also mounted a political full court press in the matter, enlisting Canadian Prime Minister and former U.S. President George H.W. Bush to write letters to Suharto on Barrick's behalf.

In November, Barrick's work appeared to pay off, when Ida Bagus Sudjana—the Indonesian minister of mines—instructed Bre-X and Barrick to develop the site jointly. Sudjana decreed that Barrick ultimately should own 75 percent of the project, with Bre-X's ownership falling to a mere 25 percent. It was up to the two companies to work out a settlement in what had by then come to be known as "the Battle of Busang." It looked like Bre-X had lost. Meanwhile, Merukh was getting ready to sue the company for more than $2 billion, and McLucas was back, asking for more cash.

Through December, Bre-X kept reporting favorable test results from the mine, including the discovery of another large, high-grade deposit.

By the end of 1996, despite the bumps in the road, Bre-X mania had spread to the United States. Fidelity's mutual funds owned more than 7 percent of its outstanding stock, and trading on the NASDAQ was heavy. Bre-X's continued rise had attracted the attention of other mining majors, and in January 1997, Placer Dome president John Willson suggested a "merger of equals" between Placer and Bre-X (subject to due diligence, of course) that would give the smaller company a 40 percent stake, instead of the 25 percent it stood to get from Barrick.

January also saw a fire break out at Bre-X's Jakarta office. Many of the company's geological records were destroyed. No cause was ever determined and no fault assigned, but the timing of the fire left many suspicious. The Indonesian government, though, just wanted to get a deal done, and appointed Bob Hassan, an influential businessman and friend of Suharto, to help resolve the matter.

Hassan quickly developed a personal interest in the mining industry, taking a 10 percent stake in PT Freeport Indonesia, a subsidiary of New Orleans-based Freeport McMoran Copper & Gold. Hassan also took a 50 percent stake in Bre-X's Indonesian minority partner in Busang's southeastern zone.

Not surprisingly, Hassan was soon able to announce that it would be Freeport McMoran that became Bre-X's partner in the Busang project, with a 15 percent ownership stake. Bre-X would retain a 45 percent interest, the Indonesian government would hold 10 percent, the Indonesian company Hassan now owned half of would get 10 percent, and PT Nusantara Ampera Bhakti, a company owned by Suharto and managed by Hassan himself, would take a 20 percent stake. Barrick and Placer were out of the picture.

Felderhof summed up the Battle of Busang in characteristic style: "I think what happened here is that we found too much gold, so therefore it becomes an issue of national interest. If we had found a lot less, this would have never happened." In fact, they had found none at all.

Rather than hurt the stock, the dramatic public battle over Busang's ownership only convinced the public that Bre-X was the real thing. The company's stock had taken some hits during the skirmish, but by the late winter Felderhof was telling analysts that Busang could contain anywhere from 70 million to an astounding 200 million ounces of gold. The amounts were staggering, completely unbelievable; and yet, investors continued to pile on. Freeport's due diligence team, meanwhile, had arrived at Busang and were busying themselves drilling ghost holes in an attempt to confirm Bre-X's results.

The weekend of March 10, 1997, was to be the highlight of Felderhof's career. At the annual convention of the Prospector and Developers Association of Canada, Felderhof was to be named "Prospector of the Year," the mining industry's Nobel Prize. In his speech, Felderhof accepted the award with typical brashness, excoriating Barrick for trying to wrest an interest in Busang for a song.

In Indonesia, things weren't shaping up quite as well. Freeport's due diligence was producing troubling results—so troubling that the company's CEO, Jim Moffett, was moved to contact Walsh at the Prospectors convention. Moffett insisted Felderhof or de Guzman be dispatched back to Indonesia immediately to help clear up what were "real problems" with the initial results. Less than a week later, de Guzman departed for Busang.

A little more than 12 hours after that, de Guzman was dead, having fallen from a helicopter on the way from Samarinda to Busang while traveling 150 kilometers per hour, 240 meters above the ground. His body was found four days later, and his death officially ruled a suicide.

When rumors of de Guzman's untimely end began to surface, Freeport knew it was over. "I've been around this business too long," Moffett told reporters, "You don't fall out of helicopters. Once [de Guzman] disappeared, I had an airplane in Balikpapan and I had my guys out of there two hours later. Because you never know what's going to happen next. When people get desperate you have to assume desperate things might happen."

For Bre-X, it was all downhill from there. Abiding by its confidentiality agreement with Bre-X, Freeport refused to comment on anything it had (or hadn't) found at Busang, but rumors that it had come up empty-handed circulated widely in the aftermath of de Guzman's death. And with questions about salting starting to surface, two executives at Bre-X's Jakarta office, Bryan Coates and Roly Francisco, called in a company known as Strathcona Mineral Services to provide yet another independent review.

Wall Street was unimpressed. One Lehman Brothers analyst downgraded Bre-X's stock from "outperform" to "neutral" on the basis of the rumors, and other analysts began to follow suit. Slowly but surely, Bre-X shares began to fall.

Both Freeport's and Strathcona's analyses, of course, turned up no trace of the 200 million ounces of gold that were supposedly lying in wait beneath Busang. As Graham Farquharson, who ran Strathcona, reported to Bre-X, "There appears to be a strong possibility that the potential gold resources on the Busang project . . . have been overstated because of invalid samples and assaying."

Bre-X had no choice but to pass along Strathcona's findings to the public. Trading of Bre-X stock was halted on the Toronto Stock Exchange until the statement could be released. When it reopened, the stock fell $13 in half an hour to $2.50.

Despite the news, many optimists continued to believe Busang would produce something, even if it wasn't the 100 million or 200 million ounces that Bre-X executives had spoken of. But signs of fraud continued to come to light. A newsletter called *The Northern Miner* had uncovered a 1995 metallurgic study de Guzman had commissioned from an outfit known as Normet Ltd. Based on the report, *The Northern Miner* was convinced Busang had been one big salting operation, and published details of how the scheme had worked, including the fact that the gold needed to salt the samples had cost Bre-X just $30,000. By now, stock analysts had grown more than skeptical. "Quite frankly, if you own Bre-X, dump it," advised Yorkton Securities.

The final blow was laid by Strathcona in May. In analyzing its new samples from Busang, Strathcona had taken elaborate measures to protect the integrity of its work. Core samples were placed into a steel box as soon as they were extracted. The box was further secured with a steel strap and the strap painted over so that any tampering could be easily detected. The boxes were stored in a locked container on the site, guarded by the Indonesian police. At a lab in Australia, Strathcona then divided the samples in half to preserve a portion for future corroboration, and further divided the remaining sample into thirds, which were then shipped to three different labs on three different continents. To further protect the reliability of the results, Farquharson arranged to have the assaying results delivered to him by the three labs virtually simultaneously on the evening of May 1, 1997.

His report, delivered on May 4 to the full board of Bre-X as well as the company's lawyers and other outside advisors, was more than damning. The report's cover letter said it all: "We very much regret having to express the firm opinion that an economic gold deposit has not been identified in the Southeast zone of the Busang property, and is unlikely to be....We realize that the conclusions reached in this interim report will be a great disappointment to the many investors, employees, suppliers, and the joint-venture partners associated with Bre-X, to the government of Indonesia, and to the mining industry everywhere. However, the magnitude of the tampering with core samples that we believe has occurred and resulting falsification of assay values at Busang is of a scale, and over a period of time and with a precision that, to our knowledge, is without precedent in the history of mining anywhere in the world."

The Strathcona report sent Bre-X shares plummeting to 3 cents each. The next day, the company was delisted from the Toronto Stock Exchange, and numerous board members and officers, including Felderhof, resigned their positions over the course of the next week. On May 8, Walsh's companies received bankruptcy protection from the courts. Lawsuits—including a class-action suit against Bresea, Bre-X, Felderhof, Walsh, and more than a dozen other parties—began to fly.

Both Walsh and Felderhof escaped any punishment, though. Felderhof fled to one of his three mansions in the Cayman Islands—which does not have an extradition treaty with either the United States or Canada. Walsh himself made away with over $150 million from his sales of Bre-X stock, and moved his money and himself to the privacy and protection of the Bahamas. Less than a year later, he suffered a stroke and died. A week before his death, a court in the Bahamas ordered a freeze on his assets. His family still lives off a monthly stipend permitted by the courts. Felderhof, for his part, remains a recluse, protecting the secrets of Busang and maintaining his innocence. Shareholder lawsuits continue to this day.

Lesson #7: Listen to the Skeptics

The debate still rages as to whether David Walsh was the mastermind of the Bre-X scandal or just the unwitting accomplice of Felderhof and de Guzman. The answer, though, is unimportant, and will not help replace the billions of dollars lost by investors. However such frauds take shape, the warning signs that can give them away repeat themselves.

In many cases, it can pay simply to listen to the skeptics. In the case of Bre-X, the skeptics were there from the start. In fact, they were there even before the company formed. A number of mining companies had assayed the Busang site previously, and found little of interest there. Those reports were publicly known and repeatedly cited during Bre-X's early forays into Indonesia. Analysts continued to be skeptical as Bre-X began to make the first of its series of stunning reports. Also publicly known was the fact that Bre-X had had trouble finding a major mining company to partner with during its early work at the site; every company Walsh had contacted had been skeptical about whether much of anything lay beneath Busang. Forewarned investors might have noted this and stayed out of the way, but in Bre-X's case, not many people listened.

The early results from Busang, in fact, caused even more skepticism in the industry. The coarse-grained gold recovered in Bre-X's early tests indicated to many people that the find might not be quite what it seemed. Many mining veterans looked askance at Bre-X's assay methodology, and were not shy about saying so. Bre-X's ownership problems also had been disclosed in the company's financial statements. The signs were there for all to see.

Even for investors who rode the stock all the way up, the signs of Bre-X's collapse might have left some sitting on a nice pile of cash, if they'd only gotten out as soon as the skeptics piped up. When the Financial Post reported on Bre-X's nonstandard testing methods, many did, sending the stock down almost 25 percent. But many bought in again, unable to believe that Bre-X really was too good to be true.

As Bre-X's stock finally began to plummet, Walsh started to blame short-sellers for the collapse. For wary investors, that should be as good a sign as any that it's time to get out. Whether people are shorting the stock or simply selling it, the fact that a company executive is complaining about the shorts is generally a sign that he or she is trying to distract attention away from the company itself.

Other Lessons From the Bre-X Scam

Always take a hard look at what a company is promising, as compared to what other companies in its sector have been able to deliver. Bre-X bandied about gold discoveries that were stratospherically greater than anything that had ever been discovered anywhere in the world, and from a site that other, larger companies had already found to be uninteresting. Too good to be true? You bet. But any doubt was met with promises of ever greater deposits. A simple reality check could have saved many investors a great deal of pain and money.

A background check would have revealed worrisome facts as well. On the eve of Bre-X's investment in Busang, all the major players in the scene were on the brink of financial catastrophe. David Walsh had a disastrous history as a CEO and was laden with debt at the time, and both Felderhof and de Guzman had been unable to hold steady jobs exploring the mountainous regions of Indonesia. Busang was their last chance; they had to make it work, even if it meant lying.

Walsh's lack of moral rigor might have been uncovered as well. He had already been sued by his own broker for taking advantage of a clerical error, and by a former employee for failing to deliver a promised bonus. Whenever Walsh had been forced to choose between the value of his word and the value of the dollar, the dollar always won.

While many fraudulent companies hide their scams behind complex accounting shenanigans, Bre-X hid its underhanded dealings behind the complexity of its operations themselves. Whenever questions emerged about the assay methods Bre-X was using, Felderhof dismissed them as the musings of under-educated analysts. He boasted of the company's sophisticated drilling techniques when asked to explain how they had found gold where none had been found before. And when questions came up about the type and quality of the gold at Busang, Felderhof simply declared that the mine was like no other in the world. In a way, he was right. But investors who want to keep their money safe should make sure the companies they invest in are working on the same basis as other companies in the same industry. If they are truly innovative, other companies should be following in their footsteps. At the very least, investors should demand clear, simple explanations of how a company operates. If an executive is unable to provide such explanations, chances are that either there is no good explanation, or the executive himself is in the dark. Either way, investors should take it as a warning sign.

Look out for the influence of accountants and numbers-crunchers as well. Financiers manage finances—not gold mines. When a stockbroker like Walsh takes the reins at a junior exploration company, it should raise questions about whether he's the best person for the job. Walsh openly proclaimed (when queried about technical details of Bre-X's drilling results) "I am not a geologist." Indeed, most of Walsh's job seemed to consist of jumping Bre-X's stock from one exchange to the next, raising money, and pumping up the share price. And when a CEO is singularly focused on the price of a stock, the risk of fraud increases dramatically. A CEO should be focused on the health of his business; if he's doing that well, the share price will follow.

The most important skeptics to pay heed to are company insiders. Though Walsh and de Guzman went to their graves proclaiming their innocence, they somehow managed to unload more than $100 million in Bre-X stock at or near its peak. And Felderhof would have you believe that he, too, simply lucked into selling more than $30 million in stock in the same period. Despite the reporting requirements of public companies, insiders often have far more knowledge about a company's operations than the public does—especially in the case of a fraudulent company such as Bre-X. When a CEO sells in vast quantities, it is because he knows something that tells him the stock is overpriced. Investors should follow his lead and find a better place to park their money.

Though most of the companies profiled in this book dealt in things (such as insurance or carpet cleaning) that are closer to the things we deal with every day, the Bre-X scandal illustrated that commodities such as oil and gold also can make great bait. Rogues love to prey on investors who hope that they too will stumble on the opportunity of a lifetime—just as the Beverly Hillbillies stumbled onto "the bubbling crude." So before you plunge into the next "find of the century," put aside greed, grab hold of reason, and assess the offer with a clear and forewarned mind.

Chapter 8

Beware Too Much Focus on Stock Price

Rarely in the history of public markets has one man created such a huge stir out of such a small and seemingly trivial company as Al Dunlap did at Sunbeam Corporation. Known as "Chainsaw" Al for his take-no-prisoners approach to cost cutting, Dunlap ran appliance maker Sunbeam for just two years in the mid-1990s. Yet despite its brevity, his tenure there has become the stuff of legend. Dunlap ran Sunbeam with an iron fist, putting into place an impossible turnaround plan and summarily firing executives who failed to do his bidding. It was all about the numbers—ultimately, *making up* the numbers.

At first, Wall Street couldn't get enough. The day Dunlap took control of Sunbeam, the stock jumped from $12.50 to almost $20. At its peak, it reached $57. But in the end, the company's aggressive accounting practices couldn't mask its increasingly troubled position. When the numbers could be propped up no longer, the company's perilous state was exposed. Dunlap's famed turnaround was revealed to be nothing more than a mirage, fabricated with a host of accounting tricks and cover-ups. The stock price collapsed and the company soon followed, quickly descending into bankruptcy.

Similar dangers lie in wait at any company where the executives are too focused on the price of the company's stock. Building profits and bolstering share price are too different things. Though the latter often follows from the former, the reverse is not the case. Investors buy stock because they believe the company's underlying business is sound enough to attract more investors, thus causing the share price to rise and their investments to show a profit. But a rising share price can't help contribute to the health of the underlying business. Executives who focus too much on inflating their company's stock probably are too little focused on building the bottom line—unless it's through gimmicks that ultimately obscure the true state of affairs.

Executives can be led to this turn by any number of things, though it's usually out of pure greed. This need not always indicate fraud—many executives' compensation packages are contingent on the share price rising under their tenure—but it often indicates an increased level of risk that should put investors on the alert. The number one job of any executive is to build his or her company's business; any other focus simply distracts. And if the incentive to focus elsewhere is too great, the core business can become a vehicle for the executive's personal enrichment. When signs of that happening begin to show up, as they did at Sunbeam, it's probably time to get out.

Firing Up the Chainsaw

Albert J. Dunlap was born on July 26, 1937 into a middle class New Jersey family. His parents and grandparents doted on him. "Al was the shining light of everyone's existence," his sister recounted. He enjoyed monogrammed outfits as a child and trendy clothes as a teenager. Until he was 11, Al and his family lived in a three-story house in Hoboken, close to Frank Sinatra's childhood home. In 1948, the family moved to a suburban neighborhood in nearby Hasbrouck Heights, which was populated by a large contingent of German and Italian immigrants.

Throughout his youth, Dunlap spent much of his time alone. Instead of socializing, Al turned to the gym (much as Stanley Goldblum and Barry Minkow had) and his studies. In high school, he was known to lift weights up to three times a day, developing an impressive physique—

which he was never shy about showing off to his classmates. He earned varsity letters in both football and track and field, and he excelled academically. Without fail Al's report cards would come home replete with A's.

After high school, Dunlap was accepted to West Point, but the academy was a struggle for him. In 1960, Dunlap graduated 537th out of his class of 550. His father was so proud that he made a shrine to Al in the family home.

To get through West Point, Dunlap had had to keep the temper that had plagued him since childhood in check. But as he entered his three years of military service, his hot temper would come to the fore. Perhaps its most unfortunate manifestation was in the context of his marriage to a stunning redheaded model named Gwyn Donnelly. Dunlap's controlling, belligerent manner dominated their marriage. He was a martinet who required the absolute obedience and submissiveness of his wife. Dunlap ran his home like a military barracks, allowing Gwyn only $15 a week to buy food for the family and insisting that she lock their young son in his room all day so that he wouldn't mess up their apartment. When he pulled a knife on her several years into their marriage, Gwyn finally decided it was time to leave.

By then, Dunlap had landed a $650 a month job as a trainee with paper goods manufacturer Kimberly-Clark Corp., working on the plant floor. Dunlap immersed himself in the work, taking on any task assigned to him with enthusiasm. After his marriage had imploded, Dunlap threw himself even harder into his job, eventually being promoted to superintendent of the Kimberly-Clark plant in Neenah, Wisconsin. As the most junior supervisor, Dunlap was assigned the worst shifts. But he didn't complain. He relished the opportunity to try out every job on the factory floor and gain a hands-on education, sure that this would propel him up through the ranks of management.

After four years with Kimberly-Clark, Dunlap was hired away by Ely Meyer, the owner of a private tissue maker, Sterling Pulp & Paper, for $25,000 a year. Dunlap's new boss was intent not only on making an executive out of his latest protégé, but also on helping him find a new bride. Meyer set Dunlap up on a blind date with a beautiful woman named Judy Stringer, and within six months the two were engaged. Dunlap wanted to marry Judy before the end of the 1967 so that he could claim a $600 marital tax deduction. Stringer objected—it was just too unromantic—

and the pair was eventually married on March 30, 1968. Dunlap and his new bride were a solid fit. Judy was comfortable with her place in Al's life. "There are three things that are important in Al's life: his business, his dogs, and his wife, in that order," she would say. "Being third isn't all that bad."

As the general manager of Sterling, Dunlap had a tremendous challenge on his hands. The company was immersed in debt and struggling to survive. As if by instinct, Dunlap decided that the solution to Sterling's woes was to cut back expenses and streamline the 1,000 employee workforce. Immediately, he started slashing jobs.

The approach did not go over well among the residents of the small Wisconsin town where Sterling was located. Dunlap received hate mail and anonymous death threats. The stress wore Judy down as well. But when she began to cry uncontrollably one night, Dunlap sat her down for a talk. "I came here not to win a popularity contest. I came here to save a company," he told her. "If I have to get rid of 30 percent of the people so that 70 percent of the people have job security, that's what I'm going to do. If you can't live with what I'm going to tell you, then maybe we're not meant to be." Judy never questioned her husband's business decisions again. She remained by his side, and became his most ardent defendant.

At Sterling, Dunlap won the support and admiration of his boss. But when Meyer died and the company was sold, Dunlap moved on rather than lose control of the company for which he had worked so hard. Over the following decade he would start to build his reputation as a ruthless cost-cutter. At American Can Company in Connecticut, Dunlap remorselessly closed plants, fired workers, slashed R&D and other investments, and ditched assets. His work paid off quickly—profits jumped and upper management was impressed. But his draconian cost-cutting and profit improvements turned out to be short-term fixes. The managers who succeeded him, forced to reinvest and rebuild the businesses, resented Dunlap deeply and questioned his judgment.

Dunlap was smart enough never to stay in one place too long. He would increase operating profits by starving companies of necessary long-term expenditures and then leave before the consequences came home to roost. After seven years at American Can, he moved on to asbestos maker Manville Corporation. His term at Manville was even shorter. When his boss lost his job in a power struggle, Dunlap was out as well.

Dunlap styled himself a corporate troubleshooter able to come into any struggling company and fix its problems. Nine months after leaving Manville, Dunlap finally got what he was waiting for—the chance to be a CEO. The Lily-Tulip Company had recently been purchased by the renowned leveraged buyout firm Kohlberg, Kravis, Roberts & Co. The disposable plate and cup company needed strong leadership and focus. Dunlap was offered the job.

Dunlap jumped headlong into the company. True to form, he immediately began slashing jobs and cutting costs. In his three years at Lily, he fired 20 percent of the staff, 40 percent of the suppliers, half of management, 11 of the company's top 13 executives, and transformed the company's $11 million yearly operating loss into a $23 million dollar profit. Dunlap's draconian techniques brought him press and attention throughout the financial world. But as with his other endeavors, Dunlap quickly left Lily for a new target.

Rambo in Pinstripes

The acclaim Dunlap received at Lily brought him to the attention of the man who would become his mentor, the internationally acclaimed corporate financier and raider Sir James Goldsmith. Though Sir James had been on the brink of bankruptcy half a dozen times in the 1950s and 1960s, he managed to build his wealth through a series of bold and outrageous takeover bids. Goldsmith believed that the best executives came from modest means, as he had. He would later tell Dunlap, "You and I have an enormous respect for money because we had to make it." Dunlap concurred: "I love every dollar I have ever made like a brother," he would say.

In 1986, Goldsmith put Dunlap in charge of a company he had recently acquired, paper maker Crown-Zellerbach. At Crown-Zellerbach, Dunlap eliminated 22 percent of the workers and cut 18 of the company's 22 distribution centers. As was becoming Al's trademark, Crown-Zellerbach's costs plummeted and profits shot higher. For his effort, Dunlap was rewarded handsomely.

After less than three years, Goldsmith transferred Dunlap to Diamond International, a timber company Goldsmith had recently acquired through a hostile takeover. Again, Dunlap slashed costs and drove profits through the roof. His successes at Crown-Zellerbach and Diamond International caused Goldsmith to dub him "Rambo in Pinstripes." It was around the same time that British naturalist John Aspinall coined the nickname that would define Al Dunlap thereafter—"Chainsaw Al."

Over the years, Dunlap and Goldsmith's relationship flourished. Their mutual zest for money had brought them together, but their conservative politics and mutual dislike of the corporate establishment sealed their friendship. Dunlap became Goldsmith's dedicated soldier. When Goldsmith made hostile bids for Goodyear Tire & Rubber Co. and BAT Industries, Dunlap was his right-hand man. The pair made extraordinary amounts of money together.

For five years, Goldsmith and Dunlap were an inseparable, formidable team. But in 1991, with Goldsmith's blessing, Dunlap took an opportunity to work with Kerry Packer, an Australian billionaire and close friend of Goldsmith. Packer's media empire, Consolidated Press Holdings, was on the cusp of bankruptcy. It was losing $25 million a year and needed an aggressive turnaround plan.

Dunlap took to the company with his typical vigor. He sold or closed 300 of CPH's 413 business units, fired thousands of employees (including Packer's family and friends) and slashed costs throughout the company. Two years into his five-year contract, Dunlap had turned massive operating losses into a $623 million profit. But Dunlap's tough character clashed with Packer's equally obstinate manner. In 1993 tensions came to a head and Dunlap returned to the United States.

He did not return empty handed, of course. On the contrary, he amassed some $40 million during his two years abroad. Notoriously frugal, Dunlap loved his money so much that he could hardly bear to put it at risk, let alone spend it. Instead of investing it in the stock market, Dunlap stowed much of it in government bonds.

Despite his fortune and reputation, Dunlap had trouble finding work. U.S. companies had grown wary of him. Every company he had headed seemed to have disappeared since Dunlap's departure—either sold or liquidated when the business he had left turned out to be unsustainable.

It took Dunlap 11 months to find a job, but in the spring of 1994 he landed the post that would transform him from a successful business executive into a Wall Street icon—though some would argue that he more or less bought his way in. Scott Paper was a severely troubled company in 1993, having lost $277 million. Scott was plagued by a bloated payroll, languishing businesses, and ineffective leadership. Dunlap was the perfect fit. He had years of experience working with paper companies and the stomach to make difficult decisions, and he was eager to test his mettle with a high-profile public company such as Scott. During a short courtship, the brash Dunlap told Scott's board of directors that if he was unable to double the stock price within three years, he would be ashamed of himself. To show he meant it, Dunlap promised to buy $4 million worth of Scott shares if and when he was named CEO. On April 19, 1994, Dunlap was hired to lead a company considered a former American treasure.

In the first two months of his tenure, Dunlap did not disappoint. He put in place a plan that would eventually eliminate 11,200 jobs, including 71 percent of the headquarters staff, 50 percent of management, and 20 percent of hourly employees. Dunlap's visits to Scott's various factories and complexes soon came to be known as the "Chainsaw Massacre Tour." Dunlap "put the fear of God into a lot of people," recalled one factory worker. "When he was in the building, people knew he was there. His presence was palpable."

It soon became clear that Dunlap's goal was simply to pretty up the business for sale. Dunlap cut R&D spending in half and cancelled all plant and equipment upgrades for 1995. Scott's head of manufacturing and technology summed up Dunlap's modus operandi this way: "What he did was borrow a year, maybe two, from the future. At some point you have to pay it back. If you wait too long, you'll pay it back double because the plants will operate inefficiently and the machines will begin to break down. We strung it out as far as we could without getting into unsafe conditions."

But simply slashing costs wasn't going to make the company attractive to buyers. It also needed to show a robust top line. To pump up revenues, Dunlap pursued a strategy often known as "inventory stuffing" which inflated sales for the current period by cannibalizing future earnings. By offering large incentives, Scott was able to induce customers to make larger purchases than normal—somewhat like convincing a family to buy a year's supply of toilet paper to get a bulk discount.

Scott accomplished its task by offering unusually large rebate credits to retailers. But the rebates were made only once the product—toilet paper, paper napkins, and so on—was sold to a retail customer. Because Scott sold its goods up to six months before retailers rung up the sales at their stores, Scott could book current sales at full price, and account for the discount in future quarters when retailers applied for their credit. To inflate volume in the final weeks of a fiscal quarter, Scott would often double these discounts, from approximately 15 to 30 percent.

Dunlap's approach to executive compensation also helped pump up Scott's numbers—and its stock. Dunlap provided his management team with generous stock option packages, well beyond those offered by competitors, tying their pay to the performance of the company's stock. These options would vest slowly over time, but if the company were acquired, all of them would become immediately exercisable. The game was clear: Make your numbers at all costs and do everything you could to make the company look good to potential buyers—the retail customer came in a distant second.

During his 20 months at Scott, Dunlap became a media darling. His arrogant, self-congratulatory style was made for TV, and he reveled in the attention. Dunlap became a regular guest on NBC, CNN, and CNBC. He built friendships with his favorite anchors, Lou Dobbs and Neil Cavuto. He contributed opinion pieces to publications such as *The Wall Street Journal* and *USA Today*, and repeatedly provided *Fortune*, *Forbes*, and *The New York Times* with access to the company. The publications returned the favor with positive pieces hailing him and his management philosophy. *Barron's* declared him "America's premiere turnaround artist." And each time Dunlap opened his mouth, it seemed, Scott's stock price would jump.

On July 17, 1995, Dunlap scored the biggest coup of his career. Paper giant Kimberly-Clark agreed to buy Scott Paper for $9.4 billion. Under Dunlap's management, the market capitalization of Scott had increased by 225 percent, to $6.3 billion. "The Scott story," Dunlap boasted, "will go down in the annals of American business history as one of the most successful, quickest turnarounds ever. It makes other turnarounds pale by comparison." For his efforts, Dunlap was compensated handsomely, earning over $100 million. Dunlap also made millionaires of Scott's top 62 executives. By now, though, the size of Dunlap's ego well exceeded that of his wallet: As the deal was in its final stages, Dunlap declared himself to be the most underpaid CEO in America.

Kimberly-Clark's executives, meanwhile, were left holding the bag, discovering only after the acquisition that Dunlap's strategy had left them with an asset worth far less than they'd thought. When the acquisition was announced, Scott was projecting profits of more than $100 million for the fourth quarter of 1995. Kimberly-Clark, however, ultimately reported an operating loss of $60 million for Scott's business that quarter. Among the hidden costs Kimberly-Clark unwittingly acquired were $30 million in discounts claimed by retailers and another $30 million in equipment upgrades that Dunlap had postponed. In addition to the initial $1.4 billion charge Kimberly-Clark took to cover Scott's integration into the company, it was forced to take a second restructuring charge of $810 million in 1998. Kimberly-Clark's CFO, John Donehower, laid the blame for the problems squarely at the feet of Dunlap and his practice of inventory stuffing.

In retrospect, it seemed clear that Dunlap had done more to obfuscate the struggles at Scott than to fix them. Scott had become just another in a laundry list of companies that Dunlap had seized control of in order to liquidate or sell. To many analysts, Dunlap was not a visionary or a builder; he was a mortician, brought in to prepare a dying company for its burial.

A New Sunbeam Shining

Dunlap, of course, was unfazed by his critics. The book he wrote after his departure from Scott, *Mean Business*, unapologetically set forth the four simple rules of his management philosophy: Get the right management team, pinch pennies, know your business, and get a real strategy. Dunlap hit the airwaves to promote himself once again, and the book shot to the top of *The New York Times* bestseller list.

Dunlap cast about for his next conquest, looking for something big, something blue chip, that would launch him even further into America's consciousness. But corporate America seemed to want nothing to do with him. Recruiters shied away from his over-the-top personality, boards of directors were threatened by his power, and there was the general sense that all Dunlap knew how to do was break up companies and sell them.

The one contingent that still adored him was shareholders. Dunlap was celebrated for his singular focus on shareholder value. And while there might be disagreement about whether his motives were pure and methods were sound, no one could argue with the results: He had made his shareholders rich. Around the country, shareholders were clamoring for Dunlap to seize control of companies where the leadership was perceived as indecisive, bloated, or both. In the spring of 1996, the shareholders who dominated the board of Sunbeam decided that Dunlap was the right man to take the helm of their company.

Sunbeam was middle class America. It made the toasters, blenders, and irons found in just about every home in the country. It had invented the first automatic coffeemaker, electric toaster, and mixmaster, and its research and development unit was a model of American ingenuity.

But in the early 1980s, Sunbeam had fallen on hard times, and a series of buyouts, mergers, sales, and management changes didn't seem to help. By 1996, it had been in and out of bankruptcy, seen control of the company change hands twice and been under the guidance of four different management teams. Though its fortunes had improved briefly in the early 1990s, the company was struggling again by 1996, its stock price languishing below $15.

By that time, the company was under the control of its two largest shareholders, investment managers Michael Price and Michael Steinhardt, who wanted a tough, decisive executive to whip the company into shape, someone with a religious dedication to building shareholder value. Dunlap was their man.

But getting Dunlap to agree to run Sunbeam wasn't easy. Dunlap insisted on having control over every facet of the business, including three board seats (he replaced every director other than Michael Price's sole representative, Peter Langerman), and would accept nothing less. Sunbeam agreed to meet his demands, giving Dunlap a $1 million a year salary, $2.5 million in stock options, and one million shares of restricted stock. Dunlap was also permitted to buy $3 million worth of stock at $12.25 a share, the closing price on the day before he was announced as CEO. Sunbeam also agreed to buy the Mercedes that Dunlap already owned and to replace it with a new car every two years. The company hired him a bodyguard and driver, and gave him an unlimited expense account that included first class travel, a country club membership, and a bullet-proof vest. Sunbeam also agreed to pay all taxes Dunlap would owe the government because of his special perks. Dunlap not only was guaranteed riches, he also gained "without limitation the power of supervision and control" over Sunbeam, to ensure that Price would not meddle in Dunlap's affairs.

The news of Dunlap's hiring sent the markets into a frenzy. Sunbeam's stock soared from $12.25 to almost $20, rising more than 60 percent, then the biggest one-day jump in the history of the NYSE. Dunlap's supporters flocked to get into what they expected would be another success story. Analysts roared, praising Sunbeam's bold move. "It's like the Lakers signing Shaquille O'Neal," an excited analyst from Oppenheimer & Co. declared. Scott Heymann at NatWest securities upgraded the stock to a buy, as did Dean Witter's William Steele. There was but one lonely voice questioning the wisdom of Dunlap's hiring—Andrew Shore, the analyst from PaineWebber. Shore expressed his doubts to *The Wall Street Journal*: "Al Dunlap is the perfect announcement to give the Street, because the Street wants to believe he can do with Sunbeam what he did with Scott Paper. But his history is as a cost-cutter and not a brand-builder—and Sunbeam's problems are more sales-related."

At 9 a.m. the following Monday, Chainsaw Al marched into a room filled with Sunbeam's senior executives. It was his first day on the job. "The old Sunbeam is over today," he declared. "You guys are responsible for the demise of Sunbeam! You are the ones who have played this political, bullshit game with Michael Price and Michael Steinhardt. You are the guys responsible for this crap, and I'm here to tell you that things have changed. The old Sunbeam is over today. It's over!" Dunlap continued, "This is the best day of your life if you are good at what you do and willing to accept change. And it's the worst day of your life if you're not."

The meeting lasted more than three hours, with Dunlap berating each executive in turn. The executive team was left stunned, but in his first morning at the company, Dunlap had successfully changed the tone. His control was evident the next day, when he fired Sunbeam president and COO Jim Clegg, who was widely respected and considered untouchable. Clegg's firing was remarkable not only for the speed with which it was completed but because, of the almost 10,000 employees Dunlap would eventually cut, Clegg was the only one Dunlap fired personally.

By the end of his first week at the company, Dunlap had brought in a team that had served him well for decades. C. Donald Burnett from consulting firm Coopers & Lybrand was hired to advise Dunlap on a turnaround plan. Burnett had advised Dunlap at every company he'd run since American Can in 1977, and quickly deployed his consultants throughout Sunbeam.

As CFO, Dunlap hired Russell Kersh, another man with whom he'd worked with repeatedly through the years. Kersh, though, was not an operations man with industry experience but was Dunlap's chief accountant. Dunlap knew Kersh would bring with him what he called his "ditty bag." Sailors use ditty bags to hold various pieces of small gear, but in Kersh's case, his ditty bag contained a collection of accounting tricks that could be used to inflate sales and reduce expenses. It was crucial that Dunlap have Kersh in position before the company reported its 1996 earnings. That year would be the one against which the company's future performance would be measured, and Dunlap needed Kersh and his ditty bag to ensure that the benchmark was not too high. To lower expectations, Kersh would have the company write off much larger amounts than Sunbeam would ever need for its actual restructuring. This would artificially deflate 1996's numbers, and create a reserve which Dunlap and Kersh could use to offset any earnings shortfalls that might emerge later.

Dunlap filled out the rest of his management team with old cronies, including marketing chief Donald Uzzi, sales chief Newt White (who had worked with Dunlap at Scott) and several execs from Sunbeam whom Dunlap trusted, including general counsel David Fannin.

For the next several months, everything went according to plan. Sunbeam's stock price continued to advance and by November had hit $26. Dunlap's team suffered only one set-back, when Fannin had a mild heart attack. While Fannin was resting in his hospital bed with his wife nearby, Al lamented to Fannin that "this same thing happened to me at Scott Paper."

"You had a heart attack?" replied Fannin's wife.

"No, not me. My corporate counsel at Scott had a heart attack."

From that point on, Al became found of telling the press, "I don't get heart attacks, I give them."

On November 12, Dunlap presented the details of his restructuring plan to the world. Expectations were high. Wall Street analysts estimated he would cut about 30 percent of the workforce. But Dunlap announced he intended to get rid of half of Sunbeam's 12,000 employees. He would cut 87 percent of the company's products and eliminate 39 of its 56 facilities. He also decided to sell several business units including the outdoor furniture operations, clocks, scales, and decorative bedding. He would close six regional offices and consolidate all corporate operations into a single headquarters in Delray Beach, Florida. At the same time, Dunlap promised to introduce at least 30 new products a year in the United States and expand sales abroad. On the sales side, he told Wall Street that revenues would double to over $2 billion by 1999. Dunlap promised to spend $12 million on a new advertising and marketing program, entitled "There's a New Sunbeam Shining." He estimated the plan would require a one-time charge of $300 million, but save the company $225 million annually.

Dunlap's hand-picked board of directors took to the plan immediately, but the rest of the world was less enthusiastic. Managers and analysts could not understand how Dunlap was going to pull it off. To meet his goal of $2 billion in revenues by 1999, Sunbeam would have to perform five times better than any of its competitors, and to meet his profitability targets, Sunbeam would have to increase operating margins from 2.5 percent to 20 percent, an increase of 1,200 percent. To achieve the $600 million in sales of new products, Sunbeam would have to pull a blockbuster out of thin air. Skeptics worried that Dunlap's plan would destroy morale, reduce efficiency, and lower productivity. Wall Street questioned its wisdom, the Secretary of the U.S. Department of Labor took great exception to its brutality, and numerous management experts were left scratching their heads.

Even Dunlap's chief of operations, Newt White, was dubious. "He was trying to put ten pounds in a five pound bag," he said. "You can't turn around a billion-dollar company in six months." White left the company soon after the plan was announced. Executives who stayed had no choice but to make the plan work.

Privately, Dunlap was secure in the knowledge that Kersh had provided him with a $30 million cushion by inflating the write-offs necessary for the turnaround. This gave Dunlap almost 40 cents worth of leeway for every share outstanding, money that could be added to earnings whenever he felt like it. Dunlap believed he would be able to declare his turnaround a success within a year, and then sell the company to a competitor.

Dunlap kept brutal pressure on his executives and managers, and also designed a system of stock options and compensation packages intended to control the behavior of his employees, as he had done at Scott. Generous option packages went to the top 300 executives, managers received at least twice as many options as they would have elsewhere, and every employee with a minimum of a year's experience received at least 100 options.

However, the options vested over three years, meaning that if Dunlap fired someone for not hitting their targets, it would pack a sizable wallop as their options reverted to the company. In addition, the options included a clause preventing the recipient from speaking with the press or stock analysts, all but gagging potential whistle-blowers. Dunlap had laid out a gauntlet of incentives and disincentives to ensure that Sunbeam employees did everything possible to hit their numbers.

And they did. To the surprise of his detractors—and of the market—Sunbeam's earnings exceeded expectations by 2 cents for the first quarter of 1997, coming in at 24 cents per share. Sunbeam's stock climbed to $41 by July. Even skeptics such as Paine Webber's Andrew Shore hailed him. "Dunlap might pull it off," Shore wrote.

To the outside world, Dunlap's strategy seemed to be working. But behind the numbers, the organization was in disarray. Managers were getting the axe. Suppliers were being fired. Computer systems were starting to fail. Assembly lines shut down as key employees were laid off. Factories closed because nobody remembered to order key parts from suppliers.

And the upheaval was starting to hit Sunbeam's customers. Wal-Mart threatened to cancel its account when Sunbeam failed to deliver an order of 300,000 irons. Sears complained it had to deal with three different sales reps in six months because they kept getting fired. Sunbeam shipments went out late, to the wrong companies, and with the wrong products.

The meltdown soon began to affect Sunbeam's financial performance. It was time to reach into the ditty bag. In the second quarter of 1997, Sunbeam reported earnings of 30 cents a share, in line with Wall Street expectations. But it had taken a bit of finessing. First, Kersh changed the way the company accounted for the cost of its manufacturing supplies. Rather than expense the supplies in the current quarter, he capitalized the cost, spreading out the expense over a number of years and reducing costs in the current quarter. Second, he skimmed $4.5 million from the inflated reserve account, boosting earnings an additional 20 percent. Both of these practices were disclosed in Sunbeam's financial statements, but most analysts were so taken with the blustery Dunlap that they did not bother to read the fine print. The stock jumped again.

But one analyst, William Steele of Buckingham Research Group, did go through the financial statements carefully, and was troubled by what he saw. Inventory had grown by $60 million to $208 million. "That told me that orders were not as strong as the company indicated or that its gross margin performance was artificially inflated because the plants were running faster than the orders received," Steele said. He also noticed that the company's working capital had sunk from a positive $1 million a year to a negative $36 million. "When your working capital is going negative, you are not efficiently selling your goods," Steele reported to the market. Steele downgraded the stock from buy to neutral in July of 1997. Other analysts, such as Shore, also noted these warnings, but the market as a whole paid no heed.

Dunlap pushed his managers hard through the third quarter of 1997, driving them to all kinds of aggressive sales tactics in an effort to push inventory at customers at any cost in an effort to meet the numbers. Vendors would go unpaid or underpaid, commissions would be withheld, products discounted dramatically, and credit extended on unbelievably favorable terms—anything to pump up sales. Dunlap's harried managers figured that the future of the company didn't matter, only the next quarter's numbers, because the company would probably be sold to an unwitting buyer before any consequences had to be paid.

But by the fourth quarter of 1997, managers still were struggling to hit their numbers, even with all the finagling. Kersh went to the ditty bag again.

This time, Kersh devised a "bill-and-hold" scheme that was really a sophisticated version of inventory stuffing. To convince retailers to purchase barbecues and other products months before they would be sold, Sunbeam offered deep discounts and did not demand payment until the products were actually delivered for sale. After the initial "purchase," Sunbeam would "deliver" the products to third-party warehouses it had leased in Missouri, to be held there until they were needed by retailers. The scheme allowed Sunbeam to recognize revenue from such "sales" immediately, even though no actual sales would take place for another six months, and then at prices far below what had been recorded.

Kersh and Dunlap, of course, were unconcerned that bill-and-hold schemes were frowned upon by the SEC. If they made it possible for the company to hit its numbers, it was okay by them. The market, meanwhile, remained blind to Sunbeam's troubles. In October, Sunbeam stock was trading for more than $40 a share.

Dunlap had promised that Sunbeam would make earnings of 48 cents per share in the fourth quarter of 1997. But it soon became clear to Dunlap and Kersh that the company would fall short. Operating performance was deteriorating, and Kersh's charge-off reserve would not be able to make up the difference.

As far as Dunlap and Kersh could figure, the only way out of their bind was to sell the company. Dunlap spent the fourth quarter of 1997 desperately seeking a suitor, switching investment bankers, and setting up a due diligence file at the law firm of Skadden, Arps, which potential acquirers could use to look over the company's books.

But not a single suitor even bothered to look over Sunbeam's files at Skadden, Arps. Dunlap had been so successful at hyping the stock that the price was now too high to attract any interest. To make matters worse, some people simply didn't trust Sunbeam's numbers. Rumors grew that Sunbeam's "turnaround" was all smoke and mirrors. Executives at other companies remembered how Kimberly-Clark was left holding the bag when it had purchased Scott from Dunlap. They were not willing to repeat that error.

It soon became clear Dunlap was not going to be able to escape from Sunbeam as easily as he had from Scott. It was time for a new approach. Instead of trying to find a buyer, he decided to use the inflated stock price as currency to acquire other consumer product companies. If he completed enough deals, Kersh could obscure Sunbeam's actual performance behind the complex accounting of the mergers.

But no one wanted to sell to Dunlap either. Dunlap's "chainsaw" moniker was well earned, and executives didn't want to feel its bite.

Finally, Dunlap found an opportunity that made sense: Coleman, the camping equipment maker, which was owned by billionaire financier Ron Perelman. Perelman was a legend, having built an empire through ruthless dealmaking, taking over businesses ranging from Marvel Entertainment Group to Revlon. Perelman respected Dunlap, had once considered hiring him to run one of his companies, and Perelman had even agreed to write a blurb for the cover of his book: "Lively, funny and provocative. No one feels neutral about Al Dunlap—you either love his ideas about running a business or hate them."

Investment manager Michael Price, Sunbeam's largest shareholder, set up a meeting with Perelman and his attorney, Howard Gittis, at Perelman's Florida house at 5 p.m. on December 18, 1998. Dunlap and Price had agreed they would pay up to $24 a share for Coleman, whose stock was mired in the low teens. But Perelman wouldn't let the company go for less than $30.

Dunlap grew furious almost immediately. "Ron, you're a pig," Dunlap shouted only minutes into the meeting. "You know your company is a piece of shit. You'll never see it worth thirty dollars a share in your lifetime. It's only worth twenty bucks and that is an early Christmas present."

"It's Hanukkah." Perelman quickly responded, mildly amused by Dunlap's threats.

Gittis attempted to reduce the tension. "This is only business," he said. "Whether we make this deal or not, Ron is not going to be any more or less rich, and I'm not going to be more or less rich. It's not going to change any of our lives."

But Dunlap was off and ranting. "Fuck you guys. You'll never make a deal. I told you, Perelman, you should never listen to lawyers." Dunlap stood up and left the house shouting, "Fuck you and fuck your company." Price, Perelman, and Gittis remained in the room in silence. Their meeting had lasted but five minutes, and Dunlap had killed any hope of a deal. "We thought the guy was crazy," Gittis later recalled. "We were just trying to do a deal. He went off like a wild man. We were mystified."

The Sun Sets on Sunbeam

What Perelman and Gittis didn't realize was that this was not, in fact, "only business" to Dunlap. Dunlap knew Sunbeam's performance was suffering, and he knew that without a major deal the world would soon know it too. He needed a deal and he needed it badly. With the collapse of talks with Perelman, Dunlap was more desperate than ever.

Meanwhile, Sunbeam's fourth quarter profits were looking horrendous. Earnings were not going to reach even 20 cents per share—less than half the 48 cents the market was expecting. Dunlap and Kersh decided to empty the write-down reserves, pouring an additional $21.5 million into income and enabling them to hide Sunbeam's deteriorating performance for another quarter.

Though Sunbeam had begun to suffer the ravages of Dunlap's management style, Chainsaw Al picked this moment to demand a raise for himself and his two chief lieutenants, Kersh and Fannin. In little over a year, Dunlap had sent Sunbeam's stock into the stratosphere, and had successfully hidden the company's deteriorating condition from directors and most investors. Although his antics infuriated people throughout the company, the fact that his managers all held millions of dollars of unvested stock options silenced any criticism. And in late 1997, rumors had emerged that Dunlap was being courted by another company, Waste Management. Although he was never offered a job, the talk gave him substantial leverage with Sunbeam.

As usual, Dunlap's demands were outrageous. For running a company with only $1 billion in revenues, he wanted a contract larger than that of his counterparts at GE, GM, Microsoft, and Intel. In the end, Price agreed to double Dunlap's salary to $2 million a year, and give him 300,000 free unrestricted shares worth more than $11 million, plus options to buy an additional 3.75 million shares. Under the contract Dunlap would make $46.5 million if Sunbeam's stock rose only 5.5 percent a year. Kersh and Fannin were to receive similar contract upgrades. The contract meant that Sunbeam would have to take a $31 million charge to earnings in the first quarter of 1998, but the boards knew the company would lose $1 to 2 billion in market capitalization if Dunlap left the company, as he was threatening to do.

By now, though, even insiders were growing skeptical. At a review of the company's fourth quarter operating results, Philip Harlow, the Arthur Andersen partner in charge of the audit, questioned the bill-and-hold sales and other aggressive accounting practices. One director asked whether the bill-and-hold transactions were within the Generally Accepted Accounting Principles. Kersh and controller Robert Gluck assured the room that all transactions were legitimate and that they had asked the company's internal auditor to work with Arthur Andersen to ensure that things were handled as conservatively as possible. Nor was the board told of concerns raised by a junior member of the company's internal audit unit, Deidra DenDanto. A steadfast critic of the bill-and-hold practice, DenDanto's concerns had previously been brushed aside by Kersh and Gluck. Even when she alerted Arthur Andersen to the practice, no concrete action was taken.

A week later, Dunlap reported fourth quarter earnings of 47 cents per share, one cent below estimates. Given Dunlap's enormous new contract, the market was shocked that the company didn't hit its numbers. The news sent the stock tumbling 10 percent to $37 a share. Talk on Wall Street was that Sunbeam's turnaround was an illusion. Dunlap, on the other hand, blamed the poor fourth quarter sales figures on the weather.

The sour reaction to Sunbeam's fourth quarter numbers made it all the more important that the company meet expectations the following quarter. But Dunlap knew that Kersh had depleted his write-off reserve, and the situation inside the company was only getting worse. Sales were plummeting. Retailers were overloaded with products. Only by acquiring another company and taking an enormous restructuring charge could Dunlap hide Sunbeam's poor performance.

Dunlap did so in spades, first mending fences with Perelman and accepting his price of $30 a share for Coleman. But Dunlap knew it would be too easy for analysts to separate Sunbeam's operating performance from Coleman's, so he also arranged to acquire both the First Alert and Signature Brands, two consumer products companies owned by Boston financier Thomas Lee. This way, the market would have no way of unraveling all the numbers and Sunbeam would be able to take larger than necessary write-offs and rebuild Kersh's reserve fund. To finance the purchases, Sunbeam was forced to increase its debt load by three-quarters of a billion dollars.

Dunlap announced his "triple" on March 2, 1998, and Wall Street loved it, sending Sunbeam's stock soaring to $45.625. Two days later, the stock hit $52. Coleman's management team, however, sensing Dunlap's plans, sold the stock they received in the deal immediately.

Sunbeam's management had even less confidence in the company. Executives were fleeing as if headquarters had caught fire. From December to February, five senior executives left the company. Less than two weeks before the end of the first quarter, only $169 million in sales had been booked. The market was expecting close to $300 million. In addition, Sunbeam was preparing to issue $500 million in new debt to pay for its recent acquisitions.

On March 18, less than three weeks after the "triple" was announced, Dunlap was forced by his lawyers to issue a statement warning the market that sales were likely to fall short of expectations "due to changes in inventory management and order patterns at certain of the company's major retail customers." But the statement promised that revenues would exceed "1997 first quarter net sales of $253.4 million," and added that

Sunbeam remained "highly confident" about the full year's sales numbers. Nonetheless, the market began to worry. Sunbeam's stock price dropped 10 percent to $45. The *New York Post* responded with a story saying, "Dunlap's failings as a manager are becoming abundantly clear."

When they read of the earnings warning, lawyers at Skadden, Arps became furious, and began watching results all the more closely. As the days passed, it became clear that there was no way Sunbeam's first quarter revenues would reach the promised $250 million. Skadden demanded yet another warning be released.

In fact, it was looking like Sunbeam would lose money for the quarter, an absolute disaster. But Dunlap was not about to take another public lashing. Instead he lay the blame squarely at the feet of COO Donald Uzzi. The press release flagging Sunbeam's poorer than expected results now had to include Uzzi's firing as well, the company's number three man. More trouble developed as the executive team sought out Rich Goudis, Sunbeam's investor relations chief, to draft the release. Goudis had decided Dunlap and Kersh were providing the markets with misleading information, and he had had enough. Having found a position at drugstore company Rexall-Sundown, Goudis told his boss that he couldn't help with the press release. Adding insult to injury, the release would now have to include the news of Goudis's resignation as well.

Rumors of the troubles quickly spread. Internet chat sites were filled with talk of Uzzi's departure and Goudis's resignation. When PaineWebber analyst Andrew Shore called the home phone number he had for Goudis, he was amazed to find Goudis was there. "I just resigned," Goudis told him, though he refused to provide any information about Uzzi. Shore was concerned. Uzzi was a respected operations man, and his departure was a red flag.

At 7:50 a.m. on April 2, Andrew Shore's voice came over the PaineWebber squawk box, announcing that he was downgrading Sunbeam. PaineWebber's sales force was stunned. Shore could hear people on the other end groaning. Shore understood that he would likely be fired if he were wrong. His downgrade sent shockwaves throughout Wall Street. Within minutes of Sunbeam's opening, the stock shed $2 to $43.

At 11:01 a.m., Fannin put out the release. Sunbeam's stock continued to fall. Soon thereafter, Dunlap held a news conference where he read a prepared statement that claimed the loss "had nothing to do with ongoing operations," implying that costs associated with his contract and the acquisitions were driving the earnings shortfall. By the end of the day, Sunbeam's stock had dropped by 25 percent to $34.375.

Over the next week, more analysts began to turn against the stock. William Steele of Buckingham Research advised his clients to sell immediately. Constance Maneaty at Bear Sterns, R. Scott Graham of CIBC, and Lisa Fontenelli of Goldman Sachs also issued downgrades. Only a few true believers remained. Nicholas Heymann of Prudential and Justin Maurer of McDonald & Company bought Dunlap's excuses hook, line, and sinker.

There was no quit in Dunlap, however. Dunlap insisted there "had to be a way for [Kersh's] finance people to find an operating profit." And indeed, Kersh, the company's biggest profit center, had a final trick in his ditty bag. Kersh noted that although Sunbeam's quarter had ended on March 30, the first quarter of the three acquired company's ended on April 1. These extra two days would provide Dunlap a lifeline. The acquisitions closed on March 31. In order to include them in Sunbeam's first quarter results, Kersh simply changed the end of Sunbeam's first quarter to match that of the companies it had acquired. This departure from common practice enabled Kersh to muddle Sunbeam's financials beyond recognition. By reporting the combined performance of the three companies and taking write-offs for expected acquisition and restructuring costs, Sunbeam's sales numbers would be buried in the report. Any market expectations also would be rendered meaningless, because they had been based on Sunbeam's stand-alone numbers.

To integrate the new acquisitions, Dunlap brought back consultant C. Donald Burnett, who recommended closing seven more plants and 13 more manufacturing sites, and selling three of Coleman's businesses, which accounted for approximately $150 million in sales. Dunlap set May 6 as the date by which to have the work done and deliver the final first quarter results to the board.

A few days before the board was to meet, *Forbes* printed an article that was surprisingly critical of the accounting practices at Sunbeam. The story's author, Matthew Schifrin, had received a tip from a short seller about disclosures in the company's public filings, and he pounced. The article reported disclosures from Sunbeam's March 6 financial statements that described the company's bill-and-hold sales and other financial gimmicks. Schifrin openly accused Dunlap of playing "hocus pocus" with the numbers to obscure the company's deteriorating operating results. "This time," concluded Schifrin, "it's not only the employees who get a taste of Al's chainsaw. The shareholders and debenture holders are likely to shed more blood before this is over."

As Schifrin's article reverberated across Wall Street, Dunlap dismissed the story as "a sloppy piece of journalism." He reported his newest restructuring plans to the board as planned. He would eliminate some 6,400 jobs and close 75 out of 120 facilities. Dunlap figured he would save $250 million annually. Dunlap let Kersh deliver the bad news. For the first quarter of 1997, Sunbeam would report a loss of $44.6 million, or 52 cents a share. Sales would be $244 million, more than 20 percent below the market's initial estimates. Even Dunlap acknowledged his excuse sounded implausible. "I can't believe I'm doing this. I always said I never would, but it was the weather. It was El Nino. People don't think of buying grills during a storm."

As depressing as Kersh's news was, the board found his projections to be optimistic. He still was calling for a profit of $1 per share for the year. But given the company's enormous debt load—$2 billion—and the difficulties of integrating three new companies into the organization without disrupting sales, they were baffled by how Dunlap planned to meet Kersh's projections.

The following week, Dunlap made the same presentation at an analyst meeting that would be remembered more for the epic confrontation between Dunlap and his loudest critic, Andrew Shore. At the meeting, Shore was given the microphone for a question. "Al, earlier you mentioned that a lot of the problems were your doing, or you take responsibility. Are you willing to give back your bonus and work for a dollar this year?" Shore recalled that Lee Iacocca had agreed to work for a dollar the year he asked Congress to help bail out Chrysler.

"No," Dunlap shot back. "I am not willing to give back my bonus and work for a dollar this year. That's a vintage Andrew Shore question. I accomplished what I accomplished last year. It was a tremendous turnaround. I also was the person who led the three acquisitions. And we have acquired three great companies. And we have put together a great strategy, and I'm quite sorry if you don't like that, Andrew. That is your problem, not our problem, not the shareholders' problem."

But analysts were not impressed by Dunlap's performance at the meeting. Sunbeam's stock continued to fall—almost 10 percent more that day—sinking below $25. And inside the company, the situation was dire. On June 4, Dunlap and Kersh received an apocalyptic memo from Lee Griffith, president of the household products group. It showed that every single category of business was underperforming its targets. Further, it declared that retail channels remained stuffed from the bill-and-hold sales. Kmart had 20 weeks of inventory on hand, Costco had 12 weeks worth. The company, the memo said, would be lucky to miss earnings estimates by only $80 million. Dunlap now faced the embarrassing reality of having to go back to Wall Street and lower the company's already pessimistic expectations yet again. To make matters worse, the sales staff was defecting en masse. With their options losing value by the day, and morale abysmal, there was no reason to stick around. At least 25 of the 30 sales people Dunlap had not fired now quit.

Two days later, *Barron's* piled on, running a devastating article outlining Dunlap's fraudulent accounting practices and painting the picture of a company teetering on the verge of collapse. "Sunbeam's financials under Dunlap look like an exercise in high-energy physics, in which time and space seem to fuse and bend," the article proffered. "Income and costs move almost imperceptibly back and forth between the income statement and the balance sheet like charged ions, whose vapor trail has long since dissipated by the end of any quarter, when results are reported." In excruciating detail, the article listed the financial shenanigans conducted by Dunlap and Kersh.

Dunlap blasted the *Barron's* article in a Monday-morning press release, declaring there was "absolutely no factual support for [the article's] outrageous accusations." But the release provided no direct rebuttals. Sunbeam's stock continued its free-fall, losing 6 percent to $20.625. It now stood at 40 percent of its peak.

Dunlap defended himself at a board meeting the next day. But he also told the board they should either give him their full support, or fire him and Kersh. The demand blindsided board members, who felt they were being asked to provide Dunlap with a face-saving way out of the situation. After Dunlap left, the board spent another three hours pondering their next move. They agreed to reconvene at the end of the week for a final decision.

General Counsel David Fannin was disturbed by what had transpired. Fannin felt Dunlap had misled the board as to the extent of company's problems. Fannin had been in on one of the meetings when Dunlap was told of a potential $80 million shortfall in revenue. Fannin knew—as did

Dunlap—that turning a profit was out of the question for the current quarter. As Fannin spoke to more people within the company, he soon discovered that Sunbeam's updated sales projections for the current quarter fell short of expectations not by $80 million, but nearly $200 million.

On June 13, 1998 the board met to determine Dunlap's fate. Peter Langerman, Michael Price's representative on board, invited Fannin to share what he had learned through his recent investigations. It quickly became clear that Dunlap and Kersh had to go. Dunlap was due to leave for London that afternoon—not on Sunbeam business, but on a tour to promote his book. The board called Dunlap immediately. Within 15 minutes, both he and Kersh were out of the company.

The day only continued to get worse for Sunbeam, though. The board suffered its biggest jolt when Ronald Richter, the company's new treasurer, informed the board that if it were true that the company faced a $200 million revenue shortfall, Sunbeam would be at risk of violating some of its debt covenants—an event that would surely tip the company into bankruptcy. Dunlap had saddled the company with debt that required $150 million in earnings just to cover interest payments. If net income weren't positive for the quarter, Sunbeam's banks could call in their $1.7 billion in loans.

The board contacted Robert Gluck, Sunbeam's controller, and asked how much cash was on hand. Gluck mentioned the company's revolving credit line. A Sunbeam director gasped. "You are meeting the payroll with revolving credit?" he asked in horror.

A shocked silence engulfed the board room as the full extent of the company's troubles finally became clear. Sunbeam would soon be in technical default on its loans, it was hovering on the edge of bankruptcy, and it didn't even have money on hand to pay its employees. Dunlap's "cost-cutting" measures had left Sunbeam more gutted than any other company he'd "saved" in the past. His reign had been a disaster.

In the months after Dunlap's termination, the public was treated to a steady stream of revelations about his misconduct while at Sunbeam. Arthur Andersen retracted its support for the company's financial statements and the SEC became involved in sorting out the mess. Finally, 10 days after Dunlap left, the lone analyst still supporting Sunbeam cut his rating. The stock price dropped to $12.25—the same price it was the day before Dunlap took over.

Though Dunlap defended himself in the press, the stock continued to slide. In the end, Michael Price was Dunlap's biggest victim. Sunbeam shares soon were trading at $5. The value of Price's position had fallen by more then 90 percent from its peak, costing his fund $850 million.

As Sunbeam's true numbers came to light, it turned out that Dunlap's "turnaround" was in fact an illusion. The company had not actually earned $109.4 million in 1997, the year its stock soared from $12 to $57 a share. In fact, it made less money that year than it had in any year under either of Dunlap's predecessors.

After collecting $26.9 million for his efforts, Dunlap sued the company for $5.3 million in severance pay, plus stock options and legal costs. A judge ruled in his favor in July of 1999. Sunbeam ultimately succumbed to bankruptcy in February of 2001. In July, the SEC filed formal fraud charges against Dunlap, Kersh, Gluck, Uzzi, Griffith, and Arthur Andersen. Gluck and Uzzi agreed to pay $100,000 fines to settle the charges; Kersh and Griffith paid $200,000. Arthur Anderson came out of it with a $110 million fine for its role in the fraud. In September 2002, Dunlap settled the SEC charges against him. He agreed to a $500,000 fine and promised not to serve again at a public company.

Dunlap never publicly apologized or admitted to any wrongdoing at Sunbeam. Chainsaw Al now lives in Florida with his wife. His lifestyle, presumably, is an easy one. Whether or not the same is true of his conscience can't be known.

Lesson #8: Beware Too Much Focus on Stock Price

Chainsaw Al Dunlap's modus operandi was similar to that of a magician who uses sleight of hand to distract his audience from what's really going on in front of their eyes. With all his arrogance and bluster, Dunlap was able to draw the attention of otherwise credible investors and analysts away from glaring warning signs that should have exposed his management technique as a fraud. In fact, Dunlap's unsophisticated tactics left danger signs artlessly exposed. Uncovering the truth behind Sunbeam's "turnaround" required neither mystics nor an MBA. Instead, it simply demanded that an observer set aside Dunlap's imprimatur and pay close attention to information distributed to the public at large.

Disciplined investors could have exited Sunbeam repeatedly at a price of well over $25 a share if they had acknowledged the ever-more-urgent warnings. These signs increased in number and regularity as Dunlap became more and more desperate, but they began the moment Dunlap took over.

The clearest and most immediate warning sign was Dunlap's single-minded focus on the company's share price. His compensation package and the packages of almost all of Sunbeam employees were closely tied to the fortunes of the company's stock. Though similar situations arise at many companies, they rarely run so deeply and broadly as they did at Sunbeam, where there was little incentive for anyone at the company to do anything other than hit their numbers in order to attract more investors to the shares.

That singular focus on share price is often a sign that something else may be wrong at a company. At the least, it's an indication that investors should look more closely at the company in order to determine whether executives are focusing on anything else—such as the fundamentals of the business. In Sunbeam's case, if investors had subjected the company to a proper examination rather than being blinded by the bright light of Dunlap's personality, they might have spotted a number of other warning signs that all was not right at the appliance maker.

Other Lessons of the Sunbeam Debacle

To begin with, Dunlap's restructuring plan promised results that were too good to be true. To meet Dunlap's targets, Sunbeam would have had to improve its margins by 1,200 percent, performing five times better than any of its competitors. With no operating history to justify the belief that Sunbeam could do significantly better than anyone else in the field, investors should have been highly skeptical of such promises.

Investors also should have been skeptical of Dunlap himself. Had they looked into the facts of his background rather than relying on the hype of his headlines, they would have seen that, while Dunlap had indeed helped pump up the share price at several companies, his successors regularly criticized his management, all but accusing him of financial fraud. The CFO of Kimberly-Clark, which purchased Scott after Dunlap "rebuilt" it, acknowledged that the company was in much worse shape than Dunlap had portrayed. Earnings were $160 million less than Dunlap had projected at the time of the sale. By digging a little deeper, investors would have discovered that as far back as American Can, managers who succeeded Dunlap condemned his tactics, claiming that all he had done was cut costs to increase short-term profits and share price, leaving the companies on much weaker long-term footing.

Dunlap's demand for total control of the board should have set off alarm bells as well. A board of directors is supposed to serve as a check and balance to the management team, not as a set of "yes-men." A board stacked with cronies lacks the independence necessary to keep an out-of-control CEO in check.

Other levels of management presented similar concerns. The mere fact that Dunlap demanded that Al Kersh, his CFO, be by his side from the first moment of his tenure was suspicious. The role of a CFO is to enforce GAAP and accurately track the company's balance sheet. Prior to Dunlap's arrival, Sunbeam's problems were not in accounting but in its sales. Putting a numbers man in as a solution is a good sign that real problems may be going unaddressed in favor of tactics that may be dishonest. In Sunbeam's case, those tactics were evident in the company's financial statements—if only investors had bothered to look. Anytime a company changes its accounting practices—as Sunbeam did when it instituted bill-and-hold sales and changed the end of its reporting quarter—investors should demand to know exactly what inspired the changes, and just what the ramifications of such change are.

Had investors been paying closer attention to Sunbeam's statements, they also would have spotted the company's bloated inventories, another warning sign of trouble. Analyst William Steele issued a report pointing out a dramatic increase in inventories and a reversal in working capital requirements. Grills were sitting around because the company had been pushing them on buyers who didn't actually want them, and accounting for them as if they had been sold already. This was a clear indication of "inventory stuffing"—the physical evidence that Kersh's ditty bag couldn't erase—and a sign that something was grievously wrong.

Another clear warning sign could have been found in the three mergers Dunlap scrambled to complete in a single day. Sunbeam's buying binge had no purpose other than to obfuscate the company's dire straits. Investors should always be skeptical when companies start snapping up other companies, especially if there is already a suspicion of trouble. Weak companies rarely become strong through acquisitions; rather, they need to start strong to successfully integrate other companies into their business. When a company embarks on an aggressive acquisition strategy, there's a chance that, like Sunbeam, it may be trying to hide something.

At the very least, investors should have listened to the skeptics. By the fourth quarter of 1997, rumors were swirling that Sunbeam's turnaround was merely smoke and mirrors. Short sellers were actively trading Sunbeam stock, journalists were casting aspersions on the company's accounting practices, and management was unable—or unwilling—to respond in substance or explain the stock price's slow deterioration.

In addition, insiders were bailing out of the company like rats leaving a sinking ship—as investors should have done. Newt White was regarded as the second most important man at Sunbeam and widely heralded as a remarkable COO. That he departed "for personal reasons" less than six months after joining the company was troubling. The mass defections in the first quarter of 1998, when dozens of salespeople, managers, and executives resigned, leaving potentially valuable stock options on the table, was another sign of trouble. Here were people who had been on the inside and yet did not believe in the company's future. Investors would have been wise to follow their lead.

Chapter 9

How Safe Are the Safeguards?

The first part of this book illustrates the great lengths rogues will go to in order to profit from unsuspecting investors. It's often surprising just how many hoops a corporate fraudster will be willing to jump through—or simply sidestep—in order to defraud people. But the fact is, it's not easy being a rogue. To succeed, a crooked businessperson must dismantle, dodge, or co-opt a battery of investor safeguards. Government regulators, law enforcement agencies, accountants, executive watchdogs, company employees, a board of directors, research analysts, legislators, and the media all erect barriers to keep the bad guys out.

And it gets tougher with each successive fraud. Each time a rogue commits a crime, the authorities respond with laws designed to prevent a similar breach in the future. The press gets a little wiser, investors grow a little smarter, the next rogue must think a little harder and come up with a more elaborate plan in order to pull off the same kind of scheme. Since the bank failures that inspired the Federal Reserve Act of 1912, all the major investor safeguards that have been put in place in the 20th century have been inspired by financial disasters in which corporate rogues played some part. The massive market manipulation of the 1920s ushered in the Securities Act of 1933 and the Securities Exchange Act of 1934; insider trading scandals prompted the Williams Act of 1966; and, most recently, the collapse of Enron, WorldCom, and the other 1990s darlings brought about the Sarbanes-Oxley Act of 2002.

While each investor safeguard has inherent strengths and weaknesses, they collectively present an imposing defense. And yet, rogues still manage to get around them. Even now, it's a good bet that somewhere, at a company whose name you know—and which you may even be invested in—there's a corporate rogue scheming up new ways to bypass whatever laws he or she thinks are holding the company back from making them big money.

The fact is, the legal safeguards that are in place make things more difficult for rogues, but they are simply not enough. Every system has its cracks. The lesson of this chapter is not to be lulled into a false sense of security just because new laws constantly appear to protect investors. Ultimately, each investor is responsible for protecting him or herself. Investor safeguards help, but in each case, rogues have found ways to get around them. As you look for the warning signs of fraud, keep this information in mind.

#1. The Regulators

The most obvious form of protection for investors—and possibly the biggest hurdle for would-be rogues—comes from the Federal government. America's modern regulatory framework is rooted in the scandals of the roaring 1920s. The rampant speculation and lack of regulation during that decade created an environment ripe for notorious rogues such as Charles Ponzi, C.C. Julian (who led a stock fraud based on largely fictional oil finds in southern California), and Samuel Insull. Tempted by the availability of easy credit and their rags-to-riches dreams, some 20 million investors set out to make their fortunes in the stock market. Most didn't fare so well. Of the $50 billion in new securities offered during this period, half were worthless by the early 1930s.

The Federal Reserve was partly to blame for the depth of the crisis. When stocks started to sink, the Fed panicked and reduced money supply, turning a recession into a stock market free-fall and the worst economic depression in U.S. history. From 1929 to 1932, 11,000 banks failed, gross national product fell approximately 10 percent per year, and unemployment soared to 25 percent. From a high of 386 in the fall of 1929, the Dow Jones Industrial Average tumbled to 41 in 1933.

Stocks failed to recover, in large part, because of a massive loss of investor confidence and a general belief that the market was rigged. Bold action was needed to restore public faith in the capital markets. Congress held hearings to identify the problems and search for solutions, passing the Securities Act of 1933 and the Securities Exchange Act of 1934. These new laws helped increase transparency and level the playing field for all investors by compelling companies to disclose accurate and timely financial information, restricting the use of insider information, and banning fraudulent trades. To enforce the new laws, Congress established the Securities and Exchange Commission in 1934.

Using the theory that "it takes a thief to catch a thief," President Franklin Delano Roosevelt appointed Joseph P. Kennedy to head the new agency. Kennedy was a Wall Street insider who built his wealth through stock manipulation, price pumping, insider trading, and the full complement of 1920s stock scams. Upon his appointment, he used his experience and knowledge to guide the implementation of the new regulatory framework, and confounded his critics with his exceptional service. Under his stewardship, the SEC became, in the words of Kennedy's successor Justice William O. Douglas, "the shotgun behind the door—loaded, well-oiled, cleaned, ready for use—but with the hope it would never have to be used."

While the SEC has jurisdiction over every element of the securities business, from brokers and mutual fund managers to accountants and executives, its broad mandate has historically exceeded the capacity of its limited staff and resources—leaving the door open for rogues, if not quite as widely as before. Moreover, while it can enjoin companies to comply with securities laws, levy fines against them, and charge them in civil court, the SEC's enforcement division cannot impose or seek criminal sanctions. Instead, the SEC is required to refer any criminal misconduct to federal and state prosecutors.

The U.S. Attorney's office has the power to bring in the cavalry. Periodically, it has secured high profile and typically politically motivated convictions, such as then-New York State Attorney General Rudy Giuliani's prosecution of Michael Milken and Ivan Boesky. But the Justice Department often lacks the expertise and patience to deconstruct complex financial crimes. Rogues often settle for paying a small portion of their ill-gotten gains in return for not having to admit their guilt. Consequently, the conviction rate for white-collar financial crime, and the corollary deterrent effect, is shocking low. Bob Dylan was right: "Steal a little, and they throw you in jail. Steal a lot, and they make you a king."

Securities laws are also regulated on the state level. Besides New York State Attorney General Eliot Spitzer's recent campaign to prosecute a number of prominent Wall Street players, state regulators tend to be understaffed and relatively unsophisticated. As a result, they focus on less complicated violations, letting the most sophisticated rogues—who are also the ones who do the most damage—run free.

The latest brick in the wall of agencies and legislation that's meant to hold back boardroom thieves is the Sarbanes-Oxley Act of 2002. Passed in the wake of the scandals at Enron, WorldCom, and other high-flying companies of the late 1990s, Sarbanes-Oxley is designed to compel more corporate accountability from top executives at publicly traded companies. Among other things, it requires chief executives to personally sign off on a company's financial statements, making it harder for them to dodge responsibility and pass the buck, as it were, to their subordinates.

Sarbanes-Oxley also creates a new layer of reports outlining the effectiveness of the company's internal accounting controls, the mechanisms that are meant to insure that no accounting "errors" creep into company statements, whether by accident or by design. While many corporations have complained about the added expense of both generating these reports and improving the security of their accounting procedures, most such expenditures are now out of the way. Besides, corporate America had little choice but to comply.

While it's too soon to tell just how effective Sarbanes-Oxley will be in ferreting out rogues before they can do much damage, it is no doubt too optimistic to think that any piece of legislation can clamp down on underhanded practices completely. In the new atmosphere of heightened scrutiny, you'd think that a rogue would have to be crazy to try to fool regulators or carry off an elaborate scam. But as we've seen throughout this book, the hubris of the corporate fraudster knows no bounds. Soon enough, if it isn't happening already, someone will decide they've found a way around the Sarbanes-Oxley Act and launch yet another complex corporate crime. When that happens, the best way to protect yourself and your investments will be to rely on the danger signs we outline in this book, which haven't changed despite the many new regulatory regimes that have been put in place, and which will still be the same under Sarbanes-Oxley and beyond.

The final line of defense on the regulatory front are the self-regulatory organizations of the securities industry and the accounting profession: the National Association of Securities Dealers, the New York Stock Exchange, and the American Institute of Certified Public Accountants. If a rogue gets this far, though, he is probably home free. These self-governing organizations have historically protected their own interests, rather than those of investors. Regulators can help stem the tide of corporate fraud, but they cannot prevent it entirely. The best way to guard against it is to be forewarned.

#2. The Auditors

The passage of the Securities Acts of 1933 and 1934 required companies to file audited financial statements, and made accountants into an integral part of the corporate team. Auditors must be brought into a company's inner circle, but at the same time must maintain their impartiality. Investors rely heavily on an auditor's stamp of approval, and there is no doubt that numerous frauds have been squashed or discouraged by the threat of an audit. Would-be rogues must shiver at the thought of a team of accountants descending on their companies to pore over every shred of paper. It's worth remembering that half of FBI agents are accountants or lawyers.

Nonetheless, such protection is not enough. Auditors have had front row seats for all the major frauds in the 20th century. After every financial disaster—including the bankruptcy of Equity Funding, the S&L crisis of the 1980s, and the collapse of Enron—investors have asked the same question: Where were the auditors? There has never been a uniform answer.

Just as they do with regulators, rogues generally find ways to take advantage of structural weaknesses in the auditing process. There is a limit to how deep auditors can dig and just how much checking they can do. Otherwise, audits would cost hundreds of times more than the millions of dollars they cost today.

Auditors examine every piece of relevant documentation they can find—bills of sale, bills of lading, payment receipts, and so on—to make sure the numbers add up. If a rogue can create fakes that are good enough to pass muster, it is possible to fool even an exacting auditor. This is exactly what happened in the McKesson & Robbins scandal: Philip Musica fabricated supporting documentation for $20 million worth of nonexistent drug inventory.

The McKesson & Robbins scandal led to a reevaluation of basic auditing practices and the initiation of physical inventory checks as standard operating procedure. These improvements made it harder to scam the auditors, but not impossible. Auditors serve a broad range of businesses, and their expertise in any one business is necessarily limited. Rogues take advantage of this knowledge gap by falsifying evidence. It is difficult for an auditor checking items as varied as precious metals, pharmaceuticals, natural gas, and oil to confirm their authenticity, and the fact that they exist in the volumes claimed. In most cases, the auditor will examine the physical inventory to the best of his ability and rely on validating documentation.

Additionally, given that the auditing process relies on spot checks and random visits, a resourceful rogue can fool an auditor by throwing money at the problem. Barry Minkow of ZZZZ Best spent over $1 million to lease a building and fake an insurance restoration project to convince his auditor that he had a multi-million dollar contract. The deception worked, and it is not clear that the auditor could reasonably have been expected to uncover the fraud. In the words of a senior partner at a rival "Big 8" accounting firm: "It could have happened to any of us." Again, this scandal triggered a change in accounting rules. Accountants are now required to actively look for fraud.

Sometimes auditors fail to uncover frauds for less benign reasons: they are compromised by conflicts of interests. In the Equity Funding scandal, the auditors were indicted for knowingly accepting false financial reporting. There was an unprofessional relationship between the auditors and the financial officers at Equity Funding: The company's financial officers had previously worked for the company's accounting firm.

Such relationships are not uncommon: Accountants frequently take senior positions with clients they've audited in the past. This can diminish the effectiveness of subsequent audits, since the accountants tend to trust their former colleagues and pursue concerns less vigorously against their friends. In the case of Equity Funding, the conflicts of interest didn't stop there. The auditors took personal loans from company officers, owned company stock, and helped the son of one of their firm's partners get a job at the company.

The evolution of accountants from bookkeepers to businessmen helps explain some of the problems that have arisen. The blurring of roles began decades ago, but the conflict has intensified in recent years, as accountants have branched out into other businesses, such as consulting. This has required accountants to play both the independent role of an auditor and the supplicant role of a salesperson. Enron's auditor, Arthur Andersen, also provided consulting services for tax matters and financial compliance. Both projects put the auditors in the awkward position of assessing their own company's work. This conflict was exacerbated by Andersen's internal compensation practices, which generously rewarded the cross-selling of services.

The profession may have reached its nadir in 2001, when PriceWaterhouseCoopers admitted that its accountants had been making personal investments in companies that they were auditing. The firm settled with the SEC for $5 million, acknowledging 8,000 legal and ethical violations. More recently, the indictment and subsequent bankruptcy of Arthur Andersen has been a stern wake-up call to the accounting industry. The partners there lost their jobs, millions of dollars in personal capital, and generous pension plans. The remaining accountants now realize that the failure to conduct comprehensive and thorough audits will place their own firms—and their own net worth—in harm's way. As a result, accountants are far less apt to get bullied by their clients into accepting overly aggressive practices. Although auditors may be more willing to do their jobs these days, problems of capacity and the ability to verify every last detail of a company's operations still remain. If you're seeing the warning signs of fraud at a company, don't be fooled into complacency just because an auditing firm has given the company its seal of approval.

#3. The Analysts

It may be hard to believe today, but once upon a time, research analysts played a meaningful role in protecting investors. Ray Dirks, an analyst at Delafield Childs, Inc., almost single-handedly uncovered the massive fraud at Equity Funding Corporation in 1973. Dirks flagged potential problems at the insurer to a number of institutional holders, who proceeded to dump the stock. Unfortunately for Dirks, his sleuthing didn't pay off professionally. Charged by the SEC for misuse of insider information, Dirks spent 10 years fighting a conviction for insider trading. The United States Supreme Court ultimately overturned the charge.

In theory, analysts are supposed to scrutinize companies and generate detailed reports and opinions to assist investors in making stock purchase decisions. But in practice, to do their jobs effectively, analysts need access. And corporate management doesn't tend to be too open with those who publish unfavorable opinions. It's the Wall Street equivalent to the White House pressroom, where reporters who ask harsh questions are given a back seat or are sometimes completely ignored. Management does what it can to quash negative opinions. One consequence is that the vast majority of Wall Street research opinions have historically been "buys," with very few "sells." More recently, that has changed. Prompted by regulatory and press scrutiny, investment banks have found religion, and issued a raft of "sell" recommendations. But it's too soon to tell whether this show of candor will generate superior returns for investors making decisions based on that research.

The pressure for analysts to produce rosy outlooks doesn't come only from the companies they cover. Banks have long used analysts to win investment-banking business from the companies they cover, in return for favorable coverage. New York State Attorney General Eliot Spitzer recently made headlines by exposing the practice at Merrill Lynch, dredging up a series of e-mails sent by its star Internet analyst Henry Blodgett, among others. Even while maintaining an enthusiastic "buy" on Internet company At Home, Blodgett was writing to colleagues that "ATHM is such a piece of crap." But Merrill had recently taken the company public and was vying for a piece of upcoming banking deals. The firm could hardly afford to have Blodgett give an honest opinion—or so it thought. In the end, Merrill settled with the New York Attorney General's office, paying a $100 million fine and promising never to engage in such practices again.

The root of the problem has been the way in which research analysts are compensated. Rather than pay analysts based on how well their stock picks perform, banks look at how much analysts contribute to their investment banking business, and at their ranking by *Institutional Investor* magazine. Determined by the votes of Wall Street leaders, the *Institutional Investor* analyst rankings tend to be more of a popularity contest than a quantitative measurement of stock picking prowess. At the dinner celebrating *Institutional Investor*'s 31st Annual All America Research Team, Spitzer said the awards were "essentially a sham" and that, on the basis of his research, virtually none of the honorees merited praise.

As part of the global settlement Spitzer won from leading Wall Street firms, the firms agreed to stop paying analysts based on their contribution to investment banking and instead measure the performance of their stock recommendations. But if research analysts cannot serve as quasi-investment bankers, their compensation levels will almost certainly plunge—dragging the value of their numbers down along with it. A number of top research analysts have already left the profession. It will be some time before it can be determined whether this brain drain will offset the benefits of the much needed compensation reform.

If equity analysts aren't much help, what about the debt world? Because fraud tends to occur most frequently at companies with weaker balance sheets, credit analysts at the three major credit rating agencies—Moody's, Standard & Poors, and Fitch—should be on the front lines of defense, flagging deteriorating operating trends and over-leveraged balance sheets. But all too often, these analysts miss the warning signs. Credit downgrades tend to follow, not precede, the public discovery of bad news. The barn door gets shut after the cow is already out.

Why the poor showing? At the risk of being uncharitable, the credit analyst's position has traditionally attracted candidates that are just not that good. They are poorly paid (by Wall Street standards) and thus tend to be equity analysts who couldn't cut it on Wall Street. Credit analysts are often criticized for relying on the word of corporate management, and for conducting very little in-depth research of their own.

Credit analysts often find themselves compromised by the very way that debt is structured. Many debt covenants contain "triggers" which allow a bank to retract a company's credit line should its debt be downgraded, an event that often leads to increased costs of borrowing for the company. Credit analysts are often wary of downgrading debt when they know it could send an otherwise stable company into a fiscal crisis. That was the excuse the credit rating agencies used to explain their failure to downgrade Enron: Cutting their rating would only have accelerated the demise of the already troubled company.

Finally there's the problem of competition. The credit agency business is an SEC-sanctioned oligopoly, with just three firms rating all publicly-traded companies. SEC approval is necessary to get into the business, yet the agency has failed to publicly delineate the standards it expects. A number of potential market entrants, including the highly regarded firm of Egan-Jones, have been unsuccessful in securing SEC approval. Presumably, some competition would exert pressure on the "Big 3" to improve the quality of their analysis. For the moment, in both the credit and equity sectors, there remains no way to truly rely on the information coming from analysts' desks. It's good as far as it goes, but all too often it doesn't do enough to flag the warning signs that can indicate when it's time to get out of a sinking investment.

#4. Corporate Governance

Investors have had the opportunity to invest in public companies for more than two centuries. In 1814, Francis Cabot Lowell, a Boston merchant, could not afford to pay for the construction and installation of machinery for his textile factory, so he sold stock in his company to 10 friends. Within seven years, these stockholders had received a cumulative return of more than 100 percent. The public company was born—and with it, the potential for corporate corruption.

Adam Smith spotted the problem early on: "The directors of such companies. . .being the managers rather of other people's money than of their own, it cannot well be expected that they should watch over it with the same anxious vigilance with which the partners in a private company frequently watch over their own."

To ensure as much vigilance as possible, modern companies have set up a series of internal checks. The CEO is flanked by two watchdogs: The Chief Financial Officer and the General Counsel. These executives provide oversight and look out for the interests of shareholders. The CFO, historically a bean counter with an accounting background, is supposed to act as a check on the more aggressive sales and operating practices that executives may want to put in place, and also be the eyes and ears for the Board of Directors. Similarly, the General Counsel, also inherently conservative, is expected to ensure procedural and substantive compliance with the law.

In most frauds, these watchdogs don't live up to their conservative billing. Enron CFO's Andy Fastow, for example, was a gun-slinging, financial-engineering salesman who self-promoted his way to 1999 CFO of the Year at *CFO Magazine*. Similarly, Tyco's General Counsel Mark Belnick seems to have lost the script for the role of in-house lawyer, jumping head first into the company trough with Tyco CEO Dennis Kozlowski and CFO Mark Schwartz—despite the fact that the rewards they were reaping had been produced through very illegal means.

From a purely logistical standpoint, a successful fraud requires the participation of top management, several middle managers, and a number of lower level employees. But the corruption of an organization doesn't happen overnight. Rather, it occurs through a combination of cronyism and what William Laufer, director of the Zicklin Center for Business Ethics Research at the Wharton School, calls "winking." With each wink and nod, the message gets conveyed to the troops. According to Laufer: "Of all the factors that lead to corporate crime, none comes close in importance to the role top management plays in tolerating, even shaping, a culture that allows for it."

The corruption, however, is usually not complete and total. An honest soul with enough courage, commitment, and ability can expose even a vast and complex fraud, though usually too late to prevent much damage. Enron Vice President Sherron Watkins warned CEO Ken Lay that she feared that the company would "implode in a wave of accounting scandals." But Lay was more concerned with selling his stock than saving his company. WorldCom Vice President Cynthia Cooper assembled a team of finance people to internally audit the company's books. When she alerted the WorldCom Board of Directors of her concerns and allegations—all of which proved to be correct—the Board responded by commissioning a memorandum on the pluses and minuses of firing Cooper. The Board ultimately retained Cooper and fired CFO Scott Sullivan when he could not defend the company's accounting strategy. While Watkins and Cooper exhibited tremendous bravery, neither was able to prevent the damage caused by the misdeeds they exposed.

In the absence of watchdog executives and whistle blowers, the Board of Directors is the final protection against fraud. The board is charged with looking out for the interests of the shareholders by overseeing management and participating in major corporate decisions. To be effective, the board must consist of directors who have independence of spirit, intellect, and character.

But there's a rub: At most companies, the CEO plays a key role in selecting board members. That means critical qualifications can include attending prep school or college with the CEO, belonging to the same golf club as the CEO, vacationing in Martha's Vineyard with CEO, or maintaining a longstanding business relationship with the CEO. Barry Minkow's Board of Directors at ZZZZ Best included his girlfriend's father, a former weight lifting instructor, and the owner of the company's building. The principal at the elementary school attended by Walt Disney CEO Michael Eisner's children served on the Disney board for a decade. It has historically been in the nature of corporate boards that their members tend to be close to management, whether through friendship, personal or business association, or family relations. Though corporate boards are meant to provide an independent check on the powers of management, their proximity to those in charge of the company profoundly undermines their effectiveness, in most cases. Even when a board is largely independent, they are often so intimidated by an executive's superior experience or, as in Al Dunlap's case, outsized personality, that they can fail to do their job.

The oversight process can truly break down when board members experience conflicts of interest. Most conflicts are small and seemingly harmless, but some are overtly absurd. Tyco director Frank Walsh received a $20 million finder's fee, which was not disclosed to other board members, for assisting in the disastrous acquisition of CIT Group. How could he possibly remain impartial when assessing that deal?

There is hope, however. A new New York Stock Exchange regulation requires that each board contain a majority of independent directors. At best, this will transform corporate boards from blank checks to true shareholder advocates. Minimally, it will eliminate unnecessary conflicts of interest and promote greater board independence. At worst, it will fill boards with people who have little idea of how a publicly traded company is meant to be run. In the end, it still leaves investors with little additional protection against unscrupulous rogues.

#5. The Media

The final line of defense against corporate fraudsters is the media. Industrious financial reporters have uncovered a number of frauds over the years that should have been prevented by the kinds of safeguards outlined above. Herb Greenberg of TheStreet.com and *Fortune* magazine has single-handedly uncovered fraud at Lernout & Hauspie, A.C.L.N., and AremisSoft by questioning convoluted press releases and publicly disclosed financials, investigating related party transactions, conducting background checks on corporate executives, canvassing institutional investors and short sellers, and confronting senior management. Reporters such as Greenberg, Charles Gasparino of *The Wall Street Journal*, Christopher Byron of the *New York Post*, and David Faber of CNBC are relatively unencumbered in their search for the truth. Unfortunately, there are not enough investigative financial reporters on the beat.

In the aggregate, the media has a track record that is not much better than that of research analysts. The editors of *Fortune* magazine touted Enron as the "most innovative" of its "most admired" companies six years in a row. In 1999, it named WorldCom as one of 10 stocks to "grow with." *Business Week* lauded Dennis Kozlowski as America's "Most Aggressive CEO" in a

2001 cover story, hailing him as a "tax master" for his creative financial engineering. CNBC was the biggest cheerleader of the Internet era, regularly fawning over about 30 CEOs. The media often reflects the spirit of the moment—cheering when stocks go up, and only turning negative once the market declines. As a consequence, the Fourth Estate has missed some great stories, leaving investors to do the work of looking out for danger signs themselves

Together, these five elements protect investors like an NFL defensive unit. There are multiple layers or zones of defense, and numerous players on the field. No one component can do the job in isolation, but together they make it very hard for a ball carrier to reach the end zone. Still, rogues sometimes manage to score. Winston Churchill's observation that "democracy is the worst form of government except for all those other forms that have been tried from time to time" applies here. Our financial system is constantly improving, and it is tough to find one that works much better, but on balance it is far from perfect. In the end, the best way to defend against corporate trickery is for investors themselves to be on the watch. No one has a more vested interest in protecting your money than you do. By putting the lessons in this book to work for yourself, you may well be able to make more of your investments than all the safeguards we've described.

Chapter 10

Don't Get Fooled Again

The history of corporate rogues is best summed up by the old adage, "Fool me once, shame on you; fool me twice, shame on me." Corporate rogues succeed because investors fail to learn the lessons of the past.

The turn of the century has ushered in a new generation of rogues. But despite the emergence of regulatory bodies, despite the strengthening of fiduciary duties, and despite the development and codification of standard accounting practices, the strategies used by corporate fraudsters have barely changed since the turn of the 20th century.

For evidence, look no further than the first rogues of the 21st century, Enron and WorldCom. Though investors at the time were protected by more sophisticated regulations and had access to more information than had ever been available before, they still got sucked in by tricks that had been around for a century or more. As you can see from the following two studies, the shady dealings behind the scenes at both Enron and WorldCom were not all that different from those that had gone on at any number of fraudulent companies of the last 100 years. The lesson here is that the schemes don't change; it's up to the investor to know what to look for.

Enron's Innovations

High-flying energy trading company Enron had more in common with electricity tycoon Samuel Insull's maze of holdings than with any standard business model of the power industry. Both used a complex corporate holding structure to hide liabilities, pump up profits, and enrich their top executives as a result. We can perhaps be forgiven for forgetting the lessons of the Insull affair; after all, Insull worked his magic some 80 years before Enron even got its start. But Insull was hardly the only historical precedent. Much more recently—certainly well within the memory of many investors and analysts—Charles Keating swiped billions of dollars from investors using similar tactics. Like Enron, he used a complex corporate structure to obfuscate the balance sheets of his ragtag collection of companies and investments, making things look more safe and rosy than they actually were.

Looked at in that light, Enron CFO Andrew Fastow, who masterminded the company's financial shenanigans and was hailed as a genius for his innovations, wasn't doing anything new at all. His off-balance-sheet subsidiaries, which hid debts, lowered Enron's cost of capital, and enabled a series of complex intra-company trades, were direct descendents of the strategies used by his felonious predecessors.

Enron's scheme worked something like this: The off-balance-sheet entities set up by Fastow purchased assets from Enron at above market rates. Enron then booked the profits from these "sales" (which in reality were nothing of the sort, because the assets in question never really left the company), making its bottom line look more robust than it really was. The off-balance-sheet partnerships also helped hide potential pockmarks: Enron transferred many of the liabilities associated with its energy contracts and other assets to off-balance-sheet entities. That way, those debts didn't show up on reports to potential creditors, making them more willing than they might have been to lend the company funds. What Enron did not disclose was that it had secretly entered into agreements to repurchase these liabilities at pre-determined prices. These agreements guaranteed the buying entity a specific profit and meant that Enron remained, in fact, fully exposed to the liability that it claimed to have transferred.

Enron's employees (primarily Fastow and his cronies) enriched themselves by structuring the off-balance-sheet deals so that they got a cut of the payments made by Enron. In one notable instance, Fastow and his associates took $19 million of the $30 million Enron paid to repurchase assets from one of these off-balance-sheet entities.

One of the main problems with Enron was that few outside the company really knew or understood just what it was that Enron did to make money. Enron was an energy company that produced no energy. Its management bragged of the company's cash-lite structuring, but few could explain what "cash-lite" meant. But the profits kept coming in, and Wall Street was enthralled.

Fastow's creativity earned him numerous awards as the best CFO in America from individuals and organizations who seemed to think it was the CFO's role to create profits through creative accounting, rather than simply record a company's financial results. "We needed someone to rethink the entire financing structure at Enron from soup to nuts," Enron president and chief operating officer Jeffrey Skilling said. "We didn't want someone stuck in the past, since the industry of yesterday is no longer." Commentators went on to call Fastow "creative," "revolutionary," and a "genius." Defrauded investors came up with less complimentary epithets.

Enron used an old trick: Dazzle them with a structure so complex, and profits so impressive, that no one—save a couple of short sellers, hedge fund managers, and enterprising journalists—dares to question the Emperor's new clothes. It was the same strategy Equity Funding used to pump out terrific results while its competitors slumped. It was the same way Charles Keating kept several steps ahead of the regulators—for a while.

Legendary investor Fayez Sarofim was one of the few who questioned Enron's money faucet—and stayed away. Despite intense pressure from his numerous Houston clients, Sarofim, who serves as sub-advisor to a number of Dreyfus mutual funds, refused to purchase Enron stock for his clients. His reasoning was simple: He could not comprehend the financial statements. Companies should try to make their financial statements and businesses easy, not difficult, to understand. If the finances are extremely complicated, there is a good chance that the company has something to hide. And when a company's CFO becomes its chief profit center, it is probably time to sell.

WorldCom's Appetite

Telecommunications company WorldCom engaged in a slightly different brand of fraud from Enron, but much of it was also cribbed from the handbooks of rogues past. WorldCom's *modus operandi* was accounting, twisting the numbers until they came out "right." The company was especially creative on two fronts: acquisitions and capital expenses.

Any flurry of M&A activity represents a great opportunity for dishonest executives to engage in deep financial chicanery. Consider the buying binges of past rogues. When Philip Musica wanted to hide his company's skyrocketing bootlegging profits, he acquired McKesson. When Equity Funding's earnings soared and questions began to emerge over the numbers, the company began to acquire other companies and assets from all over the world in order to obfuscate the fraud. When Sunbeam was about to miss Wall Street's expectations for its earnings by a wide margin, Dunlap orchestrated three simultaneous acquisitions in order to throw the market off the scent. Just as darkness provides burglars with cover to break into houses, mergers and acquisitions have long provided cover for financial mischief.

WorldCom made more than 60 acquisitions in five years under CEO Bernie Ebbers. Ebbers used these acquisitions as an excuse to set aside reserves that could later be used to prop up earnings. As bankruptcy examiner Dick Thornburg would later report, Ebbers, like Dunlap before him, set aside larger than necessary reserves each time he made one of these deals. He would then leak the reserves back into profits over the next few years, as necessary, to guarantee that his company could hit its projected numbers no matter what happened to the business or the economy.

Such shenanigans are apparently not uncommon. In 2003, the Robert H. Smith School of Business at the University of Maryland released a study of 71 companies that the SEC had prosecuted for publishing allegedly misleading financial statements between 1992 and 1999. That study found a correlation between the frequency of mergers and acquisitions and the incidence of fraud. "An environment of excessive stock options [and] deteriorating financial conditions preceded by a history of growth through acquisitions provides the conditions for accounting fraud," according to Dr. Carmelita Troy, the study's author.

Acquisition accounting tends to be flexible in that there can be a number of legitimate ways to account for the same transaction. As a result, though, seemingly legitimate accounting can be used for illegitimate ends, often to manufacture earnings growth that simply doesn't exist. As so-called "roll-up" stories—such as a company leading the consolidation of an industry by buying up its competitors—can prosper for extended periods, as WorldCom did, but they almost all eventually hit a wall. In many cases, the law of diminishing returns rears its ugly head. WorldCom needed to make bigger and bigger acquisitions over time in order to continue to manufacture growth, because its organic rate of growth was practically nonexistent.

Acquisitive companies also have a higher propensity to explode. The University of Maryland study found that many acquisitions actually failed to contribute to cash flow, although reported earnings accelerated. "The larger the number of acquisitions, the lower the cash flow the following year," Dr. Troy wrote. As a consequence, companies resorted to "the more extreme measure of accounting fraud to maintain persistent growth."

WorldCom also managed to capitalize expenses in a way that made the bottom line seem better than it really was, another trick that had been used in the past. Ebbers took standard operating expenses and treated them, for accounting purposes, as capital expenses. This enabled the company to depreciate the expenses over a number of years instead of accounting for them all at once when the cost was incurred, as operating expenses should be. So prevalent was the practice that WorldCom's profits were artificially increased to the tune of $9 billion.

Past rogues used depreciation in a slightly different manner. Insull delayed the depreciation of capital assets until they were retired or replaced—often a delay of more than a decade. That enabled him to avoid the expense altogether for a time, artificially inflating his company's earnings. Al Dunlap at Sunbeam took a converse approach but achieved equally deceitful results. By accelerating the depreciation of equipment during reorganizations, even though the equipment was still in use, Dunlap was able to artificially shift costs to the un-reorganized company, making his reorganizations look far more successful than they were.

Ebbers had one more thing in common with the rogues of the past. Like Insull and Keating, he had trouble distinguishing between company funds and his own. In Ebbers's case, he had the company guarantee his personal investments, and he did so in such a manner that should have sent a loud sell signal to WorldCom investors.

While riding high on his successes, Ebbers began to place enormous bets on real estate investments across the country. To make these and other investments, Ebbers borrowed substantial money, pledging his WorldCom stock as collateral.

Using stock as collateral for a loan is not unusual among corporate executives with huge and concentrated positions in one company. However, Ebbers's loan had an added feature: It was structured with an "escalator" clause, which stipulated that if the value of his stock decreased, he was obligated to either add additional stock as collateral or liquidate the stock to ensure that the value of his collateral would remain sufficient to cover his loan.

When the market price of WorldCom stock sank in the early 2000s, Ebbers's net worth dropped precipitously. By early 2002 his entire position in WorldCom was not worth enough to secure his outstanding loans and he faced a margin call. Ebbers had a decision to make: Sell his investment properties or sell his WorldCom stock. A number of financial reporters, including Scott Moritz at TheStreet.com, reported on this dilemma.

Ebbers made his choice without delay: His real estate couldn't be sacrificed. His company, on the other hand, could. He approached the board of directors of WorldCom and informed them that he planned to sell his entire stake in WorldCom—unless WorldCom would guarantee his personal loans. WorldCom was in an unenviable position: Either their high-profile CEO dumps an enormous amount of stock on the public markets, sending the stock price off a cliff—or the company guarantees some $480 million in speculative loans. The board provided Ebbers with the guarantee he sought.

"This has to be the largest CEO subsidization I have ever seen," said a New England-based buy-side analyst at the time. "This is frustrating—senior executives treating companies like they are their personal piggy banks. [Ebbers] is a grown-up and should have to assume investment risk like the rest of us." Just as troubling was the fact that Ebbers chose his property investments over the company he headed. That choice should have sent a chilling message to shareholders. If the CEO isn't willing to hold onto the stock, the average investor shouldn't be either.

Don't Get Fooled Again

As you've seen in the course of this book, the modern history of major financial frauds stretches back over at least a hundred years of high-profile, high-cost thievery that has robbed millions of investors of billions of dollars of hard-earned cash. And yet investors—even sophisticated businesspeople—keep getting suckered, despite the lessons of history, despite increasing regulatory protection, and despite much greater financial transparency than ever before. Why?

Blame it on being human. Our most laudatory qualities—trust, optimism, and goodwill—are just the ones corporate rogues love to take advantage of. By and large, people want to believe in the goodness of others. Who would think that a charming kid like Barry Minkow would actually fabricate an entire line of business, complete with supporting documentation and witnesses to propagate the lie? It's tough for investors—honest, by-the-book men and women—to fathom that others are capable of such elaborate ruses, or are willing to pull them off. Thieves and con men take advantage of exactly these sentiments. Almost all the schemes described in this book relied to some extent on investors being unwilling to believe the work.

Where rogues don't rely on people's natural shortage of skepticism, they lean on our baser instincts. People get greedy. Who could turn down 50 percent returns like those Ponzi offered? Who could forego the chance to get in on "the find of the century" that was being touted by Bre-X? Investors always want to believe that they have stumbled onto the next big thing. It's why people play the lottery, it's why they invested in dot-com stocks—and it's why they bought into total frauds such as Equity Funding and Bre-X.

Greed, combined with gullibility, leads investors to speculate—rather than invest—in stocks. Adam Smith defined the speculator as a person who pursues short-term opportunities for profit, as opposed to a traditional businessman, who makes more fixed, longer-term investments. Fred Schwed, a Wall Street wit, summed it up well: "Speculation is an effort, probably unsuccessful, to turn a little money into a lot. Investment is an effort, which should be successful, to prevent a lot of money becoming a little."

While the astounding returns generated by genuine growth companies such as Microsoft, Dell, and Amgen have validated and legitimized stocks as the best investment class over the long term, these same stocks have also fueled the fire of speculation. Investors scour the landscape for the next big thing. They approach the stock market as they would a sweepstakes or a roulette table. Both of these gambles are statistically bad bets, but they offer the same potential for dream fulfillment should they hit. Similarly, trolling for "20-baggers," to use Peter Lynch's terminology—stocks that will appreciate 20-fold—usually leads investors to the next Barry Minkow. The CEOs who promise outsized returns are generally the ones who cannot deliver them.

And strangely enough, government regulations aimed at protecting investors don't always help get at the truth. Because of the massive changes in the regulatory framework—from the Securities Act of 1933 to the Sarbanes-Oxley Act of 2002—companies are now required to disclose a tremendous amount of information about their business, their accounting, and their own investments. But in some ways, these requirements simply give a would-be criminal additional ammunition with which to dupe investors. Most of the time, investors simply assume that the financial statements and declarations reported in SEC filings are truthful, giving any government-filed document an inherent legitimacy that they perhaps should not have. As the SEC only has the resources to review and audit a small portion of public filings, it is far from difficult for a rogue to make false or deceptive filings, assuming he or she can co-opt or fool the accountants and lawyers.

It can be argued that investors went from getting too little information at the beginning of the 20th century to receiving too much today. It can take a tremendous amount of time and effort to sift through all the available documents to identify clues of financial misbehavior. Like a defendant in a lawsuit, companies try to overwhelm their investors with so much information that they cannot find the handful of signs that something is amiss. How does one find the needle in the haystack?

Rather than dig in like Sherlock Holmes with an accounting degree, we recommend you set aside emotion (and greed), use common sense, and keep in mind the danger signs and lessons we've outlined in this book:

- If It Seems Too Good To Be True, It Probably Is
- Beware of Companies Run by Family and Friends
- Take a Close Look at Who's in Charge
- Beware of Companies That Go On Buying Binges
- Look Twice at Byzantine Business Structures
- Pay Attention to Company Accounts
- Listen to the Skeptics
- Beware Too Much Focus on Stock Price

By now, if you've been a careful student of the lessons in this book, you should know what to look for in the companies you're invested in and how to spot the signs that you should get out fast. The warnings come in all shapes and sizes: Some clues are financial, some are behavioral, and some are structural. Sometimes they will be there in droves. Sometimes only a few will show up. But when you can readily identify four or more, it's a fair guess that the stock you're holding is risky—certainly riskier than you initially believed it to be—and you should consider getting out before disaster strikes. If you don't, you stand the chance of losing everything. When that danger presents itself, it's better not to take the chance. As the signs begin to mount, investors should move toward the exits. At this point, there's no reason to get fooled by the next generation of corporate rogues.

Index

A

B

C

D

E

Q

R

S

T

U

V

W

Z

Bibliographic references for this work are available from the authors upon request. Please call (310) 496-5360.

About the Authors

Brett S. Messing is the Managing Partner of GPS Partners, an investment management firm specializing in income-oriented securities. He was previously a Managing Director at Lehman Brothers. Mr. Messing has contributed to *Fortune* magazine and appears regularly on CNBC. He is a graduate of Harvard Law School and Brown University and lives in Los Angeles, California with his wife, Marla, and three daughters, Natalie, Samantha, and Morgan.

Steven A. Sugarman is a Partner of GPS Partners. He previously worked with Mr. Messing at Lehman Brothers where he was primarily responsible for the management of incomeoriented investments. Mr. Sugarman began his career as a management consultant at McKinsey & Company. He is a graduate of the Yale Law School and Dartmouth College and lives in Santa Monica, California with his wife, Ainslie, and his daughter, Sierra.